DAYS THAT HAVE BEEN

A CWMBRAN HISTORY

Days That Have Been

A CWMBRAN HISTORY

by

W.G. Lloyd

Printed by
J & P Davison, 3 James Place, Treforest, Pontypridd.

ISBN 0 9520543 9 6

Published by W.G. Lloyd and printed by
J & P Davison, 3 James Place, Treforest, Pontypridd, CF37 1SQ.

CONTENTS

INTRODUCTION

The autumn of a life seems to be an appropriate time for a local scribe to put pen to paper and pass on the knowledge collected over many years of patient research. This work, coupled with the many requests for a substantial written history of Cwmbran, is for those aware of their roots to have a ready account for both interesting reading and a quick reference.

Like most others I consider it a privilege to have lived in Cwmbran for many years while enjoying the advantages of both village life and a new, modern town. For those who follow in our footsteps let them be aware of the wonderful, unique experience Cwmbran gives while applauding the endeavours of those who made it possible. It is now the turn of the young to keep the dream alive by handing down to the following generations the gift of a quality way of life.

May God and the 'love of home' be always with you.

W.G. Lloyd, 2006.

ACKNOWLEDGEMENTS

I wish to thank the following for their kindness during the long hours of research: Jack Healey, Geoffrey Page, David Roderick, Olive Smith, Jack Wheeler, John and Mary Woolway, Dennis M. Blewitt, Mr. Alun Prescott and his staff at the Newport Reference Library, the staff of the Gwent Record Office, the staff of Cardiff Reference Library, the staff of National Library of Wales, the staff of Somerset Record Office, the staff of the Public Record Office, London, the staff of Cwmbran Library, Derek Michael and Martyn Redwood of the Congress Theatre, Cwmbran.

Chapter One

A TIME LONG AGO

It was bitterly cold during the final phase of the Devensian period. Lasting from about 70,000 to 8,300 B.C., an enormous sheet of ice had stretched from the Gwent coast as far as Hereford with only the tops of the Black Mountains showing above the glacier. This was a time when land bridges connected with the Continent and as the climate became warmer, early man found their way across these pathways to our land. With mans' innate curiosity to know what is over the next hill, these early explorers probably noted the topography of the land and the all important food sources as they moved up the eastern valley of Gwent. As the climate became even warmer, the water contained in these huge glaziers would later make up the sea between Britain and the Continent, thus causing coastlines to recede and the land bridges vanishing forever.

With the appearance in Gwent of thick forests containing oak, willow, aspen, birch, hazel, pine and other deciduous trees, the stone age (Palaeolithic) hunters were soon to locate their early prey of reindeer, mammoth, bison, cave lions and woolly rhinoceros.

The arrival of the Mesolithic period summoned the appearance of new people to Britain and the invention of stone tools. The availability of animal meats had also altered with red deer, wild oxen and wild pig mostly sought after. Hunters would have come across wild boar with bristling hair and razor-sharp tusks rooting for fallen acorns among the trees, or shaggy grey wolves with yellow eyes passing quietly through the undergrowth in search of their next meal. Very little else changed during this period apart from the hunter groups awareness of migration of their prey and changing weather patterns

Proof of later Neolithic man in the Cwmbran area is now conclusive and will probably get stronger as the years go by. Around 4000 B.C. the Neolithic period in Britain began. The gradual change from a hunting and gathering way of life, to the introduction of agriculture, slowly brought about the establishment of small farming communities. At this time the low land in Llantarnam, alongside the Avon Lwyd, would have been marshy bogs with little habitation.

However, Neolithic finds in Cwmbran prove that late stone age man either hunted in the area, passed through on their way to the Black Mountains, or perhaps settled and used tools to work the land. Flints were discovered after heavy rain along the lower slopes of the Mynydd Maen and on the ancient Henllys track ways, which lead across the bare hills above the 500 feet contour line where all the Stone Age forts are situated. Archaeological excavations in the grounds of Llantarnam Abbey, during 1993, revealed nineteen pieces of flint, both flakes and artefacts, dating from the Neolithic and Bronze Age periods. This number strongly suggests the presence of a settlement in the area. The majority of the flints were recovered from the bottom of the ridge on the northern fringe of the Dowlais Brook flood plain. Although most of the flints were unstratified, they showed no sign of abrasion; it would therefore appear that, whilst they had been disturbed by ploughing, they are unlikely to have been transported very far by water or soil movement. The Dowlais Brook and Afon Lwyd river valley would have afforded fertile land for the early agricultural communities, while the ridge possibly provided a dry settlement site.[1] The following interesting finds also help considerably in building part of the picture of that early time:

ARROWHEAD FOUND ON THE MYNYDD MAEN IN 1926

Found by Mr. William Jones, of 3 Graig View, Upper Cwmbran. This arrow-head, the size and shape of a laurel leaf, was found in the hollow of the mountain, about 3ft below the surface, and beside a small stream. It is perfect in shape being about three-sixteenths of an inch thick at the centre and tapering away so finely at the edges as to be almost razor-like in sharpness. The unusual discovery was deposited at the Newport Museum. The Curator considered the arrow-head to have come from the Neolithic Age and was undoubtedly used as a missile.[2]

ANCIENT AXE HEAD FOUND IN CROESYCEILIOG

While digging a kidney-bean trench in his garden, Mr. Ken Stevens, of Steepfield, Croesyceiliog, unearthed a flat axe-head which, when later examined, was discovered to be probably well over 3,000 years old.

Mr. Stevens, who works at British Nylon Spinners, had reached a depth of about two feet when he found the axe-head.

It is believed that the axe is the first of its kind to be found in the Eastern Valley and the fact that it was found in sandy soil could mean that it originally lay in the bed of the Afon Lwyd, which ran some 200 yards from his garden.

The axe was taken to Newport Museum where it was deposited. The Deputy Director of the museum, said the find provided an important link in the establishing the evidence of movement of the people of the Neolithic Age up the valleys towards the Black Mountains. He added that it was probably used about 1800 B.C.[3]

LOOPED PALSTAVE FROM CWMBRAN

Looped palstave with central mid-rib have been acquired by Newport Museum in recent years…it was purchased in a sale of antiquities at Christies, London, during

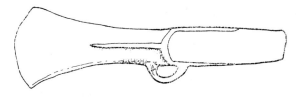

July, 1970, the provenance given being as "Cwmbran, Monmouthshire". Efforts to establish a more precise location failed, though it is known to have been sold by a local family. The previous owners had attempted to clean it, and patination only remains in such areas as recesses of the top ridges and under the loop and the whole appears to have been coated lightly with lacquer, the appearance being more coppery than is usual. The single rib is rounded and integral to the form of the blade and on one side of the blade is a small pitted hole, possibly a casting flaw. The loop is slightly askew and the narrow blade measures 5.0 cms. in width, the overall length being 17 cms and the maximum thickness 3.2 cms...a date of 1000-600 B.C., seems possible.[4]

A FLINT ARROWHEAD FROM TWM BARLWM

In 1980 Cefni Barnett wrote: 'I am indebted to Mr. David Williams, of the Holmesdale Archaeological Group, Reigate, not only for bringing to my attention a beautiful flint arrowhead in the possession of his aunt, Mrs G. Walters of Mount Pleasant, Pontnewynydd, but also for providing background information relating to the object and for the drawing of it.  Unfortunately the precise find spot of the arrowhead is not recorded. All that is known is that "it was found ten or so years ago in the Twmbarlwm, Llantarnam area by some boys", who gave it to the late Mr. H.F. Waters, then history master of Llantarnam School. In the circumstances, one might hazard a guess that it had been found on Mynydd Maen where items of worked flint have been discovered from time to time over a period of many years.

The arrowhead, of pale grey-brownish mottled flint, measures 42mm in length, with a maximum width across the shoulders of 20mm. Triangular in form, with slightly convex sides, it is skilfully worked and the point and sides are still sharp. The points of the barbs have been broken off and the square tang may have been truncated, but this is uncertain.[5]

THE FAIRWATER AXE

During some building work involving the construction of steps leading to a carpark at Fairwater Comprehensive School, Cwmbran, in 1974, a large partially polished stone axe-head was uncovered. This primitive tool made of felsite would have belonged to Neolithic man. It may have been lost when clearing the ancient forest or on a hunting expedition.[6]

St. Michael's Church, Llantarnam, 1899.

The Neolithic period lasted for around 2,000 years. By about 2500 B.C., the emergence of the Beaker people saw the introduction of copper technology. Their unusual title was introduced because they buried their dead with a distinctive bell beaker drinking vessel. Unfortunately there is no evidence of any settlement of the Beaker people or later Bronze Age settlers (around 1800 to 1400 B.C.) in Cwmbran.

However, we have the remains of an ancient Iron Age hill fort or tumulus at Twm Barlwm, which has looked out over our history for over 2,000 years, watching the successive changing generations of Celt, Saxon and Norman. Its very peculiar shape at the extremity of the long ridge of the Mynydd Maen excites curiosity. This swelling height is covered with coarse grass, moss and heath and is without a single tree. It is from this it is said to derive the name, *the hill with the summit barren or naked*. The summit is oval shaped and is crowned with a circular tumulus or artificial mound of earth and stones about eighteen yards in height and surrounded by a deep fosse or ditch. From its elevation of 1,374 feet above sea level it is in a commanding position and many spectacular views can be seen from its summit. On the right is the sight of billowy hill tops, piled one upon another; and on the left is the lovely valley of Cwmbran, backed by wooden heights and widening out beyond Caerleon and Newport into the broad level marshes, which melt into the Bristol Channel. On a fine day, far away over the gleaming water rise the shores of Somerset, with Clevedon conspicuous for the whiteness of its houses. A story of some kind or other always attaches to every part of the landscape. Twm Barlwm has its own, though a very imperfect one. None know the origin of its artificial tumulus. Some have suggested it to be a cairn marking the grave of a distinguished warrior. Others suppose the right name to be Twyn Barnol, and the place connected with the rites of the Druids, who were the priests and lawgivers in ancient Britain. It is also thought to have been a celebrated place for holding 'eisteddfodau' or bardic meetings. Around 1820, a party of navvies, it was said, endeavoured to cut into the tumulus in order to find out what lay beneath, but were obliged to desist by awful thunder and lightening that broke out every time they renewed their sacrilegious work. Due to its commanding view, it must have been used throughout the years as a lookout post. Possibly, a beacon was there waiting to be lit as a signal in the days of the first Queen Elizabeth, in readiness for the coming of the Spanish Armada. A beacon was certainly present at the Coronation of Edward VII, when it lit up the surrounding countryside and could be seen for miles.[7]

What of the occupants of this Iron Age fort? In all probability a group of Iron Age Celts arrived in the region and realised Twm Barlwm would be a good place to establish a permanent settlement. The surrounding district was fertile and held a plentiful supply of water. From a military aspect, the high position would have appeared ideal with a good view of the countryside available to give workers and farmers, on the lower slopes, plenty of time to reach the protection of the fort.

The hard work commenced to ensure that the settlement was well protected both from hostile neighbouring groups or wild animals in search of food. As a typical Iron Age fort earthen walls were built to enclose the site and the ramparts probably strengthened with boulders, small stones and timber. A stout timber fence called a palisade, and erected on top of the earthworks, gave added protection. Into this timber fence a large wooden gate would be strategically placed. This was always the weakest point in the defences and the ramparts were turned either inwards or outwards to form a long passage where any attacking force would have to fight every inch of the way. Finally, a ditch made access much more difficult.[8]

In some instances the Iron Age people lived inside their forts whilst others lived outside and only sought shelter in times of trouble. The Cwmbran Celts were members of the Silures, a southeast Wales tribe. Archaeologists have concluded that, for reasons unknown, Twm Barlwm hill fort was never finished.

A much smaller Iron Age fort found in Lower Llanfrechfa (Map reference: ST 330934 between Candwr Farm and Shaftsbury Farm) probably contained only a small number of families. The site is not much higher than the surrounding countryside and this type of fort archaeologists call a "homestead".

Another artificial mound of a later period may be seen inside Llantarnam Abbey Park, near the road, which runs from Croes-y-mwalch Farm to Caerleon. It is a round hill, like the motte of a Norman Castle, but much older, now covered with trees, shrubs and bracken, and in a line with the old hill fort at Lodge Farm, Caerleon.

The first farmers of Cwmbran made very little impression on the landscape of the area. Their small fields and herds of lean cattle barely scratched the surface of the countryside. During this period they had struggled for survival against the encroaching forest, against wild beasts and harsh weather, and it would not be long before a new enemy appeared.

The might of the all-conquering Roman Empire had descended upon Britain in AD 43 and by AD 48 Roman troops were attacking Welsh tribes. The Silures tribe in particular put up a stiff resistance to the Romans, probably carrying on guerrilla warfare from the safety of their hill forts. This resistance movement lasted for the best part of twenty-five years, but finally the Silures were defeated in about AD 75. Despite the strong Roman presence in Caerleon, they made very little impact on local life. The tribesmen made their way back to the hillfort settlement, and as long as they posed no military threat to the Imperial forces, they were left to carry on much as before. The following year the building of the great legionary fortress of Isca (Caerleon) began. The Romans had come to stay, and they remained for the next four hundred years.

There is no doubt the Romans explored the Cwmbran countryside looking for food, minerals and anything of value. Legend has it that they travelled through

Ponthir, down the hillside at the present Chapel Lane, Pontrhydyrun, and there divided to take a route to Upper Cwmbran and another over the Penyrheol mountain to Blaendare. At this time the district of Llantarnam must have been an extensive area of forest land with many marshes and swamps, and little use could have been made by them of the area. This appears to be borne out by the fact that no evidence of Roman coins, stones or pavements were ever found in the Cwmbran district. In keeping with other parts of Britain the Cwmbran tribe probably held fast to their own customs and beliefs.

The Romans left in the 5th century and occupation of hill forts had practically ceased by this time.

The following centuries are often referred to as the Dark Ages because little is known about the period. It is known that from the 5th to the 10th century there were isolated raids on Britain by Irish Celts and determined conquest by the Saxons.

During this period Caerleon must clearly have been the centre of activity in the Gwent area, and even with the advent of the Anglo-Saxon kingdoms, the Welsh managed to retain their country. At this time, in all probability, the Cwmbran area remained largely wild, uncultivated and under populated.

Although Christianity arrived in Britain with the Romans, it had largely been forgotten as the centuries past. However, it is known that by the 10th century a small Celtic cell existed at St Woolos, Newport. At Llantarnam it is very likely that there was a similar ancient cell on the site of St Michael's Church, long before the Abbey was built, and probably dedicated to one of the Welsh Saints. In 1956, Rev. John Donne pointed out to visitors where the remains of an earlier church were uncovered during restoration work some years earlier. It was Harold Brakespear, the architect at the church supervising work in 1924, who stated that these remains were the site of an early church. Unfortunately, the remains were buried again and covered with a thick layer of concrete as part of the planned improvements. Another indication of the site of the old Celtic cell is a large cross in the churchyard. The base is probably Saxon, but unfortunately the top was lost in the Reformation period and later replaced. It is also possible that Saxon walling forms part of the present nave.

By the end of the 10th century, it is now believed that the habitation of Llantarnam village had began with the establishment of the small Celtic church, which later grew into a Saxon church under the diocese of Llandaff. Originally an old Celtic saint, Arnam, lived here in his wattle church house or cell. It is believed that due to the nearness of Caerleon, afterwards the Celts and Saxons built a church on this old saint's site. The church, first named after St Arnam, who, with Saint Julian, was martyred at Caerleon in A.D. 303. Llan is the Welsh for church, so Llantarnam is explained as *The Church of Arnam*.[9]

It is important to remember that this was a church the people of Llantarnam built for themselves and in the beginning it grew up quite independent of the nearby Abbey, although they probably provided a priest. During the Norman period the small church was altered, but unfortunately there is little direct evidence of the work carried out except the crude walling of the nave. These walls were so thick as to make the church a place of defence as well as worship. Changes occurred in the thirteenth and fourteenth centuries, but the main reconstruction took place in the fifteenth century. At this time, the Cistercian monks at the nearby Abbey showed a genuine concern for this little church and took over (appropriated) the administration. Reconstruction involved altering the east end, building the tower, lighting the aisles with bigger windows and erecting the north chapel. A reference of 1535 names the church as *'The Chapel of St. Michael near the monastery'* suggesting that the church had recently received a new title.[10]

Throughout the years St. Michael's Church has revealed many interesting facts and features, the most intriguing would be the burial of the Morgan family who occupied Llantarnam Abbey after the Cistercian monks had left. An entry in a book by Archdeacon William Coxe (1747-1828), following his tour of Monmouthshire in 1798, would, as the years passed, puzzle many scholars. It reads:

> *'A chapel on the north fide of the church, is the cemetery of this branch of the Morgans; the bodies are interred in a vault, without any infcription to their memory.'*[11]

No one could throw any light on the Archdeacon's statement and many years passed before the mystery was solved.

Meanwhile, in 1802, six new bells cast by Thomas Mears at the great medieval foundry in London, replaced the old church bells. The entries in the surviving churchwardens accounts book tells of payment for the hire of a wagon to carry the old metal (old bells) as far as Bristol and return with the new bells. The cost of taking the old metal down and putting up the new bells amounted to 5 shillings.[12] These bells proved over a period of time to be too heavy and cumbersome in relation to the size of the tower. Their thrust against the structure was feared to be dangerous and sure enough, an extensive crack appeared down one side. Henceforth, except for the occasional ringing of one or two bells, the full peal of bells had not been rung since the First World War. However, this was rectified in 1973, when the tower was repaired and the bells re-cast, in a smaller size, at the Whitechapel Bell Factory.[13] Another entry in the churchwardens accounts book in 1835, lists the usual allowance of beer for bell ringers at Christmas.

It appears that whenever restoration work is carried out to this ancient church remarkable discoveries come to light. By 1869, the church presented a comfortless and neglected appearance. Traces of decay had become visible on its damp walls and the pews were heavy and old fashioned causing considerable discomfort to the congregation. This unhappy state of affairs brought about a parish meeting, which resulted in the formation of a committee to supervise the much-needed work of restoration. These gentlemen met with a ready response and with over £200 in hand, the work began. In no time the unsightly gallery over the western entrance had been moved and the choir was to occupy a place in the chancel. The new pews were of deal and provided comfortable open sittings. The clear staining effect of the arched roof of the nave and chancel corresponded with that of the pews and gave a light and pleasing effect. A decision to put a new window in the chancel caused brief excitement when during progression of the work a fine stone arch separating the nave from the chancel, and covered with whitewash, was exposed to view. With a new lighting arrangement enhancing the necessary work undertaken, re-opening services took place in September, 1869.[14]

The following year saw extensive work carried out to the adjoining annexe. This mortuary chapel, always referred to as the Morgan Chapel, is believed to have been added at the time when the Morgan family came into ownership of Llantarnam Abbey. A partition of lath and plaster, with cumbersome worm eaten doors, divided the chapel from the church. After removal of the doors, two fine flattened stone archways of ancient date were left to form an entrance. These are believed to have been brought from the Abbey at the time William Morgan purchased the estate. Around the chapel walls were found not only memorials to the Blewitt family, but also to the influential families of Kemys and Blount, but no evidence of internments. The mystery continued with no indication of the influence of the Morgan family to be found. Other ancient memorials came to light, but due to age and decay these proved not to be decipherable, although one gave the date 1591.[15]

The ravages of time caused even more thorough work to be completed in 1889. While this was in progress a very unexpected discovery was made. Steps to a rood-loft, the existence of which was unknown to any living resident in the village because no record had been left. They were concealed by the accumulation of many coatings of plaster and their presence long since buried in oblivion.

Work again taking place in 1921, produced an even more wonderful discovery. By this time the rural spot of Llantarnam had become a popular outer suburb. The church of St. Michael could be found standing back from the main highway and in what was regarded as a large graveyard. A row of tall elms formed a welcome shade from the fierce heat of the afternoon summer sun as workmen commenced their restoration work. A Newport builder by the name of William Davies received the contract for the work due to considerable experience in church restoration and he had recently carried out excellent work on St. Woolos Cathedral, Newport.

It was to some extent fortunate that this careful man remained vigilant when he scraped away some of the old plaster covering the interior of the nave walls. Many coatings of lime and colour wash were removed before an extraordinary discovery became visible. What began to take place before his astonished eyes were a number of mural paintings on the nave walls and in their original medieval colourings of dark red and brown paint.

When hearing of the discovery, Mr. Kyle-Fletcher, a Monmouthshire historian and representative of the *South Wales Argus*, immediately visited the church. Upon arrival, Rev. John Donne at once took him along to the nave and indicated to the wall on the left side where a portion of the stonework had been cleaned. Fletcher found that the wall had been cleaned down in places, but enough was revealed to give an excellent impression, which consisted of figures painted in curious long strokes. The largest section uncovered showed a figure, presumed by him to be a lady, in wide flowing robes and wearing a beaver hat, not unlike the popular Welsh hat once worn by the people of Wales. Further along the same wall, a smaller figure had been uncovered, which looked like a priest in robes.

Realising the importance of the discovery, the vicar immediately informed Archbishop Green and the well-known architect Harold Breakspear. Under their supervision the whole of the work in the nave was uncovered to reveal a magnificent set of medieval wall paintings probably completed by the Cistercian monks from the nearby Abbey.

The north wall revealed a picture of Our Lady enthroned with a boy server in robes attending and a priest in medieval costume. The south wall showed paintings of the saints, John the Baptist and Elijah in the Wilderness, while over the chancel arch were large figures of floating angels. This was thought by some to be the great picture of doom, which was generally placed in the parish church and showed the resurrection of the dead, with the last judgement, and angels carrying off souls into heaven while demons dragging others into hell. Several parishioners who witnessed these scenes later stated that the murals were painted in gorgeous blue, gold and red.

This was the bible of the people who could not read or write and was forever before their eyes as an eternal lesson. Unfortunately for the discovered paintings, after exposure to air, they gradually deteriorated and within several weeks they had crumbled away and no drawings or photographs remain to give an impression of what the nave really looked like.[16]

It was not until 1956, that the public received further information regarding the interesting, if not sombre, Morgan chapel. A group of children from the nearby Llantarnam Secondary Modern School approached Rev. Donne and requested his assistance in recording the district's past. Not for many years had the chapel doors been opened and the interior revealed everything very much as it was in 1869. However, a mystery which had puzzled local people for generations was solved when the keen-eyed scholars spotted a small hole in the chapel floor. About eighteen inches square, it was mostly covered by stone slabs. Once through the hole, and descending down seven steps, it was quickly realised that the mortuary chapel was below ground level. In earlier times there must have been a grander entrance. A report soon followed:

> '*Here there are several bricked up chambers containing coffins of the great families of Llantarnam, some of these three to four hundred years old. Parts of the brick wall have fallen exposing the coffins to view and these must have been magnificent when new. The bricks themselves are interesting, for this period, being probably made locally.*
>
> *Each coffin takes the form of a heavy lead sheet inside a wooden outer case. The wood is decayed and rotten, but we could see the remains of metal studs and carrying handles. On one there appeared to be an outer layer of leather. This had apparently covered the whole of the woodwork and fastened to it by metal studs. All the lead cases are intact and we could see four of them behind the brickworks beyond.*
>
> *Here indeed was the dead history of bygone Llantarnam before our eyes; here were the great families of our village, who had lived in the old abbey or perhaps Pentre Bach, priests, soldiers and laymen lying within a few feet of us.*
>
> '*One day when the chapel floor is repaired, the whole of this unique vault will be exposed and can be examined properly.*'[17]

It is possible that this beautiful ancient church has more hidden secrets.

REFERENCES

1. Glamorgan-Gwent Archaeological Trust Ltd, Excavations at Llantarnam Village Gwent, 1993.
2. *The Free Press of Monmouthshire,* June 11, 1926.
3. Ken Stevens, Monmouth; *The Free Press of Monmouthshire,* June 16, 1960.
4. *The Monmouthshire Antiquary* - Volume IV, (1980).
5. *The Monmouthshire Antiquary* - Volume IV, (1980).
6. C.B.A. Group 2 - *Archaeology in Wales xiv* (1974) pp.5,16.
7. Green, W.H., *Pontypool Free Press and Herald of the Hills,* June 12, 1869; Dovey, F & Waters, H.F., *Llantarnam,* 1956, pp.7-8.
8. *The Early Farmers of Cwmbran,* A Manpower Services Commission Programme Scheme.

9. Donne, Rev. John, *Western Mail,* April 1937; *Free Press of Monmouthshire,* February 1940.

10. Guy, John R. and Smith, Ewart B., *Ancient Gwent Churches.* The Starling Press Ltd, 1980.

11. Coxe, William, *Historical Tour of Monmouthshire,* 1801, p.116.

12. Gwent Record Office, D/Pa 99.59, St. Michael's Church Wardens Account Book, 1788-1888.

13. *Free Press of Monmouthshire,* July 6, 1973.

14. *Pontypool Free Press and Herald of the Hills,* September 18, 1869.

15. Lloyd, W.G., *Tales of Torfaen,* 2000, p.10.

16. *South Wales Argus ,* 1921.

17. Dovey F., and Waters, H.F., *Llantarnam.* 1956, pp.48-49.

Chapter Two

HENLLYS

Henllys possibly obtained its name, meaning 'Old Court', from the existence of an ancient Welsh chieftain who held court in the locality. The parish and village are some four miles from Newport, about two mile wide, and four miles long. It extends in a north-westerly direction from the parish of Bettws, across Mynydd Twm Barlwm to Cwmcarn dingle, where it joins the Mynyddyslwyn parish. The south-west is bounded by the parishes of Bassaleg and Risca, and the north-east by the parish of Llantarnam. The scattered hamlet lies around an old track or ancient way, which is a picturesque lane to Twm Barlwm.[1]

It is believed that over a thousand years ago Benedictine monks came to Henllys and erected a wooden cross for one of them to preach at the site every few weeks. The two streams flowing nearby no doubt would have filled the baptismal needs. In time, the wooden cross deteriorated and had to be replaced with something more substantial. A stone Celtic cross mounted on a large base, with four steps leading to it, appears to have become the fashion for the time. When the monk climbed the steps of this new design to preach, not only could the people gathered around see the orator, but it also became possible for him to be heard more clearly. The remains of the ancient base can still be seen today with just the bottom of the cross surviving. However, these open-air services could not have been comfortable to attend during winter, especially in such a mountainous parish.

In all probability a decision to make a church of mud and wattle, or timber, was welcomed by the congregation, even if built with such primitive materials. Not built to survive, no evidence of this early Henllys church remains, although it is strongly believed to have stood where St. Peter's sanctuary and chancel are found today. As was the custom, a village would have grown around the church.

It is difficult to fix even an approximate date of the foundation of the present stone structure of St. Peter's Church. For Henllys, the founding of a Benedictine Priory at Bassaleg in 1116 was of paramount importance. From this date onwards, Henllys enjoyed a close and friendly association with the neighbouring parish. The first mention of a church building on the present site is 1230-40. It is probable that the monks were gone by 1235. Henllys is again mentioned in 1254 and 1291 as belonging to the Rectory of the Church of Bassaleg.[2]

Farming had been the only way of life for the people of the parish of Henllys for many centuries. Between four and five hundred years ago more substantial

St. Peter's Church, Henllys, 1899.

dwellings, which came to be known as Welsh long-houses, began to appear in the district and gave some indication of the wealthier landowners. In some, the oak beams can still be seen today. Adjoining the living quarters was often a barn for storage, which connected to a shed used to shelter animals. This simple arrangement made it easy for the farmer to tend his animals. Usually at the back of the house was found a meat room, well supplied with iron hooks hanging from the roof timbers. Here, the proverbial pig would meet its end on the bacon and ham stone, while blood and juices were collected from a groove running along the edge. Conveniently, a connecting door lead to a cooling room and butter room. Henllys Court Farm appears to have had an additional function. As its title suggests, this farm was used many years ago as the court of the manor where disputes over boundaries were settled and thieves were dealt with accordingly. Not too long ago, when a previous tenant made some alterations to the dwelling, he found a room with iron bars at the window. This was believed to be the room where wrongdoers were kept until their crimes were dealt with.

Another significant building of great historical importance is found along Pentre Lane in the vale of Henllys. Pentre Bach, an old manor house, which later became a farmhouse, was formerly a grange of Llantarnam Abbey and known at the time as Cefn-y-Mynach, the monk's ridge. Early accounts of the possessions of Llantarnam Abbey refer to this and when William Morgan purchased the estate in 1554, he made many additions, which probably gave rise to the name Pentre Bach, or 'Little Village.'

It is divided into two distinctive parts, the older portion, which dates from monastic times, and the later 16th century great hall. This added 16th century building had a passage running from the front to the back porch and garden. Later, an oak screen separated the kitchen from the great hall, which in turn became smaller rooms. The masonry of the original building is of stone, while the newer portion is brick being nearly double the height.

The great hall is fifty feet long and twenty feet high, but narrow for its length. At one time it had a splendid ceiling. With tapestries and paintings on the walls, it became the venue of dinners and balls. Above the fireplace in the hall was once a stone, which evidently had been part of a Roman sepulchral, with an inscription to the memory of Vindutus, a soldier of the Second Augustan Legion, aged 45 years. In all probability a haulier visiting Caerleon wharf observed the stone slab and thought of a good use for recycling the material.

This ancient dwelling became a dower-house or supplementary dwelling for the Morgan family members and when the family died out the property came under the Brays, the Blewitts and the Dowlings in succession.[3] In recent times the worn-out hall took on the purpose of a barn and other farm uses.

Life in the parish carried on in many ways unchanged. Fields were ploughed, crops planted and harvested, lambing and calving, shearing, milking, slaughtering, all went on as they had always done. The Census Returns of the 19th century shows the presence of a mill near St. Peter's Church, which indicates a good crop of wheat each year. In recent years, two grinding stones with the remains of the old mill were located to bear witness to this previous exertion. Newport, Pontypool and sometimes Abergavenny markets were visited on an appointed day during each week. After various business transactions, farmers brought county or national news back to the parish. Special events such as the reading of a Royal proclamation would urge whole families to visit Newport for news of their next Sovereign.

In the parish, the hounds would often be out, ploughing matches and sheepdog trials were regular events, with the Henllys Show attracted large crowds. Winter evenings were enjoyed supporting various philanthropic societies held in the popular beerhouses. These societies raised funds for a number of good causes and also had built locally some badly needed dwellings known as the Philanthropic Houses.

For many years the parish of Henllys had been administered as part of the Newport Rural District. This was to change in 1894 when a confirming Order of the Local Government Board divided the Newport Rural District. Henllys parish, united with Bettws parish, became part of St. Mellon's Rural District Council. A later administrative change would give the title Magor and St. Mellon's Rural District Council. Twenty-one parishes made up this new rural district council each with its appointed councillor. The first rural district councillor for the

Henllys Court Farm

Duffryn Farm, Henllys - a typical Welsh Longhouse

Henllys and Bettws was Mr. Francis Cherrett, of Duffryn Farm, Henllys, but he did not remain in post for very long. By the summer of 1897, he had been adjudicated bankrupt and a legal ruling prevented him from continuing his service to the rural council. Unfortunately for Francis Cherrett, the details of his downfall were posted on the church doors of Henllys and Bettws, and other relevant buildings.[4]

This new administrative arrangement made little difference to the annual parish meeting, which had taken place for many years. In 1897, the seven elected parish councillors were: A. Knapp, publican; R. Mauk, collier; M. Williams, colliery overman; G. Giles, grocer; J.J. Hailstone, colliery machineman; E.G. Edwards, schoolmaster and J. Harris, farmer. Through their good work roads and footpaths were made safe. They campaigned resolutely until greater postal services came into use and the presence of a policeman in the parish reassured many.[5]

Records show that the Baptist cause had not been neglected in the Henllys parish. There had been occasional non-conformist preaching before 1872, but the erection of Bethesda Chapel, Tydu, brought the district under the auspices of the Baptist cause. As there was much enmity shown towards the Baptists, the houses in which members lived were licensed for holding religious services: Henllys Court, the house of James Samuel, whose wife was a member; Glansawel, the house of John Williams, who was for many years a faithful deacon of the church; and the house of Samuel Jones - he also was a deacon and his wife a faithful member. Though services were held in these houses amidst great inconveniences, yet the labour was not in vain. Mr. Thomas Jenkins, an ordained assistant minister at Bethesda since 1818, came to Henllys to live and was a great help to the early cause. A dwelling house was fitted up in 1822, it was called Castell y Bwch. Divine worship carried on here for fourteen years until a church named Zoar was erected in Henllys during 1836, where many were to be immediately baptized.

Still under the auspices of the mother-church at Tydu, by 1838, the Zoar members appeared to be at low ebb and began to be inclined to form a separate church. The mother-church eventually accorded their wishes and on Tuesday evening, February 27, 1844, the formation of the new church took place. 62 members affiliated to Bethesda Chapel, and from the Henllys parish, were dismissed to make up the congregation of the new church. During the same year the Zoar Church became free of all financial debt. The first minister was Mr. Daniel Jones, who came from Llanthewy around 1844 and left for Caerphilly in 1847. Mr. J. Jarman took charge of the church in 1852 with a membership of about forty and twenty-eight scholars. He left in 1855. Somehow the little church did not grow. The members in 1882 were twenty-eight, and fifty young people attended the Sunday school. However, an anniversary of the church in 1867 gives witness that despite its low membership, a happy atmosphere prevailed:

The anniversary in connection with the Zoar Sunday School took place on Sunday last, when Rev. William Jenkins, Risca, preached a very appropriate sermon in the morning. In the afternoon, Mr. Jenkins having taken the chair, the children recited their different pieces in a comfortable manner. The singing of the choir was very effective, the solo by Miss Cocker being very much admired. In the evening Mr. Jenkins preached to a crowded congregation. On Tuesday a general tea party took place; a number of tickets having been sold, the proceeds of which were devoted towards liquidating incidental expenses in connection with the church, and the occasion was availed of to give a treat to the Sunday School children. Sports followed, which were taken up by the children with great spirit, while visitors from the surrounding neighbourhood partook of the cup that cheers. Mr. Joshua, confectioner, Newport, supplied the cake. Upwards of 300 took tea, after which the whole assembled in a large open court adjoining the chapel, where the children again recited, and eighteen of the scholars executed a piece called "Joseph and his brethren," which was well received. After the singing of the "Old Hundred," the meeting, which will be long remembered in the neighbourhood, broke up.' [6]

In the summer of 1902, a complete renovation was badly needed. Following the work a large number attended the re-opening service and the excellent collections went towards the builder's fee.

The Zoar Baptist Church, sometimes few in numbers due to the sparsely populated parish, continued its good work until it reached its centenary year in 1936. A letter saved for posterity gives an insight into that memorable time and states:

'We had a very happy and inspiring time at the Zoar Baptist Church centenary services. Favourable weather contributed to our success, we had big crowds and a fine spirit all through.' [7]

After many years of good work the old church finally closed its doors in recent times while leaving its burial ground to bear witness to the lives of many of the respected inhabitants of the Henllys district.

Except for the coming of the Monmouthshire Canal, the way of life in this pleasant rural parish had remained uninterrupted for centuries. This was to change dramatically by the mid 19th century due to the arrival of one, Joshua Flesher Hanson.

The parents of Joshua Flesher Hanson were married in Leeds on June 26, 1777 and Joshua was born in London on February 5, 1782. He would always be known as a gentleman and entrepreneur. His career was well underway when at 36 years

Zoar Baptist Church, Henllys

of age he bought land in Brighton before dividing it into seventy plots. In 1818, these were leased out to develop the imposing Regency Square, found at the waterfront. This venture greatly added to his already substantial business capital. He married Nancy in 1820 and the happy union produced seven children.

In 1825, Joshua, of Notting Hill House, Middlesex, bought a farm house and land with mineral rights in Backwell, Somerset, for £8,985. Always on the move, he arrived in the Torfaen area in 1831, and subsequently purchased Blaengavog Farm, Trevethin, as an investment before renting out the property. Not long after arriving in the area he must have become aware of the minerals in the ground on the side of Henllys mountain and no doubt was not slow in discovering who owned the land. By the end of December 1834, Joshua had leased several plots of land in Henllys parish from Charles Morgan, Tredegar, and Charles M.R. Morgan, Ruperra. A plot on the side of the mountain measured 27 acres and 15 perch, and the 99 years lease amounted to a fee of £13 per year, plus, for each ton of coal produced and carried through the Morgans' land, an extra farthing was to be paid.[8] Joshua is named in the 1841 Tithe apportionment as living in a cottage and gardens at Penheol y Badde Fach, near a lime kiln, and at the top of the future tramroad incline. The 1841 Electoral List and Census Return shows Joshua owning property at Gelly Wastod, Machen, and his daughter Theodosia (20 years), and Mary Hanson (60 years), residing at the property while his son Cyrus (20 years), continued to look after his business interests at the Backwell Estate, Somerset.

Fully aware of the problem of transporting the harvested coal down the steep mountainside, to the Monmouthshire Canal near Two Locks, for further transport to the wharves at Newport, where it would be sold or shipped abroad, he asked the canal company to build him a tramroad. They declined, but he had followed the correct procedure and the law at that time allowed him to construct his own tramroad. He lost no time in buying or leasing land on the incline, both in the parishes of Henllys and Llantarnam. Raising a mortgage on the Backwell Estate helped considerably. In 1842, the tramroad, always to be known as Hanson's Incline, was completed and supplemented by a Coal Works and wharves alongside the canal, just below Two Locks.

On the mountainside an industry known as a level mine was soon in full production and to be known at first as Penheol y Badde Colliery. This type of mine came about by the colliers cutting into the mountain in a diagonal line. Although hard and dangerous work, many farm labourers changed their traditional occupations to earn more lucrative wages. Some Henllys farmers also combined their farming tasks with that of being a collier. At the coalface, trams were filled with coal for the younger members of the workforce to steadily guide them along the mine tunnel to the outside. Here, the coal would be sorted and the quality coal taken down the incline. The worthless material was placed on the nearby slag tip, which can still be seen today. Above the mine a shaft was dug and connected to the mine tunnel. Used mainly for ventilation purposes, some coal was removed by hauling it up with the use of a horse and pulley system.

The Hansons were never slow in making full use of their acquisitions. Limestone was dug out and washed in water before being heated in a nearby kiln and crushed into fine powder. This brought forth good revenue when sold for mortar, whitewash and fertilizer. A stone quarry above the coal mine also produced building material used for boundary walls and many of the new buildings in the Henllys and Cwmbran districts.

In the 1843 Electoral List, Joshua was found to be living in the picturesque Glan-y-Nant farmhouse, Llantarnam. Still present near the canal and it is just above where the coal distributing works existed.

Probably by March 13, 1847, he realizes that his health was beginning to fail, which urged him to produce an addition to his will. Extra to leaving his wife and Mary Jeudivine (daughter) well provided for, he gave notice that his other surviving children, Alfred, Theodosia, Cyrus and Stephen should receive the substantial sum of £2,500 each.

His premonition sadly proved correct. Always obliged to attend to his business commitments, he sailed to Jersey aboard the *Lady de Saumarez* on Wednesday,

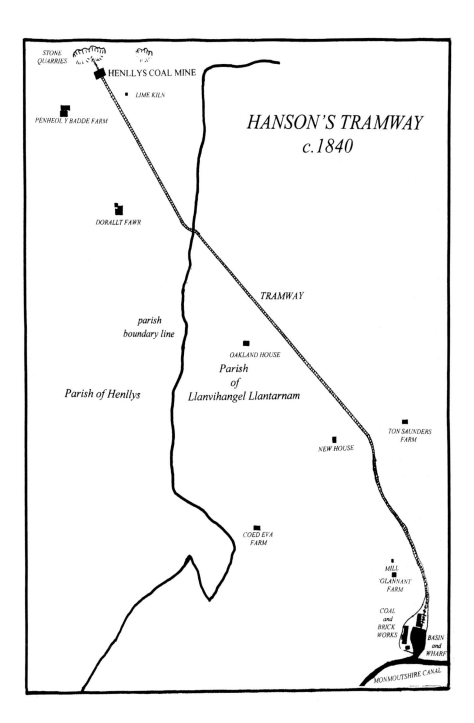

STONE QUARRIES

HENLLYS COAL MINE

LIME KILN

PENHEOL Y BADDE FARM

HANSON'S TRAMWAY
c.1840

DORALLT FAWR

TRAMWAY

parish
boundary line

OAKLAND HOUSE

Parish
of
Llanvihangel Llantarnam

Parish of Henllys

TON SAUNDERS
FARM

NEW HOUSE

COED EVA
FARM

MILL
'GLANNANT
FARM

COAL
and
BRICK
WORKS

BASIN
and
WHARF

MONMOUTHSIRE CANAL

April 7, 1847. He reserved a room at a hotel and intended to return to Southampton the next day. He dined about three o'clock, left the hotel for his business meeting and returned about six. Around half past six, the other guests at the hotel were alarmed to find him stretched across the upstairs passage. A doctor was immediately sent for, but life was extinct when he arrived. At the inquest the jury returned a verdict of 'Died by a visitation of God'[9] This unusual cause was subsequently entered on his death certificate.

At the time of his death Joshua Flesher Hanson owned a large mansion in Kensinton, London. His wife Nancy died a year later somewhere in Llantarnam, probably at Glany y Nant farmhouse. Both were buried at the modern cemetery of Kensal Green, West London.

Cyrus Hanson, born Peckham, London, in 1821, immediately took over the management of his father's business affairs. At first his main concern was sorting out the many holdings in readiness to sell off for the division among the family.

The 1851 Census Return indicates that Cyrus, then 31 years of age and unmarried, had also found good quality fireclay on his father's estate and was living at Brick Place, Llantarnam. The property was also known as Henllys Brick Works and had conveniently been erected alongside his father's coal sorting works, on the side of the Monmouthshire Canal.

Cyrus set about developing the superior quality fireclay found in abundance on his land and soon the firebricks, marked 'Hanson' or 'Henllys', and gas retorts, gained a high reputation in the district, while securing very remunerative prices. It was not long before the good name of Hanson bricks became well known all over South Wales and the West of England.

Further expansion of the Henllys Brick Works resulted in the erection of three large and substantial drying stoves, with a powerful engine and three boilers. Two large mills appeared for grinding the stone and clay. These were fitted with four iron crushers of about eight tons each. When fully operational, the new works was capable of producing 10,000 bricks per day.[10]

Over the next twenty years Cyrus prospered as a coal proprietor and firebrick and retort manufacturer. The 1871 Census Return lists him as 52 years of age and still unmarried. At this time he had twenty men and five boys in his employment, and, after purchasing land in the Henllys parish, he set about building houses to accommodate his workforce.

Unlike his father, Cyrus was not a entrepreneur and gave all his energy to the Henllys industries. By the early eighteen seventies his thoughts were turning towards retiring and enjoying the financial rewards brought about by his management skills. On May 1st, 1873, he married Mary Hare, a forty-three year old spinster and farmer's daughter, at Hastings, Sussex. The following year, and while sojourning in Germany, he made his last will and testament. It is unknown if Cyrus and his wife moved to Germany or enjoyed regular excursions to a beautiful part of the country, however, on November 21, 1877, he died at Obergape, Biebrich am Rhien. Today, people are reminded of the legacy of this remarkable family by the well-known presence of the Hanson Incline.

It was not easy for those living at the northern end of the parish, particularly the children, who had to walk a considerable distance in all weathers to have their religious needs met. To ease this difficult situation, friends from Henllys, about the year 1860, opened a Branch Sunday School in Penheol-y-badd. Friends also rendered some help from Siloam, Cwmbran and other chapels. For some years, the school flourished, but owing to the instability of trade and the removal of families from the place, the school became almost extinct. At this time, Mr. E. Edmunds, a deacon from Siloam, and one Mr. J. Griffiths, a non-member, chiefly held it up.

Due to new houses being built in the immediate area, and mainly for the colliers, about 1874, the school revived, and it numbered around sixty persons. However, the room had become too small, and it was moved to build a new chapel. The chapels of Zoar, Siloam and friends in the place were concerned in this. Failing to agree about the nature of the deed, Zoar withdrew entirely, and the matter was left in the hands of the chapel at Siloam, and its Pastor, Mr. T. Cocker.

At the Association meeting held at Beaufort in May 1876, a resolution was adopted which said: "That we encourage the brethren at Cwmbran in their effort to open a station for occasional preaching and Sunday School at Penheol-y-badd."

A site was secured for building a school-chapel under a lease of 99 years at 1d a year. In case, however, the house being turned to other than religious service, the annual rent was to be 10/-. Although the site was just over the parish boundary line, and in the parish of Llantarnam, it was, in the main, to serve the influx of workers at the northern end of Henllys parish. The new chapel was opened at Christmas 1876 and called Mount Pleasant. It sat 150 and cost £220. For many years to follow there were regular services held on Sundays, and the care in the early days fell chiefly upon Rev. T. Cocker, the later minister at Pontnewydd.[11]

The known population of the parish until the twentieth century:

Year	Population	Dwellings
1801	188	
1811	182	
1821	209	
1831	207	
1841	245	52 dwellings
1851	265	
1861	238	
1871	202	
1881	304	
1891	392	72 dwellings

Joshua Flesher Hanson 1782-1847.

Former Henllys Brickworks.

By the late eighteen-sixties, it had become obvious that vital structural repairs to the parish church of St. Peter were urgently required, although the actual work carried out has not been recorded. Fund-raising activities were soon well under way and witnessed by a picnic held at Henllys Church Farm on a Tuesday in September, 1870. A large number of people partook of the tea with many coming from outside the parish. Everything passed off admirably and all appeared to enjoy the organised entertainment. Everyone dug deep into their pockets and the profits arising from the proceedings swelled the restoration fund. A special harvest thanksgiving service followed in the evening. To suit better the convenience of the farmers and working classes, the service was fixed for 7 o'clock p.m., which, with the propitious weather continuing, caused a large assembly of worshippers, who heartily joined in the singing.[12] The final bill for the finished work was £160.

It seemed a natural decision in 1877, for the adjoining ecclesiastical parishes of St. Peter, Henllys, and St. David, Bettws, to become a single living. Henceforth, and after many centuries, Bassaleg clergy were no longer required to regularly officiate at divine service in Henllys.[13] St. Peter's Church now had its own incumbent and due to this administrative change, Godfrey Morgan, (Lord Tredegar), the brave and fortunate survivor of the legendary charge of the Light Brigade, kindly donated two acres of farm land for the building of a Rectory.

At intervals it is recorded that the children of Henllys had received some education. From as early as 1742, one of Rev. Griffith Jones's circulating schools was held periodically in the scattered community. Free lessons, given in Welsh and limited to reading and learning the Catechism, did little to improve the illiteracy among the poorer children. Another church school is recorded as present in the parish in 1818, but no details are available. The Census Return of 1841 also lists a schoolmistress living in the district and ten years later a schoolmaster is recorded as occupying a schoolroom near Henllys Church. These unsatisfactory attempts to give a full education were to change dramatically.

Early in 1878, the Rogerstone and Henllys School Board had, quite responsibly, decided that the time was right to build a school on a site in Henllys. The advertisement placed in the Monmouthshire newspapers for builders to supply a tender for the building of a school met with a good response. Messrs William Jones and Son, builders, Newport, received the contract and commenced work from the design of Mr. E.A. Lansdowne, architect. Throughout 1878, a buzz of excitement prevailed in the parish, as workmen appeared to have more than their usual purpose for erecting a modern building. The walls were built of sandstone, quarried from the nearby mountainside, and freestone sparingly used in the heads of windows and bell cote. This added to the pleasing effect as it contrasted favourable with warm grey sandstone when the building took shape.

*Mount Pleasant
Baptist Church
built in 1876.*

*Sunday School children
singing at the
anniversary service
of
Mount Pleasant Baptist
Church.*

Ample accommodation was provided for boys, girls and infants as witnessed by all the necessary classrooms and offices for each department. The timber inside was of pitch pine, and the wrought portions stained and varnished. A well-planned master's house joined the school. This contained a living room, kitchen, scullery, three bedrooms, offices and stores. Owing to the site being 800 feet above level of the sea, the views from the house windows, which all faced east and south, were most panoramic. This was supplemented by a good garden alongside the master's house. In those far off days, these were indeed grand living conditions.

Advertising posters gave notice of the impending opening of the well-built and substantial school. On Thursday, October 31st, 1878, a tea meeting heralded the special event. At three o'clock p.m., the schoolchildren of the parish received a free tea while parents and other visitors were charged one shilling. A further effort to raise badly needed money for the school was witnessed by a public meeting later in the day when speeches were made and some very good singing was gone through by various artists and children.[14]

On the morning of November 4, 1878, John Ablart, Certified Schoolmaster, admitted fifty-five scholars to the school. At first Mrs Ablart would be his only assistant and was paid to teach sewing to the girls. It was not easy for the young schoolmaster in the untried school. At first conditions were basic with pupils sitting on log bench type seats. Lessons began with the learning of the 3 R's and scripture. School fees became an immediate problem. Infants and children in Standards I and II were to pay two pence per week and the children in Standards IV, V, and VI, three pence per week. Parents with large families quite rightly complained. The School Board responded quickly and reduced the fees for these large families accordingly. In the early days poor attendance became very evident. In January 1879, few attended due to the great depth of snow found to be as high as the tops of the hedges throughout the parish. Later, in the same month, an accident occurred on Hanson's Incline, by which means several loaded trucks were upset. The children were absent making themselves busy in picking up the coal.

In spite of all the teething problems, in 1880, the first report of the new school proved favourable:

"Summary of Her Majesty's Inspector's Report"

'The infants are backward at present. They should receive object lessons and be taught four separate songs and there should be a greater show of infant's sewing according to the Schedule of the Code...Notwithstanding that this is a new school, the results, as far as they go, are creditable and the discipline is excellent.' [15]

For just over ten years John Ablart carried out his duties as headmaster with remarkable resolve, but his dedication came to a sudden end at the young age of thirty-four years. An ulcer of the stomach became malignant and he died at the schoolhouse on January 28, 1889.[16] His untimely death shocked everyone.

Evan Griffith Edwards, 2nd Class Certified Schoolmaster, took charge of the school on the morning of March 25, 1889, and remained as headmaster for thirty-four years. Assisted by all of his family throughout the years, the contribution of this man to the school, and parish, was remarkable. A much loved and esteemed man, he died aged 63 years, on August 26, 1934, during the school summer holidays. He and his wife were buried at St. Peter's Church. Throughout the years there would be many dedicated staff fondly remembered by the scholars.

St. Peter's Church continued its good work into the twentieth century despite the lack of financial funds and costs rising all the time. A description of the church in 1901 contained the following information:

'The church is built of local stone and contains 130 sittings. There is nothing to relieve the bareness of its construction. In common with many churches of early foundation the walls of the nave have an outward bend, a distinction here which is particularly noticeable. The interior is covered with the ugly yellow wash reminiscent of the times of the Reformation, and the entrance of the south porch is low and narrow, in keeping with the ancient and rude workmanship of which the edifice is a singular example.

None of the windows are stained. They all lack any of the grace and beauty introduced in after years. Especially striking is the windows within the altar rails on the south side, the ledge which is nearly on the floor. Within the Chancel and all down the aisle are memorial stones, most of them dating back nearly two hundred years. On the walls too, are many tablets, bearing the names and virtues of those long since passed away in quaintly worded phraseology. A long tombstone in the middle of the Chancel records the interment of several members of a branch of the Morgan family, the first dated so long ago as 1669 and inscribed to the memory of David Morgan.

'Among the monuments on the north wall of the nave is one in memory of Adam Thomas, of Lantiliocrossenny, dated 1729, and bearing a peculiar doggerel.

'On the south wall of the nave is a notice headed "Donations to the poor," setting forth that David Williams, Yeoman of the parish of Henllys, left by his will, dated 30th December, 1809, one hundred pounds, the interest of which to be divided annually among the poor of the said parish.

'The embattled western tower has a small pinnacle in the corner. There are three bells, but only one is now in use, the others have long since fallen into decay. The living is a rectory, with the vicarage of Bettws, in the gift of the Bishop of Llandaff.'[17]

The thinly populated parish continued through the twentieth century with its inhabitants showing great interest in the happenings of the times. In 1907, a great excitement, reminiscent of the Klondyke, prevailed everywhere in the parish with the news that gold had been discovered at Henllys. The prospector, having had considerable success finding the precious metal at Tintern, used the same method on similar strata at Pandy Farm, Henllys. His report gave good reason to believe that the valuable metal was in sufficient quantity to render work very profitable. Alas, no further information is available today regarding the startling revelation.[18]

In 1910, another event would excite Henllys folk both young and old alike. All experienced a unique moment in time when eyes were turned upwards to the night sky. To them the journey of Haley's Comet, with its tail, a luminous column extending upwards, seemed a mystical happening; while young lovers took the opportunity to watch the passing from the mountainside of Twm Barlwm. For some, it would be a great sadness when the comet eventually disappeared.

By the late nineteen fifties time had agreeably stood still for many of the residents in the ancient parish of Henllys. Its colliery had closed down in 1927, and just over the boundary line, the Henllys Brickworks, commenced by Cyrus Hanson over a century previously, had also shut its doors. In later years, most of the young people had no difficulty finding employment in the modern industries outside the parish where good wages could be earned. The gentle pace of the local folk is indicated in 1967, when some concern occurred while observing that the old Hanson tramway had become almost impassable. The mile-and-half of dead straight track down the incline, which once carried coal trams from the mountainside colliery to the Henllys coal works, had served as a walkway for many years for Henllys folk when visiting Cwmbran. It had been a long time since the narrow gauge metal track had been taken up, but the old tramway still served a useful purpose and forward looking councillors also began to realise the historical importance of the site. Soon, it was announced that the tramway must stay as an amenity and a through pedestrian route. A far greater upset was about to inflicted on the unsuspecting villagers in 1975. The planners of Cwmbran New Town had almost reached the end of their mammoth building project when they realised that around 500 acres of land was required at Henllys. This land would be used for sufficient housing to raise the population to their target of 55,000 residents. Fearful that the development would destroy the narrow green belt between Cwmbran and Newport, individuals and well-organised residents' associations protested vigorously, but to no avail. Fortunately, not too much damage was done to the countryside.

In 1978, Henllys Primary School held its centenary celebrations. The celebrations began with a service in the school conducted by the Vicar of Henllys and Bettws, and that was followed later in the week by a concert in the village hall. On a Wednesday occurred a party when each child was presented with a centenary plate, which featured an engraving of the school in the centre. This was followed on Thursday and Friday by an exhibition at the school of photographs showing how it had changed over the years and the development of the village. Among the Victorian memorabilia on show was a photocopy of the 1878 handbill advertising the opening of the school, then called Henllis Board School.[19]

In the meantime, an extensive programme of church restoration had been completed by the late 1970's. Within the walls of St. Peter's chancel, decaying plaster had become very evident and caused concern among church members. Unknown to all concerned these walls contained medieval paintings, in all probability similar to those at St. Michael's Church, Llantarnam, and with the removal of the decaying plaster, these were lost forever. However, several strokes of reddish-brown paintwork can still be seen near the chancel window. At the same time, a series of congregational ballots and decisions taken at Diocesan level, brought about the decision that St. Peter's Church, Henllys would become separate from Bettws and constitute a part of the district of Fairwater, within the Rectorial Benefice of Cwmbran.[20]

Many generations of Henllys folk received a good early education in their village school before its doors were finally closed. On April 15, 1991, the beginning of the final term of the school, pupils on the roll numbered nineteen. Early in July an Open Day and Exhibition was held to remember all the good work carried out at the school in Victorian times and until the present day. The Chairman of the Governors presented commemorative hand-made plates, made at the Rhymney pottery, to pupils and six of the staff during the day.

The last and much loved headmaster of this esteemed school picked up his pen and wrote for the final time in the school log book:

> '24th July, 1991 - This is the last day of Henllys Junior and Infant's School. My family of pupils are not at school today. The noises are of adult voices, footsteps and the clatter of packing as willing helpers set about the task of preparing for the removal men.
>
> 'I now make my way to County Hall to deposit this and other records. Henllys School has played its part in history. In my retirement I will follow the development of Henllys Village and education both in the County and the Country.
>
> Eric Atkin'[21]

Henllys Junior and Infant's School - c. 1980

Some time before the closure a young pupil wrote the following enchanting account of her life in Henllys. It gives witness to the beauty, which still endures in this ancient parish:

My Henllys

'Henllys is a lovely old village. There are old farmhouses and no air pollution. The old farmhouses are so interesting and many old things can be seen, such as old carts, cream machines, old milk churns and corn grinders. I live in an old Welsh longhouse. It is called Dorallt Fach, which is Welsh for "little forest". The house is about four hundred years old. On a summer day our village is at its very best. Wild flowers in the hedges bloom out and the colours dazzle your eyes. Fields of buttercups looks like a carpet of gold and the hay and corn sway in the breeze. The cows sit in the shade and those in the sun flick their tails lazily at the flies. The lambs in the field have grown and their woolly fleeces have been cut off for it's so warm. The view is lovely. You can see right down to the Channel. The evening comes and the cows go in for milking. The work is all done and the farmer whistles to his dog, "Come on tea is ready." The darkness falls and the barn owl can only be heard.

Sarah Baulch.[22]

REFERENCES

1. Webster's Commercial Directory, 1865; Evans, C.J.O., *Monmouthshire - Its History and Topography.* 1953. p.300.
2. Guest, Rev'd Simon Llew., *St. Peter's Church, Henllys - A History and Guide.* 1990. pp.5-6.
3. Evans, C.J.O., *Monmouthshire - Its History and Topography.* 1953. p.301; Dovey, F. and Walters, H.F., *Llantarnam,* 1953, pp. 83-86.
4. Gwent Record Office, A 132 A M 1, St. Mellon's Rural District Council Minute Book, 1895-98.
5. *Pontypool Free Press and Herald of the Hills,* March 26, 1897.
6. *Star of Gwent,* July 13, 1867.
7. Gwent Record Office, D2174.98; D1605.4, p.94.
8. Gwent Record Office, D1078.130.
9. *Monmouthshire Merlin,* April 17,1847.
10. Gwent Record Office, D32.763.
11. Gwent Record Office, D1605.4, p.103.
12. *Monmouthshire Merlin,* October 1, 1870.
13. Guest, Rev'd Simon Llew., *St. Peter's Church, Henllys - A History and Guide.* 1990, p.10.
14. *Monmouthshire Merlin,* November 8, 1878.
15. Gwent Record Office, CEA 84 1, Henllys School Log Book (1878-1914).
16. Copy of Death Certificate.
17. *Star of Gwent,* March 1, 1901.
18. *Free Press of Monmouthshire,* January 3, 1908.
19. *Free Press of Monmouthshire,* June 9, 1978.
20. Guest, Rev'd Simon Llew., *St. Peter's Church , Henllys - A History and Guide,* 1990, p.13.
21. Gwent Record Office, CEA 84.15, Henllys School Log Book (1989-1991)
22. Pontypool Museum, Henllys School Project, 1980-81.

Chapter Three

LLANTARNAM ABBEY

In the 12th century a great religious movement commenced throughout the land with the arrival of the Cistercian monks from the Continent. This became more evident by the erection of large and costly edifices for the purpose of worship. Such buildings of more or less grandeur were soon to be seen at Bassaleg, Malpas, Usk, Goldcliffe, Monmouth, Llantarnam, Abergavenny and Tintern. The ruins of Tintern, a richer abbey, still indicate the magnificence of design and wealth expended in its erection, but the majority of the buildings have long since become unnoticed, or entirely lost in time. The various monastic orders, the introduction of which into Britain had been the means of stirring up religious enthusiasm of the people, eventually became less active when the zeal for founding religious institutions calmed. This did not stop the members of these monastic orders from enjoying the delightful solitude in which their abodes were chiefly found and the rural delights surrounding them. The pleasures of good living were open to them with the charms of innocent and healthy pastimes easily in their reach. Many of the brethren spent their spare time in the study of literature and science. Perhaps through unawareness, or due to the conditions of the time, the bulk of these communities allowed the masses of the people around them to remain in ignorance or to gather their religious instruction from witnessing the colourful church ceremonies, and the scriptural pictures and sculptures adorning the walls of ecclesiastical buildings.

As farmers they made fertile their large estates. In the commercial world they excelled, trading all sorts of agricultural commodities, especially wool, and due to their shrewdness, some of their benevolence diminished. In spite of this they gave with equal readiness. It was they who attended to the wants of the poor and sick in the locality, and helped the stranger and wayfarer on the road.

The Cistercian abbey of Llantarnam was founded by Howel ap Iorwerth, lord of Caerleon, about the year 1175. At the time the lordship of Caerleon extended into the Llantarnam area. Known in history as Sir Howel of Caerleon, he appears in a undated deed, but believed to be about 1175, as giving, with the consent of his father Iorwerth, certain lands for the administration of the monks of Bassaleg. This was shortly before Sir Howel's death and his generosity is thought to have been influenced by his mother, who was the daughter of the Bishop of Llandaff.¹ However, there is no doubt that Strata Florida soon became the mother monastery when, following inspection of the site, Dafydd, its first abbot, sent an abbot and twelve monks to begin their work at Llantarnam.

The lands gifted to the Cistercian Order proved considerable and when established on the abbey site the monks set about clearing away much of the trees and foliage from the large estate in preparation for planting and sheep and cattle farming. When built, the abbey was dedicated to St. Mary Magdalene, hence their white habits to denote her purity. The monks became a familiar sight in their white habits with loose wide sleeves and partly shaven heads. Due to their apparel these new comers were known throughout Wales as the White Monks, and a very austere life they led. Deeply in earnest, the rules of their Order were obeyed in the strictest fashion; they fasted often and rarely tasted wine. Despite a small village in a field near the abbey, the site at Llantarnam, close to the Avon Lwyd, suited well their policy of building in mostly remote, desolate places alongside rivers.

The Cistercian order was often known as the "Silent Order" because in addition to the usual vows of celibacy, poverty, humility, and obedience, they added those of silence and labour. The Cistercians divided their day into twelve hours of light and twelve of darkness. At Llantarnam, stone monastic cells were built around a large church with a dorter for sleeping quarters. In each of these cells several monks lived while still part of the main establishment. Meals were eaten in the refractory, always in silence except for a reading by a brother from a sacred book. An adjoining chapter house served for business purposes and a cloister for reading and meditation. Very little meat was eaten and none on Lent, Fast Days or Fridays, so that having access to good fishing became very important. Valuable fishing rights on the Avon Lwyd and river Usk provided the monastery with an excellent supply of fish. The main physical occupation of the Llantarnam monks, particularly in the immediate area of the manor of Magna Porta, became sheep rearing.

In the early days the abbey was built mainly of wood and for a good many years became the richest religious house in Monmouthshire, maintaining some sixty monks. This profitable period lasted until 1272, when the Normans conquered Wales and the Lordship of Caerleon was taken over by the De Clares, who seized a great deal of monastic property. By 1317, the number of monks at Llantarnam had dwindled to twenty.

A troubled period for the abbey lasted for almost the whole of the fourteenth century and a great fire during March, 1398, razed it to the ground. The cause of the fire never became clear, but due to much of the building being of wood the result must have been devastating, with the loss also of furniture, records and valuable books. Only a few items remain of the early time. (See Appendix 1) Appeals for help went out and by 1400, the Abbot of Llantarnam, John ap Gruffydd, had restored his monastery in just a few years, mostly in stone with

1828. Llantarnam Abbey in the Elizabethan Style.

MONMOUTHSHIRE.

PARTICULARS

OF A VALUABLE AND IMPORTANT

Freehold Residential Estate,

Beautifully situate Two and a Half Miles North of the rising Town of Newport, with Three Railway Stations on the Property, from whence London can be reached in about Four Hours.

It comprises the Picturesque Residence known as

LLANTARNAM ABBEY,

On the site of the Cistercian Monastery, A.D. 1170, rebuilt after the Reformation, and restored in 1837 under THOMAS WYATT, who has reproduced the Tudor Abbey in all its external grace of outline, and combined in the interior commodious Reception Rooms and other modern conveniences. It is situate on a level plane in an undulated and

FERTILE PARK,

Adorned with some of the most stately Oak and Beech Trees in the County, and bounded on Two Sides by Hard Roads, and on the Third Side by the River Afon Llwyd; with

MODERN STABLE AND COACH HOUSE PREMISES,

Surrounded by tastefully-disposed Gardens and Pleasure Grounds, together with

TY ISSA FARM,

A valuable occupation in the Park, and the greater portion of the Village of LLANTARNAM. Likewise the following Six Valuable Farms :—

PEN-Y-PARK, let to J. Sawtell; **CROES-Y MYALCH**, let to W. Mumford;
PENTREBACH, let to H. Lawrence; **PANT GLASS**, let to W. Waters;
LODGE FARM, let to Mrs. Parsons; and **COURT FARM**, let to H. Thomas;

Some smaller occupations, numerous Cottages, Public Houses.

Freehold Ground Rents of £300 a Year,

Secured on 108 Houses at Cwmbrân, and about

43 ACRES OF BUILDING LAND,

The whole embracing an Area of about

1,520 ACRES,

And producing an Income exclusive of the Mansion and Lands in Hand, of

£2,000 A YEAR,

WHICH WILL BE SOLD BY AUCTION BY

Messrs. DRIVER & CO.,

AT THE MART, TOKENHOUSE YARD, LOTHBURY, LONDON,

On TUESDAY, the 14th day of JULY, 1885,

At TWO O'CLOCK precisely.

some ornate mouldings.[2] It is believed that the Cistercian brothers used material re-cycled from the then standing remains of Roman Caerleon.

By 1500, the abbey had declined with their numbers dwindling even more. This was due mainly to Government action to control wool marketing, which kept down the price. In 1535, the value of Llantarnam Abbey is shown in the Valor Ecclesiasticus as £71-3s-2d.[3] The Abbot at the time was named Jasper and only six monks remained at the abbey. At the Dissolution of the monasteries, on February 4th, 1536, the Llantarnam monastery was surrendered to King Henry VIII and the monks expelled. A further loss of valuable books and records probably occurred at this time, and, despite the 'high living' suggested as taking place in some monasteries, remaining evidence point to a laborious life for the Llantarnam monks.[4]

The subsequent history tells that only the lands were leased several times for short periods until the complete transfer of both lands and abbey to William Morgan, in 1561. Including in the acquisition was the manor house of Pentre Bach, where Morgan was living. While in possession of the Morgan family, remodelling of the religious building in the Elizabethan style, with materials from the old abbey, gradually took place. The abbey remained in the possession of the well-known Morgans of Llantarnam until the line died out.

Sir Edward Morgan, the third baronet died in 1682, at the early age of twenty-five years. No son and heir remained and this would have a large effect on the ownership of land in Torfaen during the years to follow. However, he left two daughters, Anne, the elder and Frances. In 1707 these two agreed to divide the extensive lands bequeathed to them. Frances received the manor of Wentsland and Bryngwyn, including Llanhilleth, that part of the parish of Trevethin, which lies west of the Afon Lwyd, Llanvehangel-Pontymoel and part of Llantarnam, inclusive of the abbey and grounds, all of which totalled 4,483 acres. She married Edmund Bray, of Barrington Co. of Gloucester, and it is interesting to note that it is her name which appears on plaques outside Pontypool Market:

Frances Bray
daughter of Sir Edward
Morgan of Llantarnam
in the county,
Baronet, and widow to
Edmund Bray of
Barrington, in the Counties of
Gloucester and Berks, Esquire,
built this market house
in the year
1730

Frances Bray, nee Morgan, had two daughters, Mary, who married John Blewitt, and Frances, wife of John Fettiplace.

While touring Monmouthshire at the beginning of the nineteenth century Archdeacon William Coxe (1747-1828) gave a splendid insight into the condition of Llantarnam Abbey and its management. Known at the time as Llantarnam House he writes:

'The nature of the succession has principally occasioned the decay of the mansion; it was left jointly among the daughters of Mrs Bray, and as neither would agree to relinquish the residence of her ancestors, they occupied the house alternately. Since their death the uncomfortable terms of a joint possession disgusted their descendants, who were settled in a distant county, and the house has remained untenanted for a considerable number of years. The present mansion appears to have been finished in the time of Queen Elizabeth, from the old materials of the abbey. The only remains of the ancient structure are the stone cells, converted into stables, the walls of the garden, and a beautiful gothic gateway, which is still called Magna Porta, and was the grand entrance. Within this gateway is a porch which bears the date of 1588, distinguished with a shield of the Morgan arms in stone, with nine quarterings.

'The house is a large antiquated mansion, damp, dreary, and having been long untenanted, exhibits an appearance of gloom and decay, rendered still more melancholy by a few traces of former magnificence. The large hall contains several whole length portraits of our kings and queens, particularly of Henry the eighth, of James the first, of his queen, Anne of Denmark, and of Charles the first when prince of Wales; the royal arms are also blazoned in the windows. Many family portraits are dispersed about the rooms, but no one could inform me whom they represented.

'The gardens occupy a flat, and being surrounded with high and massive walls, are lonely and secluded. The park is extensive and diversified, swelling into gentle undulations of rich pasture, and interspersed with thick plantations and dark avenues, which make a conspicuous figure in the adjoining landscape.'[5]

The lands in time passed to Edmund Blewitt, of Salford, and Charles Fettiplace, of Swinbrook, in Oxfordshire. After more family disputes the mansion came firmly in the possession of Edward Blewitt.

Edward had married towards the end of the 18th century and four children were the issue of the marriage. Sadly, his eldest son Edward was to be a lunatic, but Reginald, Edmund and Francis all led useful lives. Shortly before their mother's death in 1808, a woman by the name of Rachel Roberts was hired by Mrs Blewitt as a housemaid. She afterwards became an attendant upon Mrs Blewitt, and continued so till the death of her mistress. Afterwards, a period in the service of Major Blewitt continued till the year 1810, when she returned to her family at Caerleon. There was some suspicion that before she returned, there had been illicit intercourse between her and her master, but they were never seen together, or later, in personal circumstances. No child was born at Llantarnam Abbey, but they would have six illegitimate children, the first born in late 1808. The connexion was clandestinely carried on for a great number of years; there was no public cohabitation, either by introducing her or her children to his friends. Major Blewitt continued to live at Llantarnam Abbey, and Rachel Roberts at Caerleon.[6]

By 1810, Llantarnam Abbey estate had been let to Sir Henry Protheroe on lease for twenty one years. He was a Bristol merchant who had been knighted on March 16, 1803. During his stay at the abbey he served the office of High Sheriff of Monmouthshire in 1816. Unfortunately, during this period serious neglect to the fabric of the building occurred. Also, many of the valuable contents of the mansion disappeared during his tenancy, which resulted in Edward Blewitt having him arrested in 1817, for debts of £700. The abbey would again go through an untenanted period.

Due to Edward Blewitt's oldest son being *'Non Compos Mentus'* his second son Reginald James Blewitt became the natural heir. Reginald was bred to the law, and was articled to Messrs Stevenson and Co., Lincoln's Inn. After Mr. Stevenson retired, he became a partner, and the firm became Bicknell, Roberts, and Blewitt; but this partnership dissolved in 1827. His marriage took place in 1821, of which his father did not approve. Because of this disagreement, for a short time Edmund became heir and collected the rents on the estate, but by 1830, he went up to London to study for the bar. Due to a serious leg infection, which resulted in a near death experience, Reginald received an unexpected visit from his father, who showed tremendous concern for his plight and gave him a large amount of money to cover his medical expenses. Reginald was now forgiven and when recovered collected the estate's rents while gradually regaining his father's confidence.

Around 1830, Squire Blewitt's health began to noticeably suffer. By now he and Rachel Roberts were residing together in different parts of London, but the relationship still held a considerable degree of concealment from his family and intimate friends. In September 1830, they married. In November 1830, he changed his will. Reginald helped with the preparation and was shocked by the disclosure of his father's six illegitimate children. At the time the real estate of Llantarnam Abbey produced approximately £2,500 per annum. For other properties the value was considerable. The new terms of the will were:

'The widow is to have £600 a year for life, with benefit of survivorship to the six children; each of the six children is to have an annuity of £100 a year, with benefit of survivorship; and to the four sons, there is a power given to the trustees of advancing £400 each, for the purpose of setting them up in life; and the residue of the personal property is given to my son, Edmund Blewitt, and in the case of his death, to my son Reginald James Blewitt, and in the case of his death, to my daughter, Francis Mary Anne Blewitt.'

Within several months of making his last will Edward Blewitt suffered a serious stroke, which badly affected his right side making writing difficult. Perhaps this was fortunate for his legitimate heirs due to the fact that his wife would not allow access to him by anyone. His third legitimate son, Edmund, had married the daughter of a Mr. Protheroe, a solicitor in Monmouthshire, with the full consent of her father. Sadly, Edmund died in July 1831, and when his father died the following year, on March 8th, 1832, this made Reginald the undisputed heir to the Llantarnam estate despite various legal challenges..

Reginald James Blewitt was the great great grandson of Mary Blewitt. Born May 17, 1799, he became an important figure in the commercial, industrial and political life during the middle of the nineteenth century. Educated at Rugby School and later called to the Bar, he was a man of culture with literary tastes and is known for having founded, and for a short time edited, the first county newspaper, *'The Monmouthshire Merlin'*.

As a young man Reginald Blewitt had gained the respect of his acquaintances with his loyal and caring behaviour. This is witnessed in a letter thanking his physician after what became serious accident in 1828:

'In the month of August 1828, I was summoned from Gloucester, where I resided, to Boulogne, to receive the last dying wishes of a friend. On entering the harbour at Boulogne, the steam ship in which I had embarked from Dover took the ground, and the tide being then on the ebb, the passengers were obliged to go on shore in small boats. I leaped into the first that came alongside, and in so doing, bruised my leg. The anxiety to see my friend, to watch his dying moments, and, after the lapse of a few days, to perform his obsequies, prevented me from thinking of myself... I found that my wound did not improve and that my health became every day more debilitated...Sir A. Cooper pronounced my case to be of the most desperate of the kind he had ever seen...In this state, I, on the 3rd of February last, resorted to you, who kindly undertook my case...I now find myself in more robust health than I have experienced for years, my wounds are all healed, and I have become to my friends, really and absolutely, without any figure of language, "a marvel and show."'[7]

40

Llantarnam Abbey

41

The Tower, Llantarnam Abbey.

Upon his father's demise, Reginald Blewitt let it be known that he would reside at Llantarnam House and take a keen interest in the locality. A date and time of the new squire's arrival circulated and although not completely reliable, caused tremendous excitement among his staff and tenants.

On December 12th, 1832, all persons who knew the gentleman were anxious to ascertain where and when he would turn up. Some said he would arrive at the Newport wharf by packet (mail boat), others equally confident, reported that the route would be through Gloucester and Chepstow. The packet arrived, but not Squire Blewitt. His friends immediately set out for Chepstow road, and soon met a carriage and four, but as carriages and four were so numerous in this extra important crisis, his friends had no doubt that it would have to be decided by an impertinent peep. Soon the intelligence spread, 'Squire Blewitt was coming.' In Newport, there gathered a large muster of gentlemen and respectable inhabitants of the place before he was escorted to Llantarnam Abbey, by cavalcade, which extended half a mile in length. He was met at the parish boundary by nearly the whole of the neighbouring population. The arrangements had been made by Mr. Rees Edward Rees, in a highly creditable manner. The four horses were removed and twenty of the cheerful peasantry drew a good landlord to his mansion, preceded by flags with mottoes, and a good band of musicians, that played some of the most appropriate airs, among which was *'Home, Sweet Home,'* and *'Twas Merry in the Hall.'* When the worthy host alighted, the local people received the first insight into his great oratory skills. In front of him was perhaps the largest assemblage that ever met on the lawn at Llantarnam Abbey for such an occasion. In an animated and very suitable speech he stated that he had come to live among them for one, and only one, purpose, - that of promoting a proper feeling between landlord and tenant. He was determined to 'live and let live.' Whatever disunion had existed in the neighbourhood, he hoped would be forgotten, for now that he was to spend his days among them, he had made up his mind to do so happily, and this he hoped should not apply to himself only, but to all around him. He thanked them all for the flattering manner in which they had thought proper to compliment him, hoping that he should ever deserve their regards.

About two-hundred persons sat down to plenty of old English fare and good cwrw-da. The toasts were plentiful before the Newport gentlemen returned home and left the numerous peasantry to keep it up till a late hour.[8]

Due to damage and neglect to the roof of the mansion by Sir Henry Protheroe, the new resident had no other recourse than to immediately repair the damage at an estimated cost of fifty pounds. This began a vast rebuilding of much of the structure, and a re-routing of the road from the Three Blackbirds to the Greenhouse, with the construction of a wall alongside. The attention of the neighbourhood soon became strongly drawn to the magnificent new mansion emerging from what many described as the old ruined pile of Llantarnam Abbey. The happy mixture of Tudor towers and gables, of ornamental chimney shafts, crosses and pinnacles, with painted doors and windows, by 1835, reflected highly on the architect, Mr. Thomas Henry Wyatt. The great staircase was made at this time from oak on the abbey estate, a new dining room added, and the Great Hall, containing a polished floor, became much improved with a new ceiling. Also in the Great Hall a large stained glass window, commissioned to commemorate and show the Morgan coat of arms, was installed. Further examination revealed about twenty bedrooms, a billiard room with beautiful carved roof, a library, and an organ gallery was very evident in the noble hall. The work outside showed extensive stabling by further utilising the stone monks' cells, conservatories, vinery, pleasure gardens with terrace walk, kitchen gardens and orchards. In keeping with the style at the time a grotto, caverns, and a labyrinth were formed. Many of the outside windows were rebuilt and a beautifully improved entrance placed on the site of the old gateway at the west end, known as the Magna Porta, after the old manor of this name. At the time of restoration the initials of the owner was engraved in the drawing room and above the main entrance too commemorate the work. This work, mostly completed in 1836, and combined with the early Victorian passion for landscape gardening, is believed to have cost £60,000.

Possibly due to great many disputes between tenants and landlord prior to his arrival, Reginald Blewitt appears to have set out to be a kind and liberal landlord. Commencing on Christmas Eve, 1834, the poor in the neighbourhood of Llantarnam Abbey were treated with a 'cheer' worthy of the hospitality of ancient times. Mr. Blewitt gave upwards of two-hundred and fifty persons each a pound of beef and three pennyworth of bread. It was distributed at Mr. Tranter's *Greenhouse Inn*. Where there happened to be a family of half-a-dozen, six pounds of prime beef, and eighteen pennyworth of good bread, was a comfortable adjunct on a cottagers' table for Christmas day. The object of his bounty continued at the festive season for a good number of years with one year seeing the distribution of six barge loads of coal, taken from his coalmine, to the needy.[9]

The half-yearly collection of rents in the *Greenhouse Inn* became a little less traumatic for the tenants when Mr. Blewitt afterwards entertained them to dinner. After the cloth was removed, the health of the youthful and beloved Queen and other loyal and patriotic toasts were given from the chair. Following this, the health of their worthy squire, and success to him at the approaching election, was given by Rev. Dr. Davies, rector of Llantarnam. Further toasts to the success of Mr. Blewit's colliery brought forth from him the promise to distribute, in the ensuing winter, 50 tons of coal to the poor of the parish of Llantarnam, and 50 tons of coal to the poor of Llanfrechfa parish. The evening passed amidst the greatest harmony before the party separated late in the night.[10]

Reginald James Blewitt had commenced his political life in earnest by 1837. This new career gained momentum by the readiness of his powerful speeches. As mayor of Newport in 1837-38, and 1841-42, his popularity grew considerably. Following the retirement of Benjamin Hall as Member of Parliament for the Monmouth Boroughs in 1837, Blewitt stood as a Liberal candidate against the Tory ironmaster, Joseph Bailey, junior, and won the seat by polling 440 votes against Bailey's 386.

Soon after his address as a candidate for Member of Parliament for the united boroughs of Monmouth, Newport and Usk, he became responsible as a main co-director, for the founding of the Monmouth and Glamorgan Bank at the King's Head, Newport, on February 6, 1837. The bank paid good dividends for some years, but it collapsed suddenly in 1851, and these were the days before the concept of limited liability for companies. Many of the shareholders suddenly found themselves liable to the extent of all they possessed and great hardship and suffering was caused to many Monmouthshire families. R.J. Blewitt resigned his seat in Parliament, withdrew from public life in the county and went to live abroad, mainly in France. Although his elder brother was of unsound mind, Reginald Blewitt had cared for him while both lived at Llantarnam Abbey and it was here that Edward died on February 20, 1868, aged 71 years. Following the death of his elder brother Reginald Blewitt returned to England to dispute the title of his widowed sister to the family estates.

Frances Blewitt had married Richard Brinsley Dowling, a barrister-at-law, and with her brother very much out of the way and residing abroad, she allowed her husband to set himself up as the squire of Llantarnam Abbey. Dowling died in

1859, but by this time an irreparable rift had become fixed between brother and sister.

A long legal battle followed which Reginald lost and his connection with Monmouthshire ceased. On September 11, 1878, he died at The Priory, Roehampton, Wandsworth, Greater London, after being nursed for two years with paralysis due to brain disease. *The Times* and *Western Mail* newspapers carried his obituary. In the newspaper he had founded, *The Monmouthshire Merlin*, the following sad announcement of his demise read:

DEATH OF R.J. BLEWITT, ESQ.

'We have this week to record the death of a gentleman who in years long past occupied a prominent position in this county, viz., Mr. Reginald James Blewitt, formerly for some years member of Parliament for the Monmouthshire Boroughs. Mr. Blewitt having withdrawn from this neighbourhood more than 20 years ago, his name is familiar to only a small proportion of those now residing in the county; many who were his contemporaries and supporters during an active political career, have long since passed away. For years Mr. Blewitt took a conspicuous part in local affairs, and, as a genial friend, a man of culture, business aptitude, and extraordinary energy, was much esteemed. More than forty years ago, viz., on the 27th of January 1837, Mr. Blewitt issued his first address as a candidate for the representation of the Monmouthshire Boroughs, and was declared elected (in the Liberal interest) on 26th of July in the same year. His opponent was Mr. Joseph Bailey, jnr. Mr. Blewitt resigned the seat in the year 1852. A cloud having fallen upon his fortunes, he withdrew from the county, and his connection with it was never afterwards resumed. He had, we believe, reached his 80th year, and retained his characteristic energy of mind almost to the close of life.'[11]

Thus, the passing of Reginald Blewitt ended another chapter in the existence of the beautiful old abbey. He had felt the joys of success and the scorn of his fellow man. Of one thing there can be no doubt and that is when he left his home in 1839, and travelled the short distance to the *Greenhouse Inn*, before standing squarely in the path of hundreds of 'liquored up' chartists, ready for battle at Newport, he was indeed a very brave man. His entreaties warning of the serious consequences of their actions fell on deaf ears, but his concern for their plight on that historic day became very apparent and would be remembered by many for years to follow.

By 1872, Llanarnam Abbey was again untenanted and advertisements in the Monmouthshire newspapers gave notice of the mansion, in good repair, to be let, fully furnished, together with 2,500 acres of excellent shooting. No one appears to have taken up the tenancy and on the death of Frances Mary Dowling in 1875, the property went into chancery.

The property was again in great danger of deteriorating and losing a tremendous amount in value. In 1879, a gentleman wished to purchase the estate as a wedding present for his daughter on her impending marriage and offered nearly £100,000 for it, but the offer was declined.

While still in chancery and for the benefit of the nearby Llantarnam Church fund, caretaker staff allowed a 'Grand Fete and Fancy Fair' in the beautiful grounds of the abbey during August, 1888. Lovers of the picturesque in nature or in art found ample material to excite their interest and admiration. When arriving everyone could not help but to feast their eyes on the splendour for which the park abounded. For a small fee a rare glimpse of the interior could be had and all were enchanted by the magnificent hall, with polished floor, the stained glass windows, bearing the crests of former owners, the music chamber, the billiard hall with beautiful carved roof, and the massive staircase, believed by many of the visitors to be the finest in the county. The successful day raised £267-17shillings for the church fund.[12]

Not until November, 1889, did the news filter through that the abbey had been purchased. By now there was a considerable reduction in the size of the estate. The fine old mansion, park lands, farms and cottages, and about 200 acres of land came into the possession of Mr. William Edgar Williams, of Crumlin Hall, for the meagre sum of £15,000. The estate spent a long period in chancery, and the sale, effected by private treaty, came about by order of the court. The purchaser had been lately secretary to the South Wales Colliery Company. The depreciation of the estate within the few years prior to the auction proved very great and if it had not been for two other gentlemen, also in competition, who ran up the price, the sale price would have amounted to much less.[13]

Some six years later Mr. Williams sold Llantarnam Abbey to Clifford Cory, who would live in the mansion until his death in 1940.

Clifford John Cory was born in Cardiff in 1859. Of Cornish origin, his grandfather settled in Cardiff when it was but a small community on the Taff and depending for its future on the wealth of minerals from the surrounding hills. He founded the great firm of Messrs Cory Brothers that went from strength to strength. His son John took over the business interests and became one of richest men in the United Kingdom. Some of his great fortune went towards improving the lot of the Cardiff seamen, to relieve the sufferings of the poor, and in the good cause of education.

Mr. Clifford John Cory is the son of this millionaire and philanthropist. He was chiefly educated privately, but it is known that during his schooldays he entered into sport with great zeal leading to success; and the dining-room sideboard at Llantarnam would later be filled with trophies won in many classes of athletics. Following his education he travelled throughout Europe. Upon returning home, he adopted a business career by entering the London branch office of the firm. As a director of the large company he had not only inherited his father's personal likeness, but also many of his splendid characteristics. Probably, his marriage in 1893, to Anne, daughter of the late Albert Arthur Lethbridge, influenced his decision to purchase the Llantarnam estate in 1895. At the time of the purchase, he was considered to be among the ablest and most successful men of business to be found in the coal trade of the United Kingdom.

He would always remain a keen sportsman. Not only did he play in the first organised football match to be played in South Wales, but he also became a fine equestrian winning many prizes in the show ring while exacting great concern for his horses. Hunting and shooting became a relaxation from the huge pressure of the business world and not long after taking up residence at the abbey, within the park, he had constructed one of the best polo grounds in the kingdom. He would soon be in the first rank as a player of the game. His love of horses never ceased and in later life he became a skilled whip driving his four-in-hand in competitions.

By 1905, Mr. Cory had taken a pleasurable interest in agriculture, and farmed about three hundred acres of land mainly as a hobby. He would boast of the finest herd of Black Kerry cattle, perhaps, to be found in the United Kingdom, with some of which he took first and champion prizes at the Royal Agricultural and other important shows. Many prizes also came with his black Berkshire pigs, while on the estate could be found the only flock of pedigree Lincoln long-wool sheep in the Principality.

During his travels he sought out and conversed with many famous people of his time, and when at his beautiful Monmouthshire home, he frequently entertained those distinguished in political life.

His philanthropic gestures became well know amongst the mining communities. The founding of several miners institutes, with each holding a good stock of books, were to be attributed to him. On one occasion the workmen of Resolven Colliery presented him with an illuminated address for his efforts on their behalf. Frequent requests by religious organisations to use his park for raising badly needed funds always met with success and the picnics were a delight for all ages.

For some years he served on the Commission of the Peace for the counties of Glamorgan and Monmouth and in 1905 became High Sheriff of Monmouthshire. This work was combined with his membership of different organisations for the promotion of education.[14] Following a period as a member of Glamorgan County Council he also became a Liberal Member of Parliament for the St. Ives Division of Cornwall, which lasted for eighteen years.

A few years later, at a meeting of Llantarnam Urban District Council, on December 6, 1907, following a pleasant announcement, it was resolved on the motion of the Chairman and Councillor Lawrence, that the Clerk should convey in a letter to Sir C.J. Cory, Bart, their respective fellow parishioner, the hearty congratulations of the Council on the Knighthood, which had been recently conferred on him by His Majesty.[15]

Towards the end of the nineteenth century the Abbey Mill went out of use and by 1901 it had been converted into a meeting place by the new owner of the abbey. The conversion of the mill is a significant indication of a change in the nature of estate ownership. More and more of the large rural estates were passing into the possession of wealthy industrialists and others whose main source of income was not dependent on agriculture. Because of this Llantarnam Abbey estate became increasingly recreational and leisure orientated. The abbey was in fact a frequent weekend and holiday retreat from the business and hectic social life of London.

We can thank Mrs Theodore Cory, a former actress and wife of his cousin, for a personal insight into living at the abbey and the late autumn of the life of the esteemed gentleman. Mrs Theodore Cory became a prolific authoress who claimed to have produced at least eighteen-seven books. While using the pseudonym of Winifred Graham, in 1946, she produced a chatty book of short stories. One contained the following rare information:

> *'Naturally our family interests centred around Clifford, who also did a great deal of entertaining both in London and Monmouthshire. Theodore and I were his frequent guests at dinners and dances in town and on visits to his fascinating country seat, Llantarnam Abbey. It would take a volume to enumerate the many offices he filled in his active life. He took us to some delightful Hunt Balls in our younger days, when the lack of certain amenities in his big Abbey astonished me, especially on my first visit there as a bride. The huge fire-places blazing on all sides camouflaged the lack of central heating and were even sufficient to warm the lofty entrance hall with its Minstrel Gallery and long church-like stained-glass windows. We were given comfortable adjoining bedrooms where fires also blazed. Then, in this home of luxury, came a surprise. My astonishment was great to see an old-fashioned round bath placed on the hearthrug, with large steaming cans of water for my ablutions. The Abbey, with its numerous apartments for visitors boasted no bathrooms! The large staff seemed to make nothing of carrying cans down the endless corridors and stoking fires from morning till night.*
>
> *'The Abbey staircase always appealed to me as dramatic and would have looked well on the stage. At each turn it was guarded by a life-sized figure in armour holding up a lantern illuminated by modern electricity, which threw its beams on enormous pictures.*
>
> *'The Abbey grounds have a charming lake with a romantic looking house-pavilion..A pair of stately white swans and a pure black one, crimson beaked, added to the picturesqueness of the scene. But a*

Sir Clifford Cory-Bart, MP.

Monks' Cells, Llantarnam Abbey.

Sir Clifford Cory with his four-in-hand.

morning came when only half the body of one white swan remained, the other half having been devoured by a murderous fox who must have caught and killed the graceful bird while sleeping on the bank. In that estate of 2,000 acres the lake makes a peaceful retreat, with tall trees for a background.

'Clifford, who never refused us anything, had an extraordinary way of inspiring awe in his dependants and ran the house in a Spartan fashion. For instance, no visitor was allowed even to put a lump of coal on the fire, the bell had to be rung for the butler to perform this simple office. Early to bed was another fetish in which Clifford expected us to collaborate; so we all trooped upstairs soon after ten o'clock to listen to the wireless in our bedrooms. Occasionally we crept down again, made up the waning fire and unknown to our host broke the rigid rule of retirement.

'Every night he held a brief service in the private Chapel. Punctually the door would be flung open and the butler announced in a stentorian voice: "Prayers, Sir Clifford!" Whereupon we all rose and followed him like obedient sheep through the high hall and dingy passages to the Chapel in the Abbey. Sleepy servants sat at the back with the housekeeper in front occupying a solitary pew. I always felt this enforced custom was not welcomed by the staff after working hard all day, but woe betide any who failed to appear spotlessly clothed to listen while Clifford read the scripture and prayed from a very old-fashioned prayer book. He was extremely Low Church, no flowers were ever allowed on the altar and certainly not a cross.

'He did not have a resident Private Chaplain, but each week-end engaged a different clergyman who arrived to stay at the Abbey and conduct Sunday services and Sunday School, which the tenants on the estate and their children attended.

'When I remember the meals at Llantarnam in those early days of war, they seem fantastic and impossible, the breakfast dishes on the sideboard, the lavish display of eggs, the dessert at lunch and dinner, with as many as eight different choices at times when muscat grapes and other home-grown fruit abounded. Always bananas were put at night in Theodore's room as he was known to like them and crystallized ginger with other sweets ornamented the dining-table. We all enjoyed the good things procurable and I often wonder if Clifford missed his luxuries before the wheels of life at last stood still for him.

'Only a few years before Clifford died at the age of eighty, he decided suddenly to inaugurate bathrooms and central heating. He never did things by halves. Stately marble bathrooms were arranged and owing to the great thickness of the old Abbey walls, these alterations cost over

52

£3,000. The floor of the gunroom, when taken up for central heating pipes, revealed buried human skeletons, hundreds of years old, and probably former monks.'[16]

Sir Cifford and his wife Annie had a legal separation and while he, sometimes looking a lonely figure, remained mostly at the abbey, she went to live at 28 Belgrave Square, London. Lady Cory had packed into boxes probably all of the abbey's small treasures and they would adorn her London home while a lot of famous musical parties took place. Much esteemed throughout his life, Clifford Cory, age 81 years, Baronet and colliery proprietor, suffered a cerebral thrombosis at Llantarnam Abbey and after being in a coma for a while, died on February 3rd, 1941. Following his death, the remaining abbey treasures, consisting of rare antique furniture, Louis XV clocks, valuable carpets and an array of unique accessories, were sold at auction in May, 1941.[17] This was followed by the sale of the property to the Government during World War II and the Royal Air Force used it as a storage centre for uniforms, after which it came up for auction.

In July, 1946, the abbey, lands and properties were to have been offered for sale at an auction at the King's Head Hotel, Newport. Those who attended the auction were informed that the abbey mansion and parkland, an area of eighty and three-quarter acres, had been disposed of privately, together with four cottages and the estate's saw mill, and were therefore withdrawn from the sale. Also, at the time, abbey farms, land and cottages were sold separately to the tenants.[18]

After the passing of four centuries local people were pleased to hear that the abbey site came once more into the hands of a religious community. It became the Provincial House of the Congregation of the Sisters of St. Joseph, the headquarters of the Order in England and Wales.

During the fifty years since the Sisters bought the abbey, there were some changes. In 1952, the stable block was converted into the Noviciate building. Originally the chapel was located in what is now St Joseph's Parlour and the refectory. The altar was between the communicating doors. In 1957, the present chapel was built on the site of the conservatory. At a later date, in response to Vatican II, a new altar facing the congregation was added to the front of the sanctuary area. Again, in response to Vatican II, Our Lady's wing was opened in 1968. This provided individual study-bedrooms for the Sisters as well as the library and conference room. One of the more recent additions, in 1983, has been that of a purpose-built wing to accommodate the elderly Sisters who need special care.

Between 1978-1984, and as part of the 800th anniversary of the foundation of the Cistercian Abbey of Llantarnam, the Monmouthshire Antiquarian Association was invited by the Sisters to carry out an active programme of excavations around the abbey.

They confirmed the remains of a monastic graveyard, the position of the east end and the south transept of the monastic church, and possibly either the Prior's lodgings or the monk's lodging. The gatehouse and ditch marking the northern limit of the monastic enclave were discovered, as were the monastic fishponds and, its mill on the adjacent Afon Lwyd. However, the 'tithe barn' was shown to be post-monastic and probably early or mid-eighteenth century. Excavations next to it revealed another large barn, which proved to be a corn barn and used between 1790-1830. Both overlay a monastic graveyard, which was succeeded by sixteenth and seventeenth century agricultural or industrial activity and a building, or buildings, used probably as a stable and smithy. Just as the Cistercian brothers used material quarried from the then standing remains of Roman Carleon, so did their successors use the elaborately carved stone from the monastery to build the fine seventeenth and nineteenth century mansions, whose stable block was uncovered in the field to the west of the present buildings.[19]

In 1996, the Golden Jubilee of the purchase of Llantarnam Abbey was commemorated by the Sisters and long may these caring people live and work amongst us.

REFERENCES

1. Bradney, Sir Joseph, *A History of Monmouthshire - Llanfihangel Llantarnam*. p. 224.
2. Bradney, Sir Joseph, *A History of Monmouthshire - Llanfihangel Llantarnam*. pp. 225-226.
3. Gwent Record Office, *Valour Ecclesiasticus*, 1535 (iv. p. 365)
4. Allgood, Henry G.C., Newport Local Studies Library, qM310 (900), *Llantarnam Abbey*.
5. Coxe, William, *An Historical Tour in Monmouthshire*, 1801. pp. 115-117.
6. *Monmouthshire Merlin*, April 6, 1833.
7. Blewitt, Reginald James. Letter, M310-920, Newport Local Studies Library.
8. *Monmouthshire Merlin*, December 15, 1832.
9. *Monmouthshire Merlin*, January 4, 1834; *Monmouthshire Merlin*, January 26, 1839.
10. *Monmouthshire Merlin*, July 8, 1837.
11. *Monmouthshire Merlin*, September 20, 1878; *Western Mail*, September 1878.
12. *Pontypool Free Press and Herald of the Hills*, August 8, 1888.
13. *Pontypool Free Press and Herald of the Hills*, November 8, 1889.
14. *The Shipping World*, December 27, 1905.
15. Gwent Record Office, A 421 A M 4, Llantarnam Urban District Minute Book 1907-1910.
16. Graham, Winifred, *Observations*, 1946, Newport Local Studies Library, M310-920.
17. Newport Local Studies Library, pq M310-645, Llantarnam Abbey Auction Catalogue, May 13-16, 1941.
18. *The Free Press of Monmouthshire*, July 26, 1946.
19. Mein, A.G., Summary of Results of Llantarnam Abbey Excavations 1978-1984.

Chapter Four

LLANDERFEL AND ST. DIALS

Llanderfel, a chapel-of-ease, stood on the side of the Mynydd Maen, in the upper part of the parish of Llantarnam, at an elevation of nearly one thousand feet above sea-level. The building was constructed of local sandstone, obtained from the mountain nearby. After the chapel fell into disuse the stone from the structure helped in the construction of sheep pens and the nearby farm, which bears the same name. For many years the ruin lay in a small copse at the bottom of a pathway known as, 'The Slippery Path.'

The chapel was of an 'L' shape, and consisted of a large room, with two smaller rooms at right angles to this. It is probable that the chapel extended from its original form, since the early Welsh churches consisted merely of a depository for religious objects and services were held outside. Later, however, naves were introduced and it seems reasonable to assume that the larger room was a nave and added to the smaller of the two rooms. This then functioned as an eastern choir and a small chapel. The presence of an enclosure, adjacent to the chapel, suggests that the building served also for the collection of tithes.[1] With regard to the founding of the small church, Sir Joseph Bradney wrote the following in his extensive *History of Monmouthshire:*

> *'Derval Gadarn (Derval the Strong) a celebrated warrior in the time of King Arthur, distinguished himself at the battle of Camlan in 542. The latter part of his life was devoted to religion, and he found this church and Llanderfel in Merionethshire. At the latter are preserved what are considered relics of Dervel, part of a wooden horse and wooden crosier, called Ceffyl and Ffon Dervel. There was also in that church a wooden image said to be of Dervel, which was taken to London and burnt at Smithfield in May 1538.*
>
> *'Nothing seems to be known as to when this church came to be disused and allowed to get into disrepair. The ruins of the walls are no more than two or three feet high, out of which at the east end are growing beech trees of considerable age, giving the appearance of it having been a ruin for two hundred years.'*

In the Middle Ages, Llanderfel was in the possession of the Cistercian Abbey of Llantarnam and probably used by the monks as a chapel-of-ease for their possessions at the foot of the Mynydd Maen. This ancient Monmouthshire shrine is known to have been still in use in 1535, when the Valor Ecclesiasticus recording Capella S'ti Dervalli' as bringing 26s. 8d. to the Llantarnam Abbey in oblations.[2] It is unlikely that the chapel was used after the Dissolution and the lack of documentary evidence helps to verify this fact. Throughout the following centuries the land containing the ruin came into the possession of various owners.

It is known that the chapel was built directly over a seam of coal which outcrops very near the surface, in fact scratching about with a pick will reveal the mineral. During the great strike of 1926, this area was the scene of much activity when local people dug small pits for coal.

During World War Two, the policy of German aircraft to discard any unused bombs in order to lighten their load before crossing the Channel, and also not to return to base with explosives which should have landed on a designated target, caused them to drop their implements of death in the Torfaen Valley. Several of these landed a hundred metres from the site of the chapel and killed a few cattle belonging to the nearby Llanderfel Farm. The next day, a Sunday, hundreds of people from Cwmbran village walked up the mountainside to inspect the damage. In all probability many of them must have walked over the ancient ruin of the chapel while unaware of what it was.[3]

In the mid-twentieth century there was a small attempt at excavating the site by amateur archaeologists, but with the memories still of the local invasion of his land during the recent war, the work was understandably stopped by the land owner. Perhaps in the not too distant future a professional excavation may take place at the site and the decision of the farmer all those years ago will no doubt be regarded as an act of Providence.

St. Dial's Chapel, another chapel-of-ease, further down the valley, and nearer to Llantarnam Abbey, appears to be of less importance. All visible remains of the chapel disappeared when a house, with a few additions, was built on the original site. However, when surveyed, its plan seemed entirely different from that of Llanderfel.

It consisted of a long nave, with rooms adjoining the nave at the end. The date is probably later than that of Llanderfel, owing to the ground plan including the nave. At a time when pilgrimages were popular, many people went on at least one pilgrimage in their lifetime, with some going on more. After a warm welcome pilgrims would wend their way from Llantarnam Abbey to St. Dials, up to Llandefel, and then follow an ancient track-way to Penrys. These chapels, shrines and saints' relics were a good income for Llantarnam Abbey, bringing in the useful sum of £3-6-8 in the last year before the monastery closed in August 1536. Excellent work has been recently carried out to allow interested people to undertake this journey and follow in the pilgrims footsteps.

A house, which replaced the chapel, was entered through a large porch. It had two staircases, one being of newel style. This suggests that the chapel was converted into the house at the time of the Reformation, since newel stair-cases were plentiful during this period.[4] It is known that a fireback in one of the rooms held the date 1673. Also present was a very ancient window, glazed with horn, known in Welsh as *'Y Ffenest Gorn'*.[5]

When owned by a member of a Morgan family in the middle of the eighteenth century, the homestead and lands were considered to be of some importance. From around 1841, and until 1891, John Jones, a farmer of ninety acres, lived in the ancient farmhouse.[6] His grandfather was said to be a famous Welsh preacher and kept a pack of hounds. About 1893, the building had become worn out and John Jones built a brick villa nearby. With the building of St. Dial's Board School in 1874, the name was preserved for many years.[7] John Jones died during December, 1913, in St. Dials Farm. At seventy-six years of age he was one of Cwmbran's oldest and best known inhabitants. His burial took place in Elim churchyard. When a young man he was one of the founders and assisted in the erection of the church. He had always worshipped at the popular church and became the oldest member in fellowship.[8] In more recent times, the site of the St. Dial's ancient chapel is perpetuated by the naming of an estate, which is now part of Cwmbran New Town.

REFERENCES

1. Babbidge, Adrian V., and Murphy, Paul P., *Llanderfel and St. Dial's Chapels, Cwmbran Monmouthshire - A Preliminary Survey*.

2. Gwent Record Office, *Valor Ecclesiasticus*, 1535.

3. Dovey, F. and Walters, H.F., *Llantarnam*, 1953, pp. 76-77.

4. Babbidge, Adrian V., and Murphy, Paul P., *Llanderfel and St. Dial's Chapels, Cwmbran Monmouthshire - A Preliminary Survey*.

5. Bradney, Sir Joseph, *A History of Monmouthshire - Llanfihangel Llantarnam*. p. 243.

6. Census Returns.

7. Bradney, Sir Joseph, *A History of Monmouthshire - Llanfihangel Llantarnam*. p. 243.

8. *Free Press of Monmouthshire*, January 9, 1914.

Chapter Five

LLANTARNAM VILLAGE

Llantarnam village is located four miles north of Newport, Gwent, on the south-eastern outskirts of Cwmbran town, alongside the old Newport-to-Pontypool road. Although it is still known as a village, encroaching urbanisation has effectively turned it into a suburb of Cwmbran.

In all probability the habitation of the village began around the end of the 10th Century with the establishment of the small Celtic church. It is a well known fact for a village to grow around a church and making it possible, as time went by, for religious participation to become stronger and for the building to enlarge.

In preparation for the 800th anniversary of the foundation of the Cistercian Abbey of Llantarnam, the Sisters of St. Joseph invited The Monmouthshire Antiquarian Association to carry out an active programme of excavations around the abbey. This valuable work took place between 1978 and 1984. In addition to the important information obtained relating to the abbey, an important discovery of a deserted medieval village in a field between the present day Llantarnam Village and the abbey, came to light.[1]

No doubt this discovery caused trial excavations to be commissioned by the Welsh Office Highways Directorate in 1990, in O.S. Field 0006, on the route of the proposed A4042 Llantarnam By-Pass. These excavations also revealed the remains of three buildings and two roads all believed to be part of the deserted medieval village of Llantarnam. During this early trial, documentary and structural evidence confirmed that the examined Mill Barn was a post-medieval mill and was possibly on the site of the monastic mill associated with the abbey.[2]

In response to these recent discoveries the Welsh Office Highways Directorate commissioned the Glamorgan-Gwent Archaeological Trust to undertake further excavations in March-May 1993.

When completed, the excavations revealed a number of buildings and their unmortared wall foundations suggests they existed before 1550. Although there is some difficulty to date the origins of the small village, there were indications that it predates the foundation of the abbey. The excavations revealed that by the mid-thirteenth century there was occupation of the northern fringe of the Dowlais Brook floodplain. This area of the village displayed some sign of planning, since many of the buildings were of the same design and construction and on a similar alignment. The lack of superstructure evidence gave the appearance of the

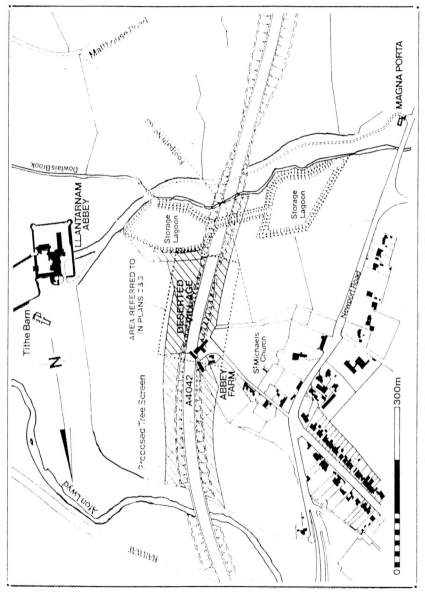

Location of deserted village and proposed A4042 Cwmbran By-Pass.

59

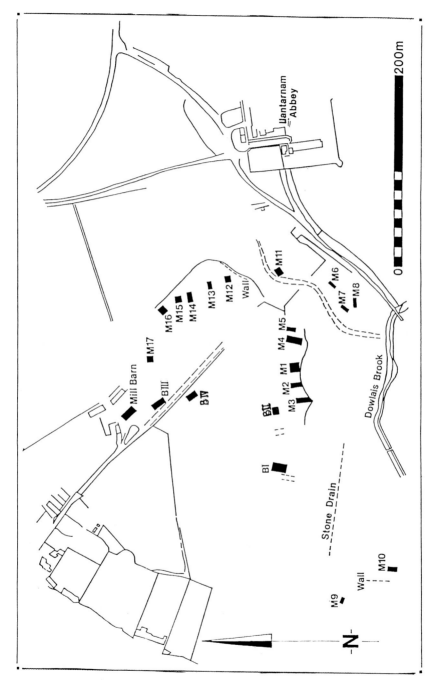

Plan showing extent of medieval village.

excavated buildings being systematically dismantled and not allowed to simply decay. Probably the stone was re-cycled.

It was customary for the Cistercians elsewhere to ensure that no settlement existed immediately at their gate, they even went so far as to remove settlements that were too close when setting up one of their houses. There can be no doubt that the White Monks sanctioned the unusual existence and development of the village in a field in front of the abbey. There would have been an intrinsic motive for its presence: it may have provided rents, tithes and a convenient labour force.

Parallel to the south-western wall of Building III and the line of the north-western wall of Building IV was a road, the line of which continued from the end of the present Abbey Lane towards the abbey. Excavations revealed a well-made metalled road, with associated roadside ditches and wall. Artefacts recovered from the road surface have a date range from the 17th century. It is likely that there has been a road in this position since the medieval period.

Excavation of the Mill Barn revealed it to be a multi-phased structure, which had undergone fundamental changes in the latter part of its history. For much of its history the mill building housed both a fulling mill (northwest end) and a corn mill (south-east end). The building was constructed mainly of split, roughly dressed river boulders with each mill having its own water supply and wheel.

The fulling mill had been constructed on top of the remains of an earlier building in which the monks no doubt produced their white robes and other garments. The mortar used in the walls of the existing building indicated it to be of the early 18th century. At the beginning of the 20th century Clifford Cory had the old building upgraded and converted into a meeting hall. It would be often used by various societies until demolished to make way for the new By-Pass.

It appears that there was a shift in the nucleus of the village from the northern fringe of the Dowlais Brook flood-plain around the southeast end of the ridge onto higher ground opposite the abbey. Medieval pottery and a 15th century groat had been recovered from this area, but no secure dating evidence established when the lower village was abandoned.

It is not certain how long the upper village survived, although it had been abandoned before the early 17th century. It is likely, although not proven, that this abandonment occurred in the first half of the 16th century, at the time of the dissolution of the abbey in 1536.[3] Perhaps William Morgan wished for a stately view from his new Elizabethan mansion.

By the 18th and 19th century the Llantarnam village began to look like it is as we know today. The church was indeed now the very centre of village life. A blacksmith's shop opposite would have carried out light industry while a wheelwright, located on the eastern side of the graveyard, made certain that transport needs were met. Local people in recent years remembered seeing the almost completed wooden wheels being rolled across the old main highway to the blacksmith shop. Here a metal tyre was put in place to complete the task.

In 1719, it must have seemed a practical enterprise to build the *Greenhouse* hostelry in the growing village. Located in an ideal position to attract growing passing trade, many a weary traveller would have been seduced by a warmth projected from the picturesque building. Most likely the erection of the hostelry alongside the southern wall of the church graveyard would have caused quite a stir in the local religious circle, but both have always existed in complete harmony. For many years a quaint sign, skilfully carved and coloured, set high in the rounded gable of the porch, invited passers-by to step inside and sample the good ale and cider. This old sign shows two jovial little men seated on opposite sides of a table set with an outsize goblet, a candle, and a jug almost as large as themselves. Beneath this convivial scene appears the Welsh inscription:

Y Ty Gwyrdd

1719

Cwrw da

A Seidir i chwi

Dewch y mewn

Chwi gewch y brofi

Which translated means: The Greenhouse, 1719, Good ale and cider for you, come in, you shall taste it.

Nearby, on the Pontypool road, is still found a substantial 18th century building named Brook House. Either owned or tenanted by the elite of the district in earlier times, it is well remembered as being occupied by Mr. Alfred William Robins, secretary to Sir Clifford Cory. Along Abbey Lane, an enchanting group of old cottages will take you back in time. These were mostly inhabited by the workers at Llantarnam Abbey with one serving as *The Cooper's Arms*, a popular small beerhouse in the 18th and 19th centuries. Here, many of the local societies held their meetings and annual dinners. Every Saturday night the solitude would be broken by the sound of music and raucous laughter. Perhaps, the noise upset the staff of Sir Clifford Cory, who lived in cottages nearby, for in April 1916, he purchased the inn and its licence, with the only desire to close it altogether. Near the old beerhouse could be found a small local police station where bars at the windows quickly reminded wrongdoers of the serious position they were in. This originated around 1870, when Police Constable James Lunick, with his wife and children, was stationed in one of the terraced houses.

Elementary education of young children appears to have started early in the village. An old cottage in Abbey Lane served as a school where local children were taught for a small fee under the 'dame school' system. Entries in the church warden's account book in 1818 and 1833, showed fees were paid for thatching the roof of this schoolroom.[4] The 1841 Census Return gives Michael Neagle, schoolmaster, 60 years of age, and his wife living at the cottage school. Sadly, he died in 1851, thus leaving his wife Mary to carry on his duties as best she could. In 1855, the school was described as low pitched, damp, and dark; and the wind playing havoc with the thatched roof, leaving the rafters in some places bare. At this time part of training up the schoolchildren included teaching them to shoot with a gun! For around forty years prior to this time, due to the church containing no vestry, parish meetings had been held in the cosy confines of the *Greenhouse* hostelry, the *Cooper's Arms* and the *Half-Way House*, at Cwmbran village, but, for reasons unknown, it was decided that the miserable hovel called a schoolroom should substitute as a vestry. A few meetings were subsequently held there, but one bitter cold night, when about thirty of the parishioners were assembled for the purpose of village business, they all felt so disgusted with their accommodation that they resolved to return to the good old custom of former times. In the first place there was no light, and one of the party had to run to the nearest public house to buy a half-penny candle, then there was no fire and lastly, only three of the number could be accommodated with seats. Due to other business at the Caerleon Petty Sessions, this particular meeting came to light and the Bench thought that the condition of the building was a disgrace to the parish. It was strongly urged that another meeting should soon be held for the purpose of putting the hovel into proper repair, for if it was unfit for men to remain in for half an hour, it must be great cruelty to confine the poor children there day after day.[5] With the opening of the British School in Oak Street, Cwmbran, during 1864, the former cottage school served as a meeting place and as late as 1874, slates were purchased for the roof. During the early 20th century, Sir Clifford Cory paid for the old building to be upgraded and used as the Abbey Sunday School for the children of Llantarnam. Some local people still treasure prizes presented to them at this old Sunday school. The prize books carry the Cory coat of arms inside the covers. Perhaps the last happy memory of this old building, worn out by years of use, is the 'Victory Celebrations', held after the 2nd World War.[6]

Much the same as other places Llantarnam Village could boast of its personalities:

The Morgans of Llantarnam Abbey were devout Catholics and their loyalty to the old faith persisted through the years of continual surveillance and persecution. A resident priest was secretly maintained by the family in defiance of the law. The Jesuit priest, Father David Lewis, was arrested on November 17, 1678, 'a little before day by six armed men' in a poor hut at Llantarnam 'under a clay floor cunningly contrived'. There was a tradition in the parish that the poor hut stood opposite the church and adjoining a blacksmith's forge. He was tried for popish practices at Monmouth and put to death in August, 1679.[7]

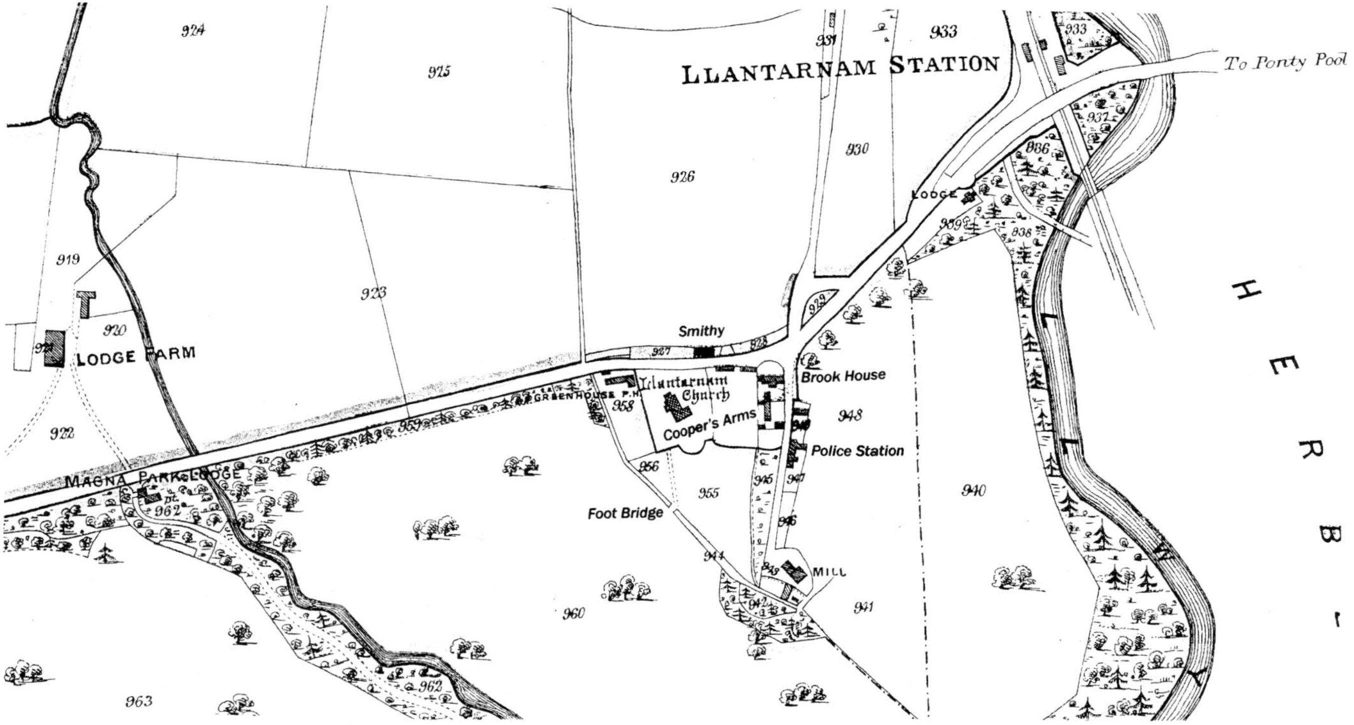
To Ponty Pool
LLANTARNAM STATION
LODGE
Smithy
Brook House
Police Station
Llantarnam Church
Cooper's Arms
GREENHOUSE P.H.
Foot Bridge
MILL
LODGE FARM
MAGNA PARK LODGE
HERB
LLWY

Llantarnam Village 1880.

Mrs Elizabeth Winslow residing in the village in the eighteen-fifties and became the object of wide-spread notoriety in consequence of numerous reputed cures she had effected, of persons suffering from almost ever description of disease, and in every stage. Her fame caused her dwelling to be visited daily by large numbers of individuals anxious to obtain advice and medicine from this sage matron. It had been a standing subject of conversation to all travellers on the recently opened Eastern Valley Railway, for the large number of people seen at Llantarnam Station with baskets and huge bottles were very conspicious. As many as between 600 and 700 arriving each week. This good lady, was held in high regard until the end of her days.[8]

Joseph Sawtell was a miller and proud of this fact. Around 1876, a series of disputes arose between the occupiers of Llantarnam Abbey and their tenants. It appears that the agents of the landlord were in the process of pinching the poor man with unreasonable demands of money owing to them. It became a tenants revolt with protest groups waiting for the agents at their rented farms and physically ejecting them when they arrived to assess the properties. Perhaps the most significant incident, and certainly the best documented, was the one involving Joseph Sawtell, of Abbey Mill. It appears to have been a fairly protracted, and often confrontational affair, and became the subject of newspaper reports when Sawtell was reported as having thrown flour over the owner's agent. He continued at the mill until 1879, and then took up the tenancy of nearby Penyparc Farm.[9] He died at Penyparc Farm, Llantarnam, on October 30, 1899, aged 78 years.

For most of the twentieth century, Llantarnam Village could compare with any picturesque village found in Britain. Travellers would see the village green containing several oak trees and cricket being played opposite *The Greenhouse* hostelry. W.H. Davies, the tramp-poet, a famous son of Gwent from neighbouring Newport, was hardly noticed as he lingered a while to quench his thirst in the local hostelries each time he passed through the village. He would at a later date remind himself of these pilgrimages to his beloved 'Llantarnam's green,' when the village became immortalised in his nostalgic poem, *'Days That Have Been.'* (See Appendix 2)

REFERENCES

1.   Mein, A.G., Summary of Results of Llantarnam Abbey Excavations 1978-1984.
2.   The Glamorgan-Gwent Archaeological Trust Ltd, Trial Excavations At Llantarnam Village, Gwent, March 1992.
3.   The Glamorgan-Gwent Archaeological Trust Ltd, Excavations At Llantarnam Village, Gwent, 1993.
4.   Gwent Record Office, D/Pa 99.59, St. Michael's Church Wardens Account Book, 1788-1888.

5.   *Monmouthshire Merlin,* March 31, 1855.

6.   Dovey, F. and Walters, H.F., *Llantarnam,* 1953, p.132.

7.   Evans, C.J.O., *Monmouthshire - Its History and Topography.* 1953. p.185.

8.   *The Newport Gazette,* April 16, 1859.

9.   Newport Local Studies Library, fm 310.347.63; Gwent Record Office, D.43.4631.M310.

Chapter Six

TREASURES OF MOTHER EARTH

In the parishes of Henllys, Llantarnam and Llanfrechfa Upper, the treasures of Mother Earth had not been fully realised in the 18th century let alone utilised. Throughout the eastern valley of Monmouthshire the bowels of the earth were loaded with minerals - hitherto unsought for and little known - merely for the need of conveyance to market.

Wealth for the few had always been obtained from what could be seen above ground and rich landowners found difficulty changing from centuries of farming their lands to that which was about to become known as heavy industry.

Since at least 1698, a few leases were taken up which permitted coal on a very small scale to be mined on the side of the Mynydd Maen. Further documentary evidence shows that the Caerleon Forge and Ponthir Works had been supplied by this means since the 1750s. No doubt the Cistercian monks had centuries before carried on outcropping for coal at Llanderfel. After filling their carts the fuel would have been laboriously transported down the steep mountainside in order to maintain the warmth of Llantarnam Abbey. In all probability this became one of the main reasons for the small number of monks living on the wind-swept mountain.

Time had stood still for those living in these old parishes until the end of 18th century, then it was realised that fortunes could be made if only the harvested, bulky minerals were to be easily transported.

By 1790, discussions among wealthy individuals led to an Act of Parliament sanctioning the building of a canal from Newport to Pontnewynydd, with a branch twelve miles long to Crumlin, which left the main line at Crindau, near Newport. The cut of the land began in 1792 and divided the parishes of Henllys, Llantarnam and Llanfrechfa Upper.

With the land rent in twain by the picks and shovels of the navvies, the Monmouthshire Canal soon became the main trade artery in the Eastern Valley rising to an elevation well over four hundred feet. The level was accomplished by negotiating forty-two locks. An average water depth of three and a half feet allowed mineral wealth of all kinds to pass along this liquid road with the narrow boats partly protected from the inclement weather by trees lining the upper bank on the opposite side to the towpath. In those early days of surveying and primitive manual labour, the canal became a monumental achievement and this is still to be witnessed by the tunnel, embankments, bridges and remains of locks in the Cwmbran district.[1] Immediately upon completion of the canal, iron ore, coal, lime, timber and other commodities were conveyed to the Bristol Channel, via Newport, and spread not only over England, but the world.

The building of the Monmouthshire Canal undoubtedly heralded the arrival of the industrial revolution to the Cwmbran area. At bridge 41, in the district of Clomendy, a tramroad leading to Caerleon had come into being. Built in 1794 by Nicholas Blannin, renter of Caerleon Iron Forge and Stone Quarries, the purpose at first was to provide materials for the building of the canal. In all probability, on the return journey, outcropped coal would have been carried to his iron works making the transport enterprise highly profitable for many years. It is interesting to note here that a Caerleon Tramroad milepost, dated 1822, was found in the Afon Lwyd river near the bridge which carried the tramroad over the river on the Pontypool side of Llantarnam Village. Found by the Sisters of Llantarnam Abbey, it was presented to Caerleon History Society and re-sited outside the town's old Charity School in 1977.[2]

Bridge 41 also provided access for the farmers to their lands below the canal and it was decided that this was the half-way point of the inland voyage from Newport to Pontnewynydd. Hence, the small *Half-Way* beerhouse came into existence and provided refreshments to thirsty canal workers and agricultural workers living nearby. A basin cut into the upper canal bank, on the northern side of the bridge, contained a wharf and provided a place for loading and unloading, and for bargees to tie up for a break, or stay the night. The wharf became busy in those early days and the new transport system brought a decent number of boatmen and canal employees to take up residence in the parish. By 1851, the Llantarnam

Caerleon Tramroad Milepost

parish housed 45 boatmen, 6 lock-keepers and 1 boat builder. With the coming of the railway, which caused a huge reduction of canal traffic, by 1861, these figures had dropped dramatically and only 8 canal employees remained in the parish.[3]

Others too quickly benefit from the new and profitable form of transport was the Conway family who commenced their iron and tinplate works on the banks of the Avon Lwyd at Pontnewydd (New Bridge) in 1802. Easy transport of their finished product no doubt encouraged the opening of another works at Pontrhydyrun in 1806.

A sign of employment becoming more available is indicated by the commencement of the Llantarnam Benefit Society in 1808. This brotherly society for the better support and relief of its members held monthly meetings at the sign of the *Canal Boat Public House*. Here it would be decided how much benefit paid up members received if unable to work due to illness or injury. The landlord of the *Canal Boat Public House*, Mr. Philip Wayne, became the treasurer of the Benefit Society and the annual dinner was always held at his hostelry.[4]

For around the next twenty-five years very little change took place in the Cwmbran area. In August 1832, the passing of the Reform Bill gave rise to celebrations in the Eastern Valley. Although the passing of the Bill proved of little consequence to the ordinary working man, he was not slow in enjoying the free attractions on the day of celebration. At the Pontrhydyrun works, Messrs. Conway brothers gave their workmen and neighbours a dinner in celebration of the national triumph. Tables were laid in an outbuilding and space made for a temporary orchestra. Around four-hundred were regaled in this manner. The evening was equally successful with the works band enlivening the proceedings with animated strains. The working men, with their wives and children, presented an appearance of cleanliness and gentility, and though so many partook of the exhilarating spirit of the malt, the whole was conducted with the greatest cordiality and good humour - not a drunken man was to be seen in the place.[5]

By 1837, employment prospects increased with a further development across the valley and opposite the Edlogan Works, Pontrhydyrun. For centuries a small dingle, with its high trees cut into the side of the Mynydd Maen was of little consequence and only the entry of the ancient homestead of Glyn (*meaning Cwm or valley*) Bran (*crow*) on old maps gave notice of its existence. With the arrival of industry, and the growth of this upper new village, it soon became known as upper Cwmbran (*Glyn Bran or valley of the crow*) after the old farm, and the name became firmly established.

The area held the remains of lime kilns used by farmers to make lime for use as a fertiliser or insecticide for whitewashing their houses. Old, small coal workings could be found on the mountainside where stone was quarried in limited amounts. A later woollen factory employing a few workers, who probably made flannel shirts for miners, but it was not until Reginald J. Blewitt turned his

Glynbran Farm and Siloam Chapel

thoughts to the potential of a coal mining site that the district began to assume some relevance. An Indenture shows that land belonging to Gelly Grafog Farm, and containing certain veins of coal, was leased by Squire Capel Hanbury Leigh, of Pontypool Park House, to Squire Reginald J. Blewitt, for a period of sixty years.[6] On this land, in 1837, he opened the Porthmawr (*Great Gate or Magna Porta*) Colliery. Soon to follow was the announcement in the *Monmouthshire Merlin* on January 1, 1838, of the opening of a new tramroad. Named the Porthmawr Tramroad, it joined the Caerleon Tramroad at Bridge 41 (near the *Half Way Inn*), which he had leased to support his new venture. In all probability any coal that had been dug by a previous lease holder was carried down the steep mountainside by horse and cart and taken to the nearest canal wharf.

Due to the influx of mainly colliers, accommodation had to be quickly supplied. Hence, a square of houses in the traditional style of the colliers' house, was built by Blewitt near the Porthmawr Colliery. Because of the topography of the land the houses were steeped and approximately twenty-nine in number. The *Squirrel Inn*, situated in the centre of the top row of The Square, could be easily visited and became a popular meeting place for many years. Here, an upstairs room served as a school from 1852-1868, then a new school was built lower down the hillside with stone from a nearby quarry.

Under the stimulus of Squire Blewitt, of Llantarnam Abbey, Upper Cwmbran development rapidly as a mining centre. Coal, fireclay and iron ore from levels driven into the eastern side of the Mynydd Maen, was now giving employment to

71

many miners. From being an agricultural district, scantily populated with bilingual people in 1837, the arrival of workers, mainly from England, caused English to become the common tongue. The following article in the March 20, 1841, issue of the Monmouthshire Merlin gives witness to these interesting times:

'Works at Cwmbran. - It has been truly said that no district in the known world would abound with such natural facilities for manufacture as South Wales. To furnish the great moving powers of the world, iron and steam, Nature has done all; human industry and enterprise are alone wanting to develop the riches of the district. Another product of mines, we find, is now added to our list of exports; and begins to assume the place of an important branch in the trade of this part. We allude to the manufacture of fireclay. About two years past a stratum of clay, bearing an exact resemblance to that found around the Lyle, in Staffordshire, and known by the name of Stourbridge Clay, was found at Cwmbran, on the estate of Mr. R.J. Blewitt, Esq., M.P. On visiting this place a few days ago, which we so late remember a lonely dell, thickly wooded, the haunt of wild fox and grouse, we found all the bustle and activity of a rising village; an extensive manufactory, with most complete machinery, in full operation. These works are, we find, erected by Mr. Ebeneezer Rogers, and carried on under the name of Stourbridge Fire Clay Company, nearly all the workmen employed have been brought from Staffordshire, and are picked hands. The work, as at present, will, we understand, turn out 60,000 firebricks per week, and when complete 110,000 per week. Notwithstanding the difficulties always attendant on the introduction of any new manufacture into a country, we are informed that the quality already stands high in the market, and we doubt not the demand for the article will be fully equal to the supply. We heartily wish success to the spirited proprietors of this undertaking, as we do to all, whose honest enterprise tends to develop the greatest natural resources of our district.'

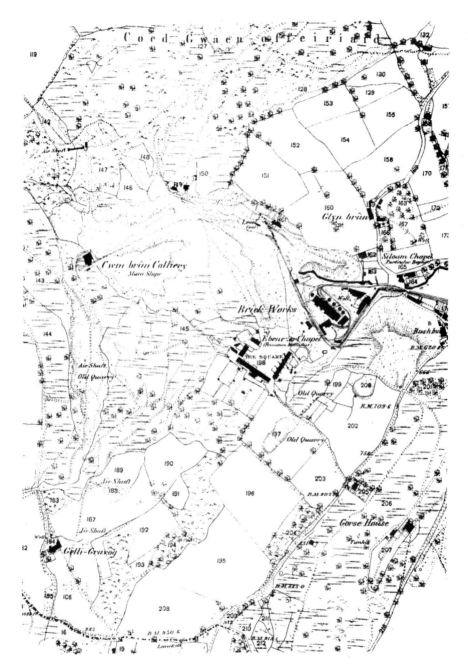

Upper Cwmbran 1882

Entrance to Porthmawr Colliery

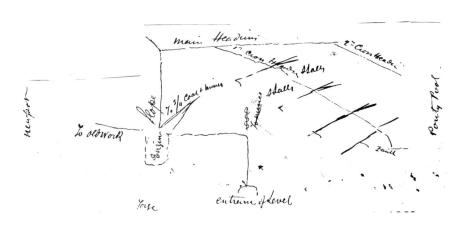

Upper Cwmbran Colliery as drawn by Henry Morgan in 1853.

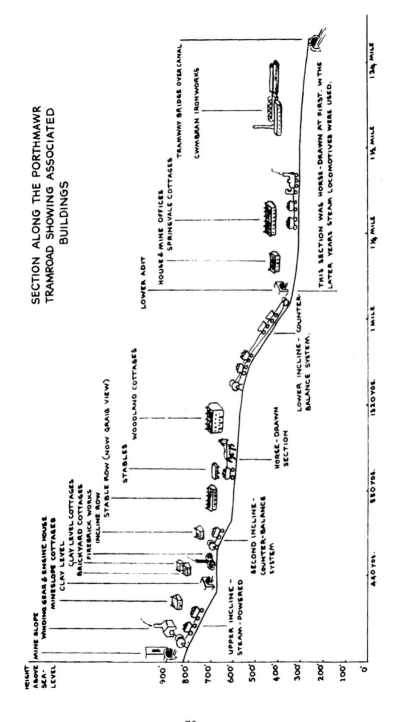

SECTION ALONG THE PORTHMAWR TRAMROAD SHOWING ASSOCIATED BUILDINGS

In 1854, this brickworks became the property of John Lawrence who leased it to Henry Parfitt, in 1867, "with the Stoves, Kilns, Smith's Shop and Cottages," for the yearly rent of £114, and the sum of 1/6d for every ton of clay taken for the following seven years from the Levels Headings, plus use of the railway sidings near the Cwmbran Furnaces.[7] With a ready supply of materials, Henry Parfitt, also became a successful builder in the last thirty years of the nineteenth century. Many of the district's private and public buildings can be attributed to him.

At this time Nonconformity was spreading its influence in the district. The Ebenezer Primitive Methodist Chapel had already been formed in the Square of the new hillside hamlet and in 1838, plans were in hand to erect the Siloam Baptist Chapel lower down the mountainside.

Nearby another house of worship came into existence perhaps more by accident than design. Learning that a beerhouse was in the process of being erected alongside the tramroad on the hillside, a worthy minister used all his powers of persuasion to defeat its accomplishment, and when a vote was taken, only one was cast in favour of a licence. The owner swallowed his rebuff and offered the house to the minister as a chapel. The deal was made at a cost of £190.[8] Bethal Congregational Chapel would assist in serving the religious needs of the community for the next one hundred and thirty-four years.

On an auspicious day in 1838, no space could be found in the popular *Half Way Inn* and many of the customers spilled out onto the narrow highway. It was the day young Victoria became the queen of all Britain. Perhaps more loyal toasts rang out than was really necessary as jugs of ale were raised time and again.

At this time most of the land of Colomendy (later shortened to Clomendy) estate, was owned by Madame de Solignac. She had been married to Charles Griffiths whose wealthy family lived for many years at Llanyrafon Farm. Charles died without issue in 1836, leaving a widow Jane, who married Frenchman, Mons. Eugene Jean Baptise de Solignac. Baroness de Solignac died in 1880.

The wharf at bridge 41, the upper terminus of the Caerleon Tram Road, had proved a good site for Joseph Meredith, landlord of the *Half Way Inn*, to sell his ales. At nearby Clomendy Farm, tenant farmer Henry Williams, employed four men to work the sixty-two acres of land. The ancient farm had been known by its Welsh name Colomendy (meaning dove-cot) for centuries. Some time during the past, in all probability, a tenant of the farmhouse must have reared doves, which was known to be a popular meat dish during winter months. In recent years, a well belonging to the farm was discovered. Built originally as a circle of latticed brickwork without mortar and backed by clay, a former owner bricked in the upper part of the well with mortar-joined bricks around 1936. Found to be about fourteen feet deep, it leads to an underground stream and contains eight feet of water. The well, found in the

Ebenezer Primitive Methodist Chapel, The Square, Upper Cwmbran

Bethal Congregational Chapel, Upper Cwmbran

garden, was covered by a concrete path and is believed to have been in existence since the farm was built, probably in Tudor times.

Prior to 1840, the district still retained a mostly rural setting, but nothing could prepare the few inhabitants for the explosion of industry which was about to take place.

Two men were the main architects of this sudden transformation. Squire Blewitt we already know, the other was a member of an old Llantarnam family. John Lawrence's grandparents lived at the well-known 13th century Llantarnam Court Farm. Believed to have been built as far back as 1291, it formed part of the old Abbey estate. In 1535, when the Abbey was dissolved, the original Llantarnam Court Farm, known as the Grange of Scybor Court, was valued at £1-6-8. After numerous tenants, around 1750, the Lawrence family occupied the farm, the first being George Lawrence, whose eldest son John was born there in 1779. An interesting fact is that around the beginning of the 19th century, the farm became known for the kennelling of a successful pack of hounds.

John Lawrence became a considerable land owner in the Eastern and Western Valleys and lived much of his life at Cwmbran House, in the parish of Llanfrechfa Upper, where he also owned a number of barges on the Monmouthshire Canal during the 1840s. It was here that his wife Ann gave birth to a son John, on November 20th, 1807. John junior took an interest in the iron industry at quite an early age. To use his own words: "The first commencement of my career in business was in the iron trade, in the year 1825, with the British Iron Company. Their works were at Abersychan. I had a great interest in those works. I first assisted in pegging out the lines of the foundations of the works; I laid the first foundation stone; I started the first blast engine; put the first blast on the furnace, and rolled the first bar of iron that was rolled there."

John married first Miss Morrison, sister of Mr. Moreton Morrison, who formerly resided at Newport, and had invested a large amount of capital in the coal trade. She lived for only twelve months. After her death he married Miss Edwards, sister of Mr. E.B. Edwards, who was magistrate's clerk at Pontypool, and under-sheriff of the county. They had four sons and two daughters.

In 1897, John Lawrence gave the interesting account of how the Iron Works came to be built at Cwmbran and not at Newport. He said: "I was always a great advocate for having an iron works at Newport; and I told my friend Blewitt that I thought of erecting blast furnaces there. 'Why not build them at my colliery at Cwmbran and I will join you?' he said; but I replied 'Newport is the right place to build them.' That was about 1840. Well one day I had a note by special messenger from Blewitt asking me to spend Sunday with him, and adding 'I think I shall persuade you to build your furnaces up here.' We were walking down his tramroad, which brought coal from Cwmbran Colliery to Newport, and he said, 'I say John, you had better make up your mind to have the furnaces up here at

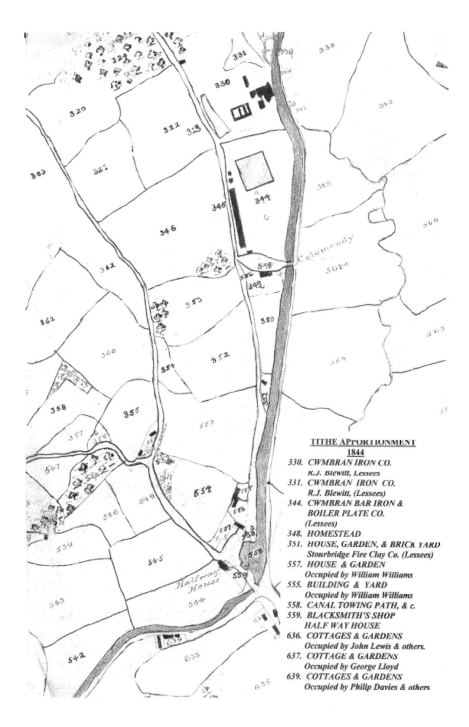

TITHE APPORTIONMENT
1844

330. CWMBRAN IRON CO.
   R.J. Blewitt, Lessees

331. CWMBRAN IRON CO.
   R.J. Blewitt, (Lessees)

344. CWMBRAN BAR IRON &
   BOILER PLATE CO.
   (Lessees)

348. HOMESTEAD

351. HOUSE, GARDEN, & BRICK YARD
   Stourbridge Fire Clay Co. (Lessees)

557. HOUSE & GARDEN
   Occupied by William Williams

555. BUILDING & YARD
   Occupied by William Williams

558. CANAL TOWING PATH, & c.

559. BLACKSMITH'S SHOP
   HALF WAY HOUSE

636. COTTAGES & GARDENS
   Occupied by John Lewis & others.

637. COTTAGE & GARDENS
   Occupied by George Lloyd

639. COTTAGES & GARDENS
   Occupied by Philip Davies & others

79

Cwmbran.' I said 'No indeed, I would not spend a shilling upon that, but if you join me at Newport I will go halves.' We walked down the tram road from the colliery to the site of the present furnaces of the Patent Nut and Bolt Company, and there, on the canal, was a boat of iron ore moored. 'There, you can see that,' he said; 'I will compromise the matter with you, if you will put the furnaces here, there's a boat of iron ore ready for you.' So I reluctantly agreed, and we built our works at Cwmbran."[9]

By 1840, John Lawrence had established the Cwmbran Iron Company a short distance north of Bridge 41, and on the upper side of the Monmouthshire Canal. Alongside this works, and nearer Bridge 41, could also be found the Cwmbran Bar Iron and Boiler Plate Company believed to be owned by R.J. Blewitt. Both companies had leased the land from Madame de Solignac. Although both works are shown on an 1840 Tithe map of the parish, the 1841 Census Return gives no indication of iron workers having recently moved to the district. It is known that one of the many unexpected slumps in the iron trade occurred at this time, or perhaps the lack of a workforce was due to both works only having been recently commissioned.

For commercial purposes these new undertakings had to have a business address and at the time they could only be identified with the recently established village of Cwmbran found at the upper end of the district. Subsequently, as the village we know today as Cwmbran expanded, it took over the name, and the small hillside community became known as Upper Cwmbran.

However, by the end of 1841, the following newspaper report indicates that all was well and the boom had began:

> 'On Tuesday last, a numerous party of gentlemen connected with the Cwmbran Iron Works, together with their friends, assembled at the house of Mr. H. Williams, Half Way Inn, to celebrate, according to ancient custom throughout the Principality, the evening called "Nas cyn-y-gayaf," when the worthy host and hostess catered bountifully for the appetite of the most fastidious, a supper consisting of every delicacy of the season; the viands were of the choicest description. The chair was able filled by Mr. John Jones, forge manager, supported by Edw. Williams, of the weighing machine. The cloth having been removed, the worthy Chairman announced the usual loyal toasts, which were heartily received. Song and sentiment went merrily around the room, and at intervals the company was much gratified at the beautiful national and other pieces played by accomplished musicians, Messrs. Silverthorne on the violin and flute; and the party, after enjoying a most pleasant evening, gave three most hearty cheers for the worthy host and his good lady, and retired to their homes highly delighted. "Prosperity to Cwmbran Works" was cheered to the echo.[10]

Another newspaper report in 1845 indicates that the Clomendy estate had become a popular site for the production of iron when yet another extension was erected. Unfortunately no information is given regarding the owner of the works or if it was an addition to the holdings of John Lawrence:

NEW IRON WORK NEAR CWMBRAN, - On the western bank of the Pontypool line of the Monmouthshire Canal, within six miles of Newport, a new iron works has sprung up, as if by magic, and is just commencing active operations. It consists of one blast furnace with all requisite conveniences; and the proprietors have the credit of being the first to introduce, into this part of the country, a new apparatus for lifting the materials to the top of the furnace, as simple and effective as it is ingenious. A passer-by standing on the opposite bank of the canal, in front of the furnace, will observe immediately adjoining thereto, and connected with it, a high stage of wood work - from the bottom of this will suddenly emerge and ascend slowly and steadily to the height of the furnace, a large iron tube or cylinder supporting a platform, covered with barrows, of mine coke, and limestone. These barrows having been emptied by a man at the furnace mouth, the tube is seen to gradually sink into the earth, and the platform descends with it. The operation above described, takes place without any noise, or apparent working of machinery, the ascent (as we are informed) being produced by the introduction of blast into the tube, and the descent by the opening of a valve which discharges it again. By means of this contrivance the large outlay usually required for making back walls and levelling ground, is entirely saved, and the duties of the furnace managers are much facilitated. While standing at the hearth of the furnace, and watching the cinder - that unerring test of quality - he can, at the same time, survey all the operations of the coke yard, and take care that his instructions for charging the furnace are rigidly adhered to. There is another advantage in this piece of machinery, which to iron masters, will be invaluable. It may be made the means of securing top room in a comparatively limited space, for almost any extent of rubbish. We do not profess to know much of iron furnaces, but it appears to us that this little work is well located, conveniently constructed, and admirably arranged. We hail it as another link in the bright chain of our country's commercial prospects.[11]

In 1847, the iron works of R.J. Blewitt appears to have been doing well as witnessed by the large metal supports produced for the canal bridges in Cwmbran. Near the *Halfway Inn*, the former bridge 41 was no more than a small humped-back stone walkway with a keystone. Known as a farmers' bridge it gave access to the animals and equipment into the lower fields. By 1847, the traffic over this bridge had increased tremendously with men reporting for work at Blewitt's iron

Cwmbran Bridge Support cast at the Cwmbran Ironworks of R.J. Blewitt, 1847.

John Lawrence　　　　*Abraham Darby*

works, on the upper bank of the canal, and the haulage of materials for the purpose of manufacture. With extra revenue going to the Monmouthshire Canal Company for transporting materials and finished iron products by barge, to and from the new iron works, they had to comply with the building of a large, new bridge for improved access and safety reasons. At the nearby Blewitt's iron works much of the metal supports were produced. Two of these supports were larger than the others and could be seen on the south and north sides of the bridge. Probably for the purpose of advertising, in the middle of each had been expertly cast 'R.J. BLEWITT ESQ^R · 1847. CWMBRAN IRON WORKS.' Fortunately, both have been preserved for posterity. The bridge was further enlarged with the coming of the railway.

In 1848, reports showed that the works in the populous and thriving locality of Cwmbran were rapidly progressing in the march of improvement. Buildings appeared to be rapidly springing up all around, while a spirit of enterprise was very much present. Added to this development a Pontypool builder received instructions for the immediate erection of a further twelve houses according to the plans and specifications of the architect and surveyor.

To satisfy the religious needs of the district in question, the former members of Penywaun Congregational Church had in fact met since 1672. In that year the church was started in the house of Margaret Jones, a pious woman, living nearby in the parish of Henllys. The descendants of these early worshippers, in the year 1741, began to hold regular prayer meeting in a Cwmbran farmhouse, which was later converted into a chapel. The land was given by Mrs Margaret Walters and her son William, of Ton Farm. At what seems to be a fortunate time to assist the formation of a new village, some of the members left Penywaun Church in 1842. These energetic people lost no time building a new church in what was to become the centre of the village. Built by 1844, Elim Congregational Church became a timely addition to the religious needs of the exploding population. By 1845, the Elim school, conducted by Mr. Davies, gave a limited education to twenty-three children. Although of mostly of a religious nature, the children were fortunate to receive some learning.

The 1851 Census Return shows that the new Cwmbran village had grown considerably with Forge Row consisting of twenty-eight houses and Foundry Row about to hold six terraced houses. Extra to these early streets, a number of single houses had taken shape. Much of the new housing held the workforce of the nearby iron works. Many had arrived from Dowlais and other far away places. Their occupations reflected the iron industry: moulders, ballers, puddlers, roll turners, blacksmiths and mill men. The region now contained the three main industries for which it would be known for many years: tin trade, coal mining and the manufacture and working of iron. Compared to most other occupations the iron workers received more money. It was argued that extra money was required to provide plenty of good food to give the necessary strength to do the heavy work required at the forge, the rolling mills and the puddling furnaces. With the better wages went an improved job status and the iron workers maintained that they were the senior work force in the district. During these times the appointed manager of the Cwmbran Iron Works lodged at the *Half Way Inn*, while John Lawrence and his family were to take up residence at his villa 'The Graig', but a short distance from the Upper Cwmbran colliery.

It is interesting to note here that for the purpose of living near the iron works, another small community, to be known as Forge Hammer, was establishing. Oral evidence suggests that this community received its name due to an enormous forge hammer found at the northern end of Cwmbran iron industries. It was reputed to be the second largest in the world!

Squire Blewitt went bust in 1852. He had made too many enemies. It was also said that he spent a great amount of money restoring Llantarnam Abbey. This, combined with his poor industrial management record, was followed by the final blow of the collapse of the Monmouthshire and Glamorgan Bank, of which he had become the principle shareholder.

The sale of Blewitt's forge and mills brought an immediate offer from the well established Ebbw Vale Company. At the Cwmbran Works, the Ebbw Vale Company, while using their vast experience, intended to produce a finished product from the raw pig iron, thus specialising more and reducing costs. In 1852, The Ebbw Vale Company also purchased the Abersychan Iron Works for a trifling £8,500, which was more than covered by the stock left behind. Abraham Darby was the main director of this expanding company. He was the descendent of the famous Abraham Darby, of Coalbrookdale, who built the first iron bridge in the world at Ironbridge. In June 1852, the Newport to Pontypool Railway opened, which improved the transport of iron goods throughout the eastern valley and would have helped Darby to make up his mind to purchase the new undertakings. His main iron works and residence was at Ebbw Vale, but he would often use the new railway service to visit his other works. It is a fact during these early days of the railway that special note would be taken by passengers of their important fellow travellers.

These were difficult times for the Cwmbran workforce with one of the iron works stopped and all hands laid off. It seemed that with Blewitt's colliery and other undertakings, also in a ruinous and unprofitable state, and about to close, great privations were about to be caused to the Cwmbran community. Fortunately, John Lawrence took over Blewitt's Upper Cwmbran operations and helped to save both the new village of Cwmbran and the Upper Cwmbran community from great hardship.[12]

Instructions from senior management of the Ebbw Vale Company, on November 29, 1852, caused John Morgan, a puddler at Blewitt's former iron works, to put on labourers. These were to be puddlers and furnace men given employment until the works reopened properly and they could resume their former occupations. With the help of the landlord of the *Half Way Inn*, twenty-one men were immediately started. At this time a young man of almost twenty-six years commenced employment in a what appeared to be a junior management position. Henry Lawrence Morgan, of Caerleon, came from an influential family and lodged at first with Elizabeth Morris, Maes-y-Rhiw, for 12/- a week. His days would be busy attending to the many small tasks necessary for the re-commissioning of the works. Mr. R.B. Roden, the senior manager at the British Iron Works, often arrived to inspect the works and took over the repair of the heavy machinery. By December 11, 1852, masons had been put to work on the furnaces and young Morgan was instructed to advertise for a skilled workforce. Puddlers were to receive 2/- per day with Ballers and Ball Rollers, Carpenters 2/9, Underhands 1/6, Strikers 1/8, Squeezers 2/-, Nightwatchmen 2/-, Railmen 2/3, Engineers 3/-, Firemen 2/- , and Blacksmiths 2/6, plus £1 per week. A track over the canal was built for the dumping of cinders and with the works becoming operational, Mr. W.R. Davies, mill manager, arrived from the British Iron Works to take overall charge, which reduced Henry Morgan to little more than a clerk.

Throughout 1853, the works progressed well with an average weekly yield of 330 tons of pig iron. On June 9, the iron works was officially closed to allow the men to go to Pontypool in the afternoon where a huge celebration took place to celebrate the birth of an heir for elderly Squire J.C. Hanbury. Henry Morgan observed that trains were tremendously full and all had a good time in the grounds of Pontypool Park House. 1854 would be very different particularly for those men who had not saved for a rainy day. At the end of summer, yields were dropping and word went around that the Ebbw Vale Company had sustained serious losses by an American financial house. Added to this, at the end of September the iron trade was beginning to get very bad. On December 9, Henry Morgan was returning by train from Newport and happened to be in the same carriage as Mr. Brown, another senior director of the Ebbw Vale Company. Mr. Brown informed him that they were reducing the establishment at their Ebbw Vale and Victoria works and the Cwmbran Iron Works would soon be completely stopped if the iron trade did not get better.[13] However, the works did survive a few more years under this management and in 1858, they successfully produced wrought iron chairs to be used only for the joints of railway tracks.

In 1857, John Lawrence, in order to receive a voluntary testimonial from his workforce and to show his fondness for the local people, decided to hold a festival at his home, the Graig, near the Upper Cwmbran Colliery. On a warm sunny day in August of that year numerous workmen in his employ, and their families, were entertained in a style of true old British hospitality by their munificent employer when arriving at his villa. The tables, benches and chairs were set on the green sward of the lawn near the house. Sometime before noon the people began to assemble, and were immediately regaled with ale. They then amused themselves, and their employer and his family and friends occasionally mingled with the crowd. The Monmouthshire Militia Band was engaged for the occasion, and were stationed on the terrace in front of the house. Soon to be heard was strains of operatic selections, stirring marches, and lively music, which invariably caused many to "trip the light fantastic." The waltz, polka, and reel were the order of the hour until the committee arrived to deliver a worthy testimonial to John Lawrence. All were quiet as the chairman spoke of the interest their employer showed in their comfort and well-being. Particular mention was given to his hard work and generosity at the time of the fall of the Monmouthshire and Glamorgan Bank in 1852. Loud cheering followed and Mr. Lawrence responded. Following his reply, upwards of four-hundred adjourned to the rural banqueting area where everyone sat down to a substantial dinner, which was washed down by good strong ale. After dinner amusements and sports were enjoyed on the lawns with everyone being well entertained until night began to draw her sable mantle over the scene. Only then did the whole party retire to their homes in a happy and orderly manner.[14]

Around this time James Gibbs, of Bristol, was researching the growing district of Cwmbran for a site to establish a vitriol works to supply South Wales. With plenty of labour and an abundance of coal available for his works, he did not hesitate in September 1858, when taking over a lease which enabled him to manufacture oil of vitriol, naphtha, ammonia, acetate of lime and sugar of lead. The site, near where the present Cwmbran Sports Stadium now stands, was at the time, a safe distance from the new village of Cwmbran, but not too far for the workers to walk to their employment. The Vitriol Works was managed at first by Mr. Edwin Selfe, and gave regular employment to local men for many years. In 1911, the works was taken over by the Cwmbran Chemical Company and a major reconstruction of the site implemented. By 1912, the chemical works had been extended and six extra sets of burners were erected in addition to the six recently completed. When fully operational again, extra workmen were needed and an increased output resulted. The chemical works continued to be a valued employer in the area. By now the village had grown nearer the works and the Cwmbran Urban District Council would regularly receive complaints of escaping fumes. A further upset for local people was the continuous acid pollution of a nearby stream. Despite the valid grumbles, the works continued and in 1926 merged into the Imperial Chemical Industrial Group. However, by 1930, the works had closed leaving a badly soiled landscape.

While the Vitriol Works was being commissioned another development had taken place in the nearby district to be known as Oakfield. Two Abergavenny gentlemen, with experience in the iron trade, and by now aware of the small, but growing industrial centre of Cwmbran, searched for a suitable site for an iron and wire works. In 1857, James Charles Hill, of the Brooks, Abergavenny, and William Forester Batt, of Kae Kenty, Abergavenny, purchased eight acres of land at Oakfield for £1,210. With a £10,000 advance to them by Henry Crawshay, they entered the locality for the business of wire rod and wire iron, tin plate bar and bar iron manufacturing.[15] In August 1860, the building of the works had been completed and a party of ladies and gentlemen, together with the workmen, assembled for a special ceremony. Mr. Hill addressed the gathering, threw a bottle of wine at the wheel, and christened the works with the name of the Oakfield Wire Works. Mrs Hill, amid much cheering, started the engine, and the first lump of iron was shingled by George Rollins, late shingler at Garnderris, and rolled by Samuel Newbury, late shingler at Pontnewynydd. At the conclusion of the ceremony, the men were regaled with a quantity of *cwrw da*, and drank 'Long life to Messrs Hill and Batt,' and 'Success to the Oakfield Wire Works.' The workmen, with their wives and sweethearts, completed the proceedings with a dance before separating much pleased at an early hour of the following morning.[16] A more comprehensive account was to appear in *The Mining Journal*:

'The New Works. - The Mining Journal in speaking of the new works recently built at this place says: They are the property of Mr. J. Charles Hill, of Wilden Ironworks, near Abergavenny, who is the managing partner, and Mr. W. Forster Batt, of Abergavenny. In the buildings and the various appliances, which are without exception of the most substantial and improved description, no expense or pains have been spared, but all has been done upon the plans, and under the personal supervision of Mr. Hill, whose experience is such that not a single shilling has been laid out unnecessarily. The Works are intended for making merchant bars, fire bars, and wire rods, all of the very best quality. There is also some very excellent wire drawing machinery, which has been in operation some time, but has been erected more with a view of testing and improving the wire rod manufacture of the firm than of entering very extensively into that department. The building, however, is laid out for carrying on, should it be found necessary, a large trade in wire. The quality of the wire rods of Messrs. Hill and Batt is already well known and acknowledged as superior by the Birmingham manufacturers; and there can be no doubt that a similar character will be obtained for all the different descriptions of iron to be manufactured at the works. The forge end is now in full operation, the enormous wheels and other machinery working beautifully; and the remaining portion will shortly be in motion.

The Oakfield works are situated close to the Newport and Hereford Railway, and are connected with it by a siding; while they are nearly on the level with the canal, communication being obtained with it by tram road with wharf abutting on the towing path. The village of Cwmbran has increased considerably during the erection of the works, and is rapidly extending itself. A large number of men will, it is expected, ultimately be employed at the new establishment.[17]

In less than twenty years the district of Cwmbran had been changed from a peaceful rural setting to that of the bustle of industry with its grime very evident and social problems increasing as each year went by. On a stroll in the country lanes near the new industries, Henry Morgan stopped and examined the discoloured hedgerow. Already it was blackened by the accumulation of industrial waste.

REFERENCES

1. Lloyd, W.G., *Sebastopol - A Local History,* 1992, p.23.
2. Elliott, Kisten & Swift, Andrew, *Archive Magazine No. 32,* December 2001, pp. 3-17.
3. Census Returns 1851 and 1861.
4. Newport Local Studies Library, pm 310-334.7, *Llantarnam Benefit Society,* 1808.
5. *The Monmouthshire Merlin,* August 25, 1832.
6. Gwent Record Office, D8C. 0010.
7. Gwent Record Office, D409.0003.
8. *The Monmouthshire Merlin,* March 16, 1838.
9. *The South Wales Argus,* June 26, 1897; *The South Wales Argus,* November 4, 1901; *The South Wales Times and The Star of Gwent,* November 8, 1901; *Western Mail,* November 8, 1901.
10. *The Monmouthshire Merlin,* November 4, 1841.
11. *The Monmouthshire Merlin,* February 8, 1845.
12. *Star of Gwent,* August 22, 1857.
13. Newport Local Studies Library, M275-920, *Henry Lawrence Morgan, Diary of a Cwmbran (Maes-y-Rhiw) resident,* 1852-1854.
14. *Star of Gwent,* August 22, 1857.
15. Gwent Record Office, D32 763.
16. *The Monmouthshire Merlin,* August 18, 1860.
17. *Newport Gazette,* September 1, 1860.

Chapter Seven

ORDER AND HOPEFUL PROSPERITY

It would be a hard earned prosperity for the men of the new industrial centre of Cwmbran. The vicissitudes of the iron and coal trade were always present and during the bad times workers had little choice but to take a ten per cent cut in wages. When trade was good wages improved, but hours were long and tiring and probably due to exhaustion, what little available leisure time existed would be spent in nearby beerhouses.

Drunkenness had always been a problem, but with regular wages it was on the increase. Workmen arrived at the iron works in a drunken state and sometimes in a belligerent manner. Despite being sent home for the day with loss of wages, the problem continued, sometimes causing a drop in the iron yield for the day. Employers everywhere became increasingly concerned about this lack of discipline and actively encouraged the formation of chapels and churches in their districts. A Cwmbran Temperance Hall, opened in 1859, with around two hundred people present, did little to solve the problem.

The Penywain Church and Elim Congregational Church were doing everything possible to bring not only religion, but also order to their expanding industrial district. This was not easy, even with the various religious faiths present. In 1860, some support appeared to be forthcoming when it became known that a new church had been discussed for the nearby Oakfield district.

With no Baptist Chapel in or near the new village of Cwmbran, after careful and prayerful consideration a committee was elected who met at New House Farm in February 1860, the chairman being Ebenezer Williams, pastor of Siloam. It took long and anxious deliberation before an unanimous decision was reached to erect a commodious chapel without delay.

Mr. John Samuel, Esq., of Penyfan, Bassaleg, kindly donated land in the Oakfield district measuring twelve perches for the use of the Baptist denomination for ever, while Cyrus Hanson, of Henllys Brickworks, provided 500 tons of stone, valued at £37, free of charge. Farmers sent teams and men, also free of charge, to haul the stone. The building contract was given to stone mason Mr. William Lloyd. It is an interesting fact that while the building was taking place two score people asked to be members and some were baptised in the nearby Cocker Brook.

The stone-laying ceremony took place on 2nd September, 1860, in the presence of a large company. On the site near the extensive new works of Messrs. Hill and Batt, the foundation stone of the new Baptist Chapel was laid by Miss Samuel, of Penyfan, Bassaleg. After reading and prayer Miss Samuel, having been presented with a beautiful hammer and trowel by the architect, proceeded to lay the foundation stone, which was done by the young lady with considerable skill, and in the midst of marked approbation from the assembled multitude. The day was beautifully fine, and many people came from several miles around to witness the historic ceremony.

The new Baptist Chapel, near Two Locks, and conveniently situated alongside bridge 40, was opened and dedicated on Sunday, 3 November, 1861, when it was named Ebenezer after Reverend Ebenezer Williams who conducted the services.

The Baptist Church became a resounding success. By November 1889, it had become too small and Pontnewydd builder Henry Parfitt was engaged to renovate it, and to put in end and side galleries. The year 1903 brought the need of increased seating capacity for the Church and Sunday School. It was decided to add to the length of the church and to build a lecture hall with ten classrooms and a minister's vestry above. In 1960 successful centenary celebrations took place and today this highly respected church continues the good work started all those years ago.[1]

With regard to law and order, the value of religious worship in Cwmbran and surrounding districts was by now becoming more recognised. Another important step in the cause of bringing order and dignity into the lives of local people occurred when another stone-laying ceremony took part in Cwmbran during September 1867. For some time the members of the Wesleyan denomination had felt the want of a place of worship in the new village. The matter languished for some years before Messrs. Hodges and Smith took up the matter, which resulted in Mrs Bytheway laying a foundation stone. Mr. Parfitt, contractor, had followed the building plans of Newport architect Samuel Hancorn, and the chapel opened to a large congregation the following year. For almost a hundred years the popular Wesleyan Methodist Church and Sunday School in Wesley Street served the community well, but by 1961, eight churches were to be found in a radius of half-a-mile. This situation, coupled with the need of the Cwmbran Council to widen the road, causing the loss of the vestry, sealed the fate of the old church. The last service in the highly respected church was held in September,1965.

The parish of Llanfrechfa Upper was experiencing similar changes to other districts in 1860. Divided into an upper and lower division, it is worth noting here the geography of this scattered parish. The Lower Llanfrechfa division stretched from Llanfrechfa to Ponthir and is out of the range of this Cwmbran history. Upper Llanfrechfa began at Pontnewydd and included Upper Cwmbran,

Ebenezer Baptist Church, Two Locks, Llantarnam.

Holy Trinity Church, Pontnewydd.

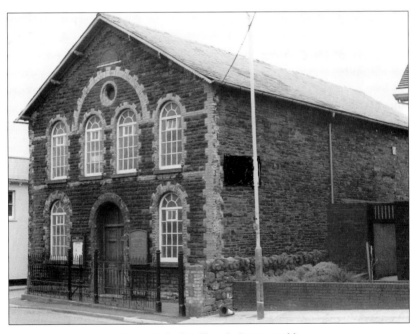

Hope Methodist Church, Pontnewydd.

Pontrhydyrun, and in the early days, Griffithstown. Some argued that Griffithstown was entirely surrounded by the parish of Panteg. For many years it was often referred to as 'the island' and again this later railway village is beyond the range of this history. Some uncertainty arises as to the origin of the name Llanfrechfa, but the most popular explanation is *'the Church of Brechfa,'* one of the Lords of the Manor of Edlogan.[2]

With the presence of the lower Conway (Pontnewydd) tin works, the Upper Cwmbran community, and the workers living at the northern end of the Clomendy iron industries, the nucleus of another village had formed to meet the many new commercial needs. Soon known as Pontnewydd, it would immediately develop its own individuality. Nearby, a Church of England schoolroom, built around 1853, had been licensed for Divine Worship, thus preventing the long trek over the Avon Lwyd to the church in the Llanfrechfa Lower division. By 1860, the populous district of Pontnewydd urgently required further religious leadership. As early as February 1858, advertisements had been placed in local newspapers by Church of England authorities for persons desirous of tendering for the building of a new church at Cwmbran. With one acre of land donated by Madame de Solignac and Mr. Thomas Brown, of the Ebbw Vale Company, the building began a little westward of the Pontnewydd railway station, just above the canal, and looking down towards the Cwmbran iron industries.

Rev. W. Powell and Mr. John Lawrence, of the Graig, chairman of the building committee, bestowed a great deal of time and effort on the project and on a rainy morning in June 1858, the exciting procedure of the stone laying ceremony took place in front of a large crowd. After the proper service, John Lawrence placed a detailed scroll in a time capsule within the foundation stone. Then, Mrs Adelaide Lucy Lawrence, of the Graig, laid the stone with precision and admirable presence of mind; and the ceremony was declared to be completed.

In July 1860, the reward of so many labours was witnessed by the following account in a local newspaper of the opening of the Holy Trinity Church, Pontnewydd:

Trinity Church, Cwmbran

'The ceremony of opening this structure was performed on Tuesday. It is a neat edifice, situated in the centre of a populous district, and is much needed, no church being within a distance of four miles. Over the entrance porch is inscribed, "This is none other than the house of God and the gate of heaven." The Church is capable of considerable enlargement with little outlay. Ample space is provided for burial, and neatly laid out. Commodious schools are also attached.

'The church was crowded in the morning with visitors from all parts of the neighbourhood, among who we noticed Mrs Hanbury Leigh and party; and the Lord Bishop of Llandaff preached an able and appropriate sermon.

'The afternoon service was well attended. Prayers were read by the Vicar of Brecon...The Rev. A. Stammer preached in the evening. The total collections for the day amounted to around £50.[3]*'*

Another opening of a religious house witnessed the growth of the village of Pontnewydd. It had proved to be a long and arduous trek for the Primitive Methodists up the mountainside to the small Ebenezer Chapel at The Square, Upper Cwmbran. Despite an enlargement of the Ebenezer in 1865, when John Lawrence laid the corner stone, the new residents of Pontnewydd, with the approval of their sister chapel, were determined to have their own place of worship nearby. On April 2nd, 1866, the trustees of the Pontnewydd Primitive Methodists: Henry Charles Parfitt, of Pontnewydd, contractor, George Milliship, Oliver Smith, William Davies, Isaac Hicks, Isaac Davies, Philip Coleman, Thomas Ephrain, William Laramy, Joseph Norton, William Davies, Paul Scott, Richard Lewis, Joseph Counsell, Robert Moore and Rev. Charles T. Harris, of the Primitive Methodist Connexion, paid Miss Leah Jones, the sum of £10 for a rectangular piece of meadow land at Pontnewydd fronting the parish road leading to the railway station. The frontage of the plot measured 35 feet while the length extended in the direction of Cwmbran for 90 feet. On a fine day in September 1866, a devotional service by the Primitive Methodists preceded the laying of a foundation stone by Mr. F.G. Grice, of the Patent Nut and Bolt Company. He generously gave £5 towards the cost of the future building.[4] Opened the following year without ceremony, it was not until 1878, that this austere group extended their church, at the rear, to include a new schoolroom. Appropriately named for the hope it brought its parishioners throughout the years, the Hope Methodist Church successfully celebrated its centenary in 1966, and through the good work of its officers over many years, it remains a fine place of worship to this very day.

The early 1860s saw a serious depression in not only the Cwmbran iron industries, but for all of Monmouthshire. Never, during the previous twenty years had an almost complete paralysis of the mineral operations of the district occurred. The iron trade had received a severe shock from the state of affairs on the Continent and in America, and either total suspension or reduction in wages became the masters only choice. The Cwmbran Iron Works of the Ebbw Vale Company closed with all hands paid off. The new Oakfield Wire Works was lucky, perhaps full order books before the trouble began helped them through the difficult period. They were even fortunate to afford constant and well re-numerated employment to a number of puddlers, ballers, rollers, and other workmen from Pontnewynydd, Pontymoile, and other comparatively deserted localities. Also to help relieve the destitution, John Lawrence took a chance and gave a few of his men work erecting a new furnace at his iron works in readiness for the end of the stagnation. After four years of depressed times the advance in the price of iron at last brought prosperity again to the Cwmbran neighbourhood.

At the end of January 1865, the news spread that the idle Cwmbran works of the Ebbw Vale Company (previously owned by R.J. Blewitt) had been purchased and would be started again at no distant future. Negotiations had been going on for some time between Messrs Weston and Grice, of West Bromwich, Birmingham, and the Ebbw Vale Iron Company, before the sale took place. The new proprietors fully intended to extend the works for the manufacture of railway parts, spikes, and nuts and bolts.

These gentlemen were the managing directors of successful iron works at Smethwick, London and Stour Valley, West Bromwich. Sir Joseph Dodge Weston (1822-1895), the son of a Bristol merchant, later married one of the daughters of the industrialist Arthur Keen. There were two Grice brothers, Frederick and Edwin James. It fell to them to come to Cwmbran to manage their new industry, but Frederick suffered from poor health leaving Edwin to be the main representative. Edwin at first lived in Cwmbran and his wife enjoyed attending many social functions in the district. Later they moved to 'The Fields', Stow Hill, Newport.

The firm of Weston and Grice was on a winner. The days had gone when forging of a few nuts and bolts proved a good days work for a skilled smith. Over a thousand hands were employed at the senior works and most attended power driven machinery. From the beginning, tons of finished hexagon and square nuts, varying in size, and railway fastenings, were ready to be sent out at a moments notice. With the railways now playing a huge part in commercial life, large orders were sent down to the Cwmbran works. Being situated in the midst of plentiful coal and the iron beds of South Wales, the excellent ports of Newport and Cardiff were soon kept busy with the Cwmbran exports. In 1864, the firm of Watkins and Keen floated as the Patent Nut and Bolt Co., before amalgamated with Weston and Grice in January 1865, but the members of the original firm retained a large interest in the joint concern.[5]

This new flourishing aspect of trade brought the number of no less than a thousand workmen employed at Cwmbran in the manufacture of iron in various forms. What was recently an almost deserted spot had again become a busy and thriving hive of industry. Unfortunately, the number of houses in Cwmbran were totally inadequate to accommodate the workmen and their families. It would be regularly observed that more than one large family were huddled together in a small cottage. Many of the workmen had to resort to Ponthir, Caerleon, Pontnewydd, and other places in order to secure habitation. Thus, in addition to their arduous labour they had to make a journey of six or seven miles a day. Alert to the problem, the iron masters soon built rows of terraced houses near the *Half Way Inn* to alleviate the problem, but unfortunately neglected to provide effective

Tenders.

TO BUILDERS AND CONTRACTORS.

LLANTARNAM SCHOOL BOARD.

TENDERS are required for BOYS, GIRLS, and INFANTS' SCHOOLS, with MASTERS' RESIDENCES, at CWMBRAN, Mon.

Drawings and Specifications can be seen, after the 20th, at the ARCHITECT's Office, Bank-chambers, Newport.

The lowest or any Tender will not necessarily be accepted.

E. A. LANSDOWNE,

17,949]   Architect to the Board.

Oak St., Cwmbran.

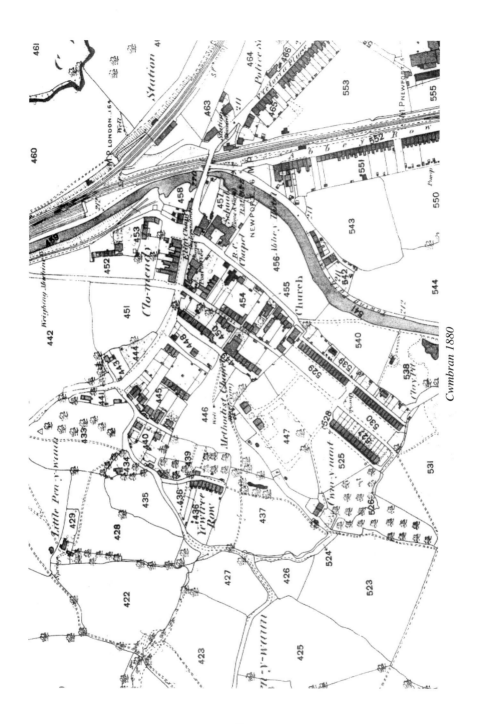

Cwmbran 1880

97

sanitary needs. In time this additional problem was rectified. Other branches of business benefited from the new found prosperity. It was reported that the tradesmen of Newport received no small share of the benefit which had arisen from the Cwmbran iron trade. No fewer than three hundred Cwmbran people found their way to this town every Saturday for the purchase of goods.

The Cwmbran neighbourhood prospered, but many did not forget the recent slump in trade. When the American Civil War came to an end, for a short time a nervousness became apparent in master and workman alike. However, the blast furnaces of John Lawrence were fully employed. Another addition to the iron manufacturing complex stretching along the western bank of the canal also had its blast furnaces fully working. Richard Stephen Roper, a Newport ironmaster, recognised the growing importance of the Cwmbran industrial site and had his first furnace blown in during 1863. This venture did not last long before it was transferred to the Patent Nut and Bolt Company at the beginning of 1866.

Despite occasional trading concerns the Patent Nut and Bolt Works Company remained hopeful. This was made obvious in 1869 when an extension became an important addition to the already large works. This addition included twelve new puddling furnaces with boilers, a new engine, new rolls and squeezer. Mr. Rafarel, the manager, presided and inaugurated the rolls by throwing a bottle of wine upon them.[7]

By 1871, various bodies representing the South Wales ironworkers were agitating for improved working conditions. In December, a large number of men met at the Cwmbran British Schoolroom to discuss the popular idea everywhere that the working day should be reduced to nine hours. Pushed to make a decision by the 'Nine Hours Movement' the men presented Edwin Grice with a petition to that effect. By this time Mr. Grice had become very respected, even much loved by the Cwmbran people, and many feared that considerable damage would be done to a good relationship between employer and employee. Mr. Grice took the 'wind out of the sails' of the agitators. His early reply delighted the men. Not only did he agree to their request, but he informed them that it would be put into force at the beginning of the following month.

Further expansion of the Patent Nut and Bolt Company occurred in 1872 when they bought the Cwmbran blast furnaces, adjacent to their works. For some time they had been negotiating with John Lawrence for the Cwmbran Iron Company blast furnaces and Upper Cwmbran colliery. Although having done well during his time as an iron master John Lawrence had experience the cruel vicissitudes of the iron industry. At one time during his career he had no problems with producing pig iron, but selling it became another matter. An accumulation of around 25,000 tons forced him to sell the manufactured article at a very low price in the market. Perhaps with thoughts of the former difficult times, and a good price agreed for his holdings, he believed the time was right to sell. Some losses in previous years had been experienced by the Patent Nut and Bolt Company for the want of iron to carry out their orders expeditiously, and having acquired the blast furnaces so near their own works, these difficulties would not again have to occur.[6] Improvements followed to their new acquisition and the retained workforce were happy to learn that they would receive weekly pay in keeping with the rest of the industrial complex. The Patent Nut and Bolt Company now owned all of the iron industries along this section of the Monmouthshire Canal and had a good supply of coal.

Much of the workers lives involved their place of work. Annual suppers of the different departments took place at the hall supplied by the company or in hostelries throughout the neighbourhood. At Christmas, Messrs Grice and Rafarel gave the wives of the workmen a tea party in the company's hall under the direction of Dr. Cousins and a committee of ladies. After the sumptuous meal, singing and dancing were carried out with tremendous spirit. Mrs Grice enjoyed giving joy to the children. Before Xmas 1870, she gave a tea to the children in the work's hall. The Cwmbran Band went to meet the children coming down the canal bank, and on their arrival they were regaled with a good festive tea. After, they were sent up to a field to play while a splendid magic lantern was prepared. Subsequently the children were delighted by amusing and instructive film slides. Before the children went home each was presented with a bun by Mrs Grice. In the summer months works trips were regularly organised and a particularly great treat was the visit to Newport to see Blondin, the famous Niagara Falls ropewalker, conducting his daring escapades on the high wire. Another favourite annual trip, which always took about three hundred to Newport, was the chartering of a steam boat to ferry the revellers to Weston-super-Mare. A works band always provided good entertainment and regular summer picnics on the nearby mountainside would be fondly remembered. An illegal gambling activity known as 'Pitch and Toss' also became a pass-time for the men for many years. Often occurring while waiting for a hostelry to open, the game would be frowned upon by people passing. An elderly Cwmbran resident remembered that when a small boy, he would be placed as a lookout. When the local sergeant appeared with his dog, a warning shout caused everyone to bolt. The narrator of the memory told indignantly of during each chase, for some unknown reason, the dog would only go after him, before inflicting painful injuries to the ankles.

Extra to the many amusements organised by works and individuals, the Cwmbran district soon boasted a leisure activity that would become famous all over South Wales. Richard Clark and his family lived alongside the canal and about five minutes from the Pontnewydd Railway Station. Originally his home had been built by the Monmouthshire Canal Company and for many years served as a depot. In 1842, Thomas Cooke, a clerk for the then busy company, lived at the substantial homestead. Later it would become the 'Company Shop' the only store where Upper Cwmbran colliers could use their company tokens to purchase the necessities of living. When Richard Clark purchased the disused company shop his large garden consisted of around twenty acres. About 1870, he commenced planting until it abounded in broad and well-gravelled walks, fringed with beautiful flowering plants, and with one and half acres taken up with strawberry beds. When entering the premises from the canal side, the visitor found himself on a neatly constructed terrace, whose *facade* took the form of rock work amongst which many very pretty ferns grew. Below this terrace a small fountain played lazily in the sunshine while a gentle slope led to numerous apple and other fruit trees. Nearby could be found a large luxurious lawn suitable for dancing. Beyond this a turbulent little stream, free at the time of rustic bridges, whose rippling waters indicated a pleasurable spot to recline. Richard Clark continued enlarging his grounds and added to the already sumptuous display of fruits of all kinds.

Perhaps urged on by people admiring his work, he decided to throw open the gardens to the public on a Monday in July, 1873. They were an instant success. Advertised at first as Cwmbran Fruit and Recreation Gardens, over two thousand people visited the first day and most partook of tea in the grounds. For the workers employed in the exhausting industries of the district, it proved a welcome break to enjoy the sunshine and fresh air with their families. Later in the evening a Newport factory band took up position outdoors to deliver a long programme of dance music. A large room provided non-intoxicating refreshments with tea having to be sold in relays. Over two hundred quarts of strawberries were sold on this opening day and everyone agreed that the venture was a tremendous success.

Richard Clark improved his undertaking and the fame of the Cwmbran Pleasure Gardens & Hotel spread far and wide. Nothing like this existed in nearby Newport and on Thursdays, when their main establishments closed at an early hour in the afternoon, the advantages offered by these gardens, and the presence of a quadrille band, attracted a great number of the large town's pleasure seekers.

With the regular introduction of new attractions many paid return visits to the gardens. The Pontnewydd Railway Station was kept busy while organised parties in horse-drawn breaks came from as far as Cardiff. Cricket matches, tennis, croquet and athletic events all added to the summer programme, while indoor suppers and dances became a winter pleasure. For many years Richard Clark showed great kindness to the poor of the locality before he died in 1885, age 59 years. His wife and children successfully continued the business until 1889, when it was sold. In 1874, Richard Clark had given up land to the Local Government Board for the building of a road through the Lowlands, Pontnewydd. Now named Clark Avenue, the road is said to perpetuate the memory of this enterprising family. The Cwmbran Gardens was eventually demolished in 1965.

At the Oakfield Wireworks events were very much the same as the works of the Patent Nut and Bolt Company. This was due in the main to Tom Leadbeater, the popular appointed manager, who always strived for a good relationship between master and men. However, there was a hitch in June 1863, when for a few weeks there was talk of strike action. All the puddlers gave notice to leave unless they were allowed a rise in pay. The proprietors declined to grant the advance, and the majority of the workmen decided to continue with their work at the old rate. The four workmen who made themselves rather conspicuous in fomenting the threatened dispute were at once dismissed.

Tom Leadbeater worked hard to repair the trust between workers and proprietors. In November of the same year, the starting of a new mill, with more hands taken on, helped his sincere quest for an amicable understanding between all parties. On the occasion of starting the new mill the men were treated to some good home brewed beer, with which they drank long life and prosperity to Messrs Hill and Batt, and Mr. Leadbeater, as well as "Success to the Oakfield Iron Works." Perhaps the earlier display of discontent had some effect for when Mr. Hill addressed the men, they were informed that he would always be happy to give them the same amount of wages as any other firm was paying, and do all he could in promoting their happiness and welfare. The remarks were received by loud cheering. A few months later notices were posted in the works to inform the men that at the next pay day they would receive a 10% increase in wages.

In 1864, the tremendous affection for Tom Leadbeater at the works was witnessed by the presentation of a splendid gold lever watch valued at thirty guineas. The watch showed the following inscription: "Presented to Mr. Thos. Leadbeater by the agents, workmen, &c. of the Oakfield Wire Works, as a token of their respect and esteem of him as a manager of the above works. April, 1864." Mrs Leadbeater was included in the proceedings when she was surprised to receive a large gold keeper. For some time to follow the respected manager of the works exercised a healthy influence among the men. He became mindful of not only their physical comforts, but also extremely solicitous in respect to their moral, religious and intellectual training. Chapels and kindred edifices were supported, penny readings, Sunday and day schools upheld; and the workmen seeing their manager concerned for their welfare, reciprocated the feeling by being attentive to his requests.

In no time the works had became a model for others to follow in Monmouthshire and neighbouring counties. Due to the fame of the finished article, particularly in the department in which wire took pre-eminence, the firm had more orders on hand of all kinds than what it could deliver. The arrangements, cleanliness, and general appearance of the works, convinced visitors that it was the most convenient and compact of its kind in the country. The steady progress had opened up the new district of Oakfield. Fortunately, the recent slump in the iron trade had not affected the Oakfield works and by 1870, a further increase in orders gave cause to enlarge and improve the premises. Another huge steam hammer was erected, together with an additional number of puddling furnaces, making nineteen in operation. At the end of a typical week, there was made at the Forge End a total of around 270 tons of puddled and charcoal bars. The Guide Mills also did well producing an enormous quantity of wire rods that passed through the rolls of the two mills each week.

Sadly, after being a friend and in the employment of Mr. J.C. Hill for twenty years, Tom Leadbeater died on December 11, 1870. Mr. Hill immediately ordered a cessation of all operations at the works until the funeral rites had been performed. A magnificent monument became a spontaneous gift of the workmen and can still be seen in the Llantarnam churchyard.[8]

Tom Leadbeater left his mark on both masters and workmen and each Christmas, when J.C. Hill gave his usual treat to his employees at the *Oakfield Inn*, glasses were raised in memory of their former manager.

Around 1874, J.C. Hill & Company purchased the Henllys Colliery and Henllys Firebrick Works of Cyrus Hanson. Later, the Henllys Firebrick Works had been closed for some time when in 1885, these undertakings were disposed of to the Patent Nut and Bolt Company. By October of the same year local people were pleased to hear that the Firebrick Works had been re-started under the direction of Mr. E. Southwood Jones, the former manager of the works.[9]

The Patent Nut and Bolt Company were by no means finished with expanding their interests in the Cwmbran neighbourhood. In 1879, their need for coal increased both for the use in their works and for export. In the Springvale district, the Adit, as it became known, was driven for over a mile through rocky strata. This was followed by the sinking of a ventilation shaft at Henllys. In May, a trial of new stationary engines, made by the Lilleshall Engineering Company, took place in the presence of Mr. E.J. Grice, the managing director and Jabez Jacob, the colliery manager. These had been erected for the purpose of drawing coal from the colliery. The engines were of 25 nominal horse power and the cylinders twenty inches in diameter, with four feet stroke. The connections between the machinery and the mine workings were at the time being completed as quickly as possible, and when completed, would save the wear and tear and working expenses of three inclines, by which means the coal arrived at the surface. The trial gave every satisfaction. The daily output at first consisted of only 150 tons, but this increased under various managements to 1,400 tons each week. The haulage system was unique, consisting of an endless chain, the links of which fitted in a bracket attached to wooden trams of that time. Journeys of sixteen to twenty trams were drawn up the inclines to the surface. To complete the journey in the later stages a tram would travel from the surface to the coal face and back again, a distance of four miles. Wooden houses were erected for the workmen excavating the Adit and many years later they were still in good condition and occupied.

The population explosion in the parishes, which would make up the district of Cwmbran as we know it today, was phenomenal. With it came many problems. Most children had only a limited education, if that. Since the eighteenth century, attempts at giving education to the fewer children in the parishes had taken place using, in most cases, any available space. Appropriate for those times, much of the teaching was of an religious nature. By the 1850s, certain responsible people became aware of the childrens plight and a determination set in to do something about it. Around 1850, in the Pontnewydd district of Llanfrechfa Upper parish, a Church of England schoolroom was set up by a reverend gentleman responsibly for that section of the community. By 1862, an impressive church school, partly sponsored by the National Society, had been built on this site and opened. Mr. Richard Baker became the first headmaster of the new school.

Meanwhile, ideally situated in Oak Street, in the centre of the new and growing village of Cwmbran, an early small Board School was sufficient for the educational needs of the children. Built in 1864, with voluntary subscriptions, it would be a number of years before the cost could be liquidated. Many years later the building became the old Conservative Club. In 1979, the site was required for redevelopment and great efforts to save the date-stone from the old building proved successful.[10]

The establishment of schools by now had become not only needed, but a trend. On a sunny day in August, 1866, John Lawrence, iron and coal master, laid the foundation stone of a new school in Upper Cwmbran. Education had been given earlier in a room above the Squirrel Inn, The Square, but this had become inadequate. In a recess in the foundation stone Mr. Lawrence placed a time capsule containing the Newport newspapers, which held the stone laying advertisements, and a new golden guinea. With enough funds eventually available, Henry Parfitt, builder, completed the work in two years. The school contained a large room in which it was hoped that about two hundred children may be educated. Attached to this could be found a retiring room, master's house, and other buildings and conveniences.[11] The school served the Upper Cwmbran community for many years and was demolished around 1977.

Among the many who flocked to Cwmbran looking for work and a better way of life were Irish immigrants during and after the great famine in Ireland. These hard working people made a great contribution to the growth of the small industrial centre both at the time and for many years to follow. After useful work at Pontypool, the Franciscan Missionaries came to Cwmbran in 1864 and were alarmed at what they discovered. About 380 members of the Roman Catholic faith were already employed in the iron works and without any leadership, had sunk into a state of utter indifference to religion. The only premises available for religious worship was a clubroom above a public house and this was engaged for Sunday service for a fee of two shillings and six pence each week. Sunday afternoons were spent teaching the children mainly religious matters. Unhappy with this poor situation every effort was made for improvements. After providing funds for the erection and volunteers giving free labour to dig the foundations, a fine, new Roman Catholic School Church opened in Oak Street, on January 1, 1867.[12] Still the space for teaching Roman Catholic children proved insufficient and this was soon rectified the following year by opening a popular Roman Catholic school next to the church. With the numbers of both Roman Catholic adults and children increasing enormously, by 1882, the small corrugated iron church and school, fronting Oak Street, had become too small. On land to the rear, an impressive new stone building was soon built and opened by May 1883.[12]

With fast rising population figures, it was not long before the first Board School, in Oak Street, had also become too small. On October 18, 1872, an advertisement could be seen in the Monmouthshire Merlin newspaper asking for tenders for a new school to be built further along the street. The new schools were appropriately named St. Dials, after the nearby farm and ancient chapel-of-ease. In April 1874, the children were ready to transfer to the new schools and an explicit newspaper report gives witness to that historic day:

LLANTARNAM SCHOOL BOARD
OPENING THE NEW SCHOOLS

The St. Dials new schools, built for the Llantarnam School Board on a half acre of land alongside the canal and close by the railway station, were formerly opened on Thursday, when a treat was given to the children and a public meeting held. The schools have been built to supply the rapidly growing wants of the populous district of Lower Cwmbran. The design of the building is in the Gothic style of architecture of the 13 century, and although generally of a plain character there are some quaint bits of detail introduced which produce a picturesque effect. The schools are divided into boys, girls, and infants schools, with large and well-lighted class-rooms to each. A comfortable master's house faces the public road from Cwmbran, and has the advantage of overlooking nearly the whole of the school premises. The plan of the school embraces accommodation for 406 children, allowing the maximum in each department required by the Committee of Council on Education. Several hat and cloak lobbies are provided to each school, near which are well-fitted lavatories. The material used in the walls are stone from Tyny Cmw and Abergavenny, with Bath stone dressings. The whole of the inside woodwork is stained and varnished; the walls and ceilings are plastered and whitened, and the roofs are covered with Bangor slate, with ornamental ridge and furrow tile crease. A bell cot is placed over the boys' school and contains a bell of nearly 80 lb. weight. The work has been carried out by Mr. Henry Parfitt, builder, of Pontnewydd, from the designs and under the supervision of Mr. E.A. Lansdowne, architect, Newport.

The public meeting took place at six o'clock in the evening. Mr. Knowles, Chairman of the School Board, presided, and there was also on the platform, Messrs. J. Parsons, Henry Cromwell, William Jones, and E. Croker, members of the School Board; Dr. Cousins, Dr. Davidson, Mr. E.A. Lansdowne (architect), Mr. Parfitt (contractor), Mr. Pennimore, Mr. William N. Johns, &c.

Numerous addresses were given, and from the remarks of the various speakers, it appears that the total cost of the new schools has been £2,540, or a fraction over £6 per head, which is less than the cost of any other School Board school in the neighbourhood. The Board has been established nearly three years, and their labours have been attended with most satisfactory results. In January, 1872, the British School was handed over to the Board, and William James appointed master. In the previous year only sixteen children passed their examinations, and only £21 was earned. At the end of 1872, the number of children examined had increased from sixteen to one hundred, and the grant earned was £68 2s. In 1873, 132 children were examined and £102 14s. earned in grants. Last week the number of children in attendance was 242, and in the present week it had risen to 280. The inspector's report spoke favourably of the improvements which had been effected in the school by the new master, and the Chairman, in the course of the evening, made public acknowledgement of the satisfaction felt by the Board at the admirable and efficient manner in which Mr. James had conducted the schools. With regard to the cost of the Board it was stated that in the three years they had expended £255 or a fraction over one and a half pennies in the £ per year on the rateable value of the parish. That was for working expenses. The money borrowed for building the schools was to be repaid in fifty years, and that could be done on the present rateable value on the parish with a rate of three pence in the £ per annum. As the population and prosperity of the parish are increasing with great rapidity it is expected that even this small sum will soon be reduced.

The school children enlivened the evening's proceedings with singing and recitations, which were most creditably given, and afforded much gratification to the visitors.[13]

William James served the small Board School and St. Dials School for over forty years. In March 1912, he passed away at St. Dial's House, the master's residence attached to the school. He had filled a big place in Cwmbran life as a local councillor and member of the Llantarnam Church committee. His genial personality made him much sought after especially with his inexhaustible fund of good stories. Scores of people went to him for help and he had written hundreds of letters of recommendation for those who had passed under his care. A little time before his death it was suggested to him that the inhabitants would like to give him a public testimonial at the end of his school career. His reply was characteristic: "I wish nothing for myself, I have my reward in the affections of the people, but if they care to hang my photograph in the schools as a remembrance of me, I should feel highly honoured." Just two years short of retirement he died leaving a widow and three sons and three daughters. It soon became know that his high esteem would qualify him for a remarkable monument to be displayed in the centre of Cwmbran village, and near the schools. To be defrayed by public subscription, the memorial committee selected a design of a beautiful drinking fountain to quench the thirst of passers-by. The Llanfrechfa Urban District Council wrote kindly offering to provide the necessary supply of water for the fountain, at a charge of five shillings per annum, subject to the type of tap used. After examining several sites the memorial took shape in a wall by St. Gabriel's Church and opposite the old post office.

A large crowd attended to see the unveiling ceremony performed by Councillor W.J. Thomas, Chairman of the Llantarnam U.D.C. The fountain which cost £35, bore the following inscription: "This fountain has been erected by public subscription as a tribute of respect to the memory of the late Mr. W.J. James, who was for over 40 years headmaster of St. Dial's Schools, Cwmbran." The fountain was then handed over as a gift by the inhabitants, to be vested in the Council as public property.[14] Due to the prominent position of the memorial, in the years that followed, frequent damage to the fountain and especially the chain securing the metal cup, caused the lot to be re-sited in Cwmbran Park during 1935. This did not help very much and eventually the drinking fountain was sadly removed before being stored in a Council workyard. However, a excellent sepia portrait of Mr. James, beautifully framed in oak, with a brass plate underneath, and subscribed for by the teachers and scholars, hung in the school until its closure many years later.

Until November 1869, the parish of Llanfrechfa Upper belonged to the Petty Sessional Division of Caerleon, but this was about to change. By this time the representatives of the parish had become extremely disgruntled at the great discomfort, inconvenience and expense of journeying to Caerleon. A petition requesting annexation to the Petty Sessional Division of Pontypool met with a good response.[15] More changes were to follow. At a parish vestry meeting on September 5, 1870, it was unanimously agreed that the Local Government Act of 1858, should be adopted within the parish. This decision brought about a Local Government Board which would be much more effective for years to follow. At a meeting on January 11, 1871, convened by Mr. Alfred Addams Williams, the Summoning Officer appointed by the Home Secretary to conduct the first election of members to form such a Board, the following gentlemen were elected officers: Charles Conway, Pontnewydd (143 votes); Charles A. Brew, Pontrhydyrun, (128 votes); John Sims Cousins, Cwmbran House (127 votes); John Lawrence, The Graig, (117 votes); Richard Clark, Pontnewydd, (112 votes); Henry Griffiths, Griffithstown, (110 votes); Jabez Jacob, Upper Cwmbran, (106 votes); Henry Parfitt, Pontnewydd, (104 votes); Frederick G. Grice, Newport, (88 votes); Richard Adams, Pontnewydd, (85 votes); John Rees Jenkins, Pontnewydd, (83 votes); Henry Knipe, Coedygric Farm, (82 votes). In the absence of John Lawrence, Charles Conway became chairman, a post held for twelve years until his death in 1884. It was agreed that the music room of Dr. Cousins be rented at one guinea per quarter for transacting the business and for the use of the members.[16] Fortnightly meetings soon led to an enormous improvement in the administration of the Llanfrechfa Upper parish.

Unfortunately, the parish of Llantarnam was slow in adopting this new and effective form of administration. With other parishes successfully implementing the concept of a Local Government Board, at Llantarnam, a number of landowners remained bitterly opposed because of the fear of a substantial rise in the cost of rates. Although two people represented Llantarnam at the meetings of the Caerleon Highways Board, the body responsible for managing the parish, they freely admitted that nothing much could be done due to other committee members not knowing their district. For some time the parish had suffered from defective sanitary arrangements, the cesspool system was still in use with a great fear of cholera breaking out at any time. This, coupled with an insufficient water supply, and the absence of a local governing body with the power to insist on stability in the erection of houses during the formation of new streets, all added up to a dangerous situation.

From as early as May 1879, Henry Parfitt had suggested that a Local Board be formed to manage their own affairs, thus seceding from the Caerleon Highway Board. An enquiry in 1881, at the *Greenhouse Inn*, led by the inspector of the London Local Government Board, was to no avail. Again the principle ratepayers of the district blocked the much needed progress. The inspector's suggestion that Llantarnam and Llanfrechfa join together to form one Local Board did not help and met with strong objections, particularly from the farmers.

By 1885, the need for a scheme to carry out sanitary drainage had become critical. Notices attached to the doors of every church and chapel legally sanctioned a meeting of inhabitants and a poll gave 723 in favour of a Local Board, with 54 against. Another Government enquiry later in the year, showed the population of Llantarnam as 3,994 residents, an increase in 500 people, and 200 extra houses since the Census Return of 1881. With the formation of so many Local Government Boards, the Caerleon Highways Board by then comprised of only eight parishes with Llantarnam being the main financial contributor. Without Llantarnam, the Caerleon Highways Board was in great danger of breaking up.

Despite this, the Local Government Board in London wanted the change and at a ratepayer's meeting a show of hands indicated only one opposed to the new administration. At a later election for board members the result showed: F.W. Rafarel, works manager, 433 votes; John Parry, farmer, 384 votes; Thomas Bennett, engineer, 373 votes; John Mumford, farmer, 323 votes; William Jones, cashier, 311 votes; Henry Lawrence, farmer, 299 votes; Alfred C. Pilliner, gentleman, 295 votes; John Place, blast-furnace manager, 289 votes; and Henry Parfitt, builder, 270 votes. The first meeting of the Llantarnam Local Government Board took place in St. Dial's School in December 1885, with A.C. Pilliner in the chair.

In the 1870s, Cwmbran and district still attracted industry. On September 5, 1874, the employees of the Tynewydd Iron and Tinplate Company Limited celebrated the opening of the new works, when around sixty of them sat down to dinner in the large room at the Cwmbran Pleasure Gardens. Loyal and patriotic toasts filled the room, the most noticeable were extolled to Mr. F.R. Phillips, managing director, and G. Batchelor, Newport. Erected near the Pontnewydd railway station, the works commenced making charcoal and coke tin, terne plates, canadas, and black and tin taggers. In the early years, the works did not do very well due to the stiff competition in the tin trade. By 1878, it had been idle for some time before starting up again with only one of the two mills operational.

Many of the workforce were of the Baptist faith and the management were all for the provision of a suitable meeting place. Mr. W.R. Williams, mill manager and roll turner at the recently opened works was the head of this movement. From as early as 1875, it was resolved to start a mission in Pontnewydd. An interesting entry in their minute book of 1877 states: "That any member of this church visiting Cwmbran Gardens for pleasure be brought under church discipline." Land fronting the later named Richmond Road cost £55, but it was decided to build a smaller chapel than the one contemplated, because the tinworks had ceased operation, and that many families were compelled to move. On July 19, 1880, the memorial stones were laid; the north corner stone by Charles Lewis, J.P., Newport, and the south corner stone by R. Cory, Cardiff. Built of stone from Bush Quarry, near Pontypool, the chapel opened on Sunday and Monday, August 27 and 28, 1882. Its first minister was Rev. Thomas Cocker, formerly of Siloam Chapel.[17]

The works had again come to a complete standstill in 1881, with some of the hands making arrangements to leave for America. It would be 1884, before the works re-started. In August 1885, the works was up for auction at the Kings Head Hotel, Newport. However, on behalf of the mortgager, who was losing money on the sale, an objection arose regarding the inclusion of machinery and other items, which adjourned the sale. It was not until 1887, before the problems were sorted out and the auction could proceed. For sale were six acres of land, tin plate works with two mills, tin house, smiths' and carpenters' sheds, stores, offices, reservoir, railway sidings, and fixed machinery. The works was purchased by the strong Pontardulais firm of Mr. E. Stanford.

Another small undertaking commenced in 1876, when the Cwmbran and Pontnewydd Gas Company secured a good site for their engineers to start on a project. The installation provided regular employment for many years.

These were indeed a hopeful signs for there had been great distress in the Pontnewydd district for a number of years. Many families only existed on the help provided by the organised Relief Committee. Regularly, twice a week, twenty gallons of soup would be distributed among the inhabitants. The children, who a few years earlier had been healthy and bright eyed, were now in a state of extreme poverty and desperately hungry. A system devised to provide some food to the children involved a team going out and assessing who was in most need, before giving them a ticket to report to the Mission Hall next day. At the Mission Hall, the limited amount of food consisted of porridge or soup and bread. Many hungry children arrived clutching a spoon. After the Divine blessing had been evoked on the repast each child was given two or three servings until satisfied. After the meal grace was again said and the feast concluded with the hymn *What a friend we have in Jesus.'* Commendable practical help was also received by the tinplate workers from the colliers of Cwmbran Colliery.

The Avondale Tinplate Works, opened by J. Williams and partners in 1877, was also struggling and had been idle for some time. However, trade temporarily picked up, but many were wary of what the future held.

1892 again brought stoppages, mainly due to the overstocking of the tinplate markets in Britain and abroad. Time would be needed to shift the excess before manufacturing could again commence. Unfortunately, time ran out for the Eastern Valley Tinplate Company who had taken over the Tynewydd Works. In 1896, the company became bankrupt with estimated gross liabilities of £14,000. Purchased by the Redbrook Tin Plate Co. Ltd., in 1898, the works would, at last, have many years of stability in future years.

By the 1880s, the population explosion had become so great that the limited public services in Cwmbran and district could no longer cope. This was most obvious in the area of public health. The water supply was exceedingly bad, particularly in the vicinity of Pontnewydd where some twenty wells were relied upon. Not more than five or six contained water fit for drinking purposes. There was one pump that had to supply 156 houses. The presence of animals nearby did not help, and contaminated water near the base of the wells was often returned back into the water supply when it rained. In some instances people had to travel half-a-mile for their supply. In the summer water was always short, giving rise to epidemics of diphtheria, typhoid and other dangerous diseases. Henry Parfitt, builder, had the necessary knowledge to know that a Public Health Act, passed in 1875, encouraged Local Boards to provide reservoirs and a water works in their districts. At a meeting of the Llanfrechfa Local Government Board in November, 1883, he urged members to take all the necessary steps to obtain an Act of Parliament to construct a water works at Upper Cwmbran. This would supply both parishes of Llanfrechfa and Llantarnam. Notices were subsequently seen in the *Evening Telegram* and *Evening Star* newspapers, and placed on church doors stating that a petition had been forwarded requiring a Bill in the next session of Parliament. This was granted and with a loan of £9,500 from the Dunmow Building Society, the Local Board had plans drawn up for the best site. The required seven and half acres of land was very marshy and on the side of the Upper Cwmbran mountain. Owned by J.C. Hanbury, of Pontypool, the Local Board generously valued it at £100, but the land was offered to them for £1,500. The matter went to arbitration and became a long drawn out affair. In September1885, tenders were invited for the work with the reservoir expected to have a storage capacity of about 11 million gallons. When work eventually commenced it was beset with further problems. In 1887, the contractors were still digging and in January 1888, the site engineer died. By September 1888, a serious 'slip' in the embankment, due to defective construction, caused the whole project to be reviewed. It was not until March 1890, when the reservoir was filled with ten feet of water to test, that at last it appeared safe to serve the people.[18]

On June 20, 1887, Queen Victoria had reigned for fifty years. In every school in Cwmbran and district excitement was fever pitch among the scholars at the thought of an extra day added to their holidays, and the promise of a treat. Improvement in attendance figures became very obvious leading up to the special day. All were regaled with tea and cake before adjourning to nearby fields for sports and various entertainments.

Ten years later, for Her Majesty's Diamond Jubilee, the events were repeated. This time the celebrations occurred on a grander scale. The works at Cwmbran became only partially operational during Jubilee week as Monday and Tuesday were observed as a general holiday in the neighbourhood. For some time a dark cloud had hung over the proceedings, but due to the kind offer of Mr. Clifford Cory, of Llantarnam Abbey, the gloom would be dispelled and the children experienced an exceptional Jubilee celebration. The main event of the special day was a visit to Llantarnam Park. At one o'clock the children assembled at St. Dial's

School, and headed by the Salvation Army Band, marched with banners to the beautiful park. The younger children had the added treat of being carried in spacious and brightly coloured farm wagons. A large marquee had been erected in case the weather proved unfavourable, but the children were bountifully supplied with their refreshments on the fresh green lawns. Nuts were scrambled for, and the distributed commemorative medals had been generously provided by Mr. Cory. The lively proceedings concluded with the children singing "God Save the Queen."[19]

At Pontnewydd, the children nearly had a bitter disappointment as a substantial donation to the new infirmary at Newport caused no public effort to be made for the celebration. Fortunately, at a late date, a tea was arranged in the church and schools. After the tea, games were organised in an adjoining field kindly loaned by Alderman Henry Parfitt. Three cheers were give for Mr. Parfitt before the singing of the National Anthem ended the proceedings. As darkness fell, mountain bonfires could be seen everywhere and the one on the Mynydd Maen did not disappoint.[20]

On December 24, 1894, the last meeting of the old Llanfrechfa Upper Government Board took place. The following year, on Thursday, the third day of January, 1895, the first meeting of the Llanfrechfa Upper Urban District Council heralded an even more effective system of management. The whole of the twelve men elected were present and comprised of: Colonel Jabez Jacob in the chair, Messrs Henry Parfitt, J.P., John Jenkins, Joseph Fisher, William Laramy, George Edwards, Zephaniah Lloyd, James Cocker, Charles Bowker, Thomas Scott, Edward James Richards and William Jones.[21]

Colonel Jacob had for over thirty years been manager of Cwmbran and Henllys Collieries. For some years he had been a chairman of both the old Llanfrechfa Upper Government Board and School Board and by virtue, he was later raised to the office of Justice of the Peace. As his title implies he was a veteran and enthusiastic Volunteer officer. In 1901, he retired from the district to be close to his four sons in Port Talbot.

Although much of the work of the new administration would be of a routine nature, the new Council got off to a good start by commissioning a new road linking Cwmbran village and Pontnewydd. This successful Council continued to do fine work until 1935.

REFERENCES

1. Gwent Record Office, D.2174.35, *Ebenezer Baptist Church 1860-1960* centenary booklet; *Good News,* The Story of Ebenezer, Llantarnam, September 1985; *Star of Gwent,* October 6, 1860; *The Pontypool Free Press and Herald of the Hills,*

October 6, 1860; *The Monmouthshire Merlin,* November 9, 1961; *The Pontypool Free Press and Herald of the Hills,* November 9, 1961.

2. Bradney, Sir Joseph, *A History of Monmouthshire - Llanfrechfa.* p. 285.

3. *The Pontypool Free Press and Herald of the Hills,* July 21, 1860.

4. Gwent Record Office, D2723.5; *Centenary Brochure 1866-1966.*

5. *The Engineer,* September, 1865.

6. *The Pontypool Free Press and Herald of the Hills,* March 4, 1871.

7. *Mining Journal,* July 1972.

8. *Star of Gwent,* May 20, 1871.

9. Gwent Record Office, D32.763, J.C. Hill & Company, Limited, Prospectus; *The Pontypool Free Press and Herald of the Hills,* October 16, 1885.

10. *The Free Press of Monmouthshire,* March 16, 1979.

11. *Star of Gwent,* August 4, 1866; *The Monmouthshire Merlin,* August 4, 1866.

12. Cwmbran Local Studies Library, *Franciscan Missions Among the Colliers and Ironworkers of Monmouthshire.* 1876. pp. 32-42; *Pontypool Free Press and Herald of the Hills,* May 18, 1883.

13. *The Monmouthshire Merlin,* October 18, 1972 and April 24, 1874.

14. Gwent Record Office, A421 A M 12, Llantarnam U.D.C. Minute Book 1913-14.

15. Gwent Record Office, Miss. Mss. 1419, Llanfrechfa Upper Parish Meeting Book, 1853-1900, November 18, 1869.

16. Gwent Record Office, A 422 A M 1, Llanfrechfa Upper Local Board Minute Book, 1871-1877, January 16, 1871.

17. Gwent Record Office, D1605.4, p. 93.

18. Gwent Record Office, Llanfrechfa Upper Local Government Board Minute Books, A 422 A M 2 (1877-1885) and A422 A M 3 (1885-1890).

19. Lloyd, W.G., *The Golden Jubilee of Queen Elizabeth II and Torfaen,* 2002; Gwent Record Office, CEA. 197.1, St. Dial's Infants School Log Book, 1875-1899; Gwent Record Office, A 4212 M 1, Llantarnam Local Government Board Minute Book, 1893-1898.

20. Gwent Record Office, CE. B24.19, Cwmbran National School Logbook, 1862-1895, (Mount Pleasant Junior Mixed School, Pontnewydd).

21. Gwent Record Office, A 422 A M 5, Llanfrechfa Upper Urban District Council Minute Book, 1894-1898.

Chapter Eight

INTO THE TWENTIETH CENTURY

In good time for the new century, the Llantarnam Local Government Board also entered into the more effective system of management. On January 1, 1895, the first meeting of the Llantarnam Urban District Council took place with F.W. Rafarel, J.P., Chairman, and elected committee members J. Parry, A.M. Pilliner, J.P., R. Sawtell, W.M. Jones, E.A. Pryer and H. Mumford.[1]

Gradually, Cwmbran and district was to form into what many remembers in more recent times. Sadly, the pioneers of this remarkable change into a thriving industrial centre succumbed to the inevitable and their names became lost in time until revealed by recent research.

Edwin James Grice, the popular director of the Patent Nut and Bolt Company Limited died on March 9, 1889, at the young age of 55 years. He had become well known and highly respected by men of all creeds and politics. His geniality made him a favourite amongst all classes. While living at Newport he became a town councillor and Mayor for the year 1885-86. A man with many noble interests he also became High Sheriff of Monmouthshire and a Justice of the Peace. His passing undoubtedly heralded major changes for the future of the Patent Nut and Bolt Works.

On the morning of December 10, 1898, Alderman Henry Parfitt, J.P., of Ashley House, Pontnewydd passed away. He had been a builder, contractor, and a brick manufacturer. With strict integrity and a great attention to detail, he succeeded in building up a good business, which gave employment to many people throughout the years. He had always taken a keen interest in the affairs of Cwmbran. This led to many of the improvements that benefited generations of Cwmbran folk. A faithful member of the Hope Methodist Church, and acknowledged leader of the Liberal Party in the district, his early death at 62 years of age became a sad loss for the people.

John Lawrence had been a giant not only in Cwmbran, but through all of Monmouthshire. His decision to build blast furnaces at Cwmbran, instead of Newport, most certainly endorsed the industrial standing of the area. At the news of his death in 1901, many older folk immediately remembered the hounds in full cry as they chased fox and hare through the neighbourhood with their athletic owner not far behind. When invited to be Master of the Llangibby Hunt, little did he know that this status position would bring him fame for the next forty-one years.[2] During his 94 years, he had served Monmouthshire well in various important positions.

Another sad loss for the district occurred when Frederick William Rafarel died at his Glencoed residence on June 2, 1903, aged 66 years. He had come to Cwmbran thirty seven years earlier to take charge of the Patent Nut and Bolt Works under Mr. E.J. Grice. Much of his energy had contributed to the small works gradually changing into the industry of great magnitude present at the turn of the century. For many years he had taken a prominent part in the life of the district and an impressive monument was erected by the officials and workmen of Messrs Guest Keen and Nettlefolds works. This can still be seen at Llantarnam Church.

There had been tremendous changes at the Patent Nut and Bolt Company since the death of Edwin J. Grice. Arthur Keen had become by far the largest single shareholder in the company. In 1901, the Patent Nut and Bolt Co., merged with the Dowlais Iron, Steel & Coal Co., to form Guest, Keen & Co., under the chairmanship of Arthur Keen.

Having created Guest, Keen & Co., he scarcely paused for breath before contemplating another merger. Whilst the merger between the Guests and the Keens had been carried through with amity and goodwill, this could not be said of the events of 1902. For a long time, Keen had cast envious eyes on the Heath Street mills of his neighbours, Nettlefolds Ltd. Despite the logical assessment by Keen explaining how much time and money could be saved by his provision of raw material, they consistently rebuffed his suggestions of a union.

Keen was a clever and persistent man and no doubt a recent fact finding tour of the United States helped him to form a plan. It was not the logic of the situation which made Nettlefolds change their minds, but a ploy by Keen to bring the matter to a head. Legend has it that Keen purchased several modern machines from America for making woodscrews and had them openly conveyed into his London works. These were then secretly removed at night to be brought back repeatedly to create the impression that he was about to manufacture woodscrews on a large scale. The threat of further competition, at a time when Nettlefold's profits had established a pattern of slow decline, was sufficient to propel a weakened management towards the negotiating table.[3] In 1902, Guest, Keen & Co., amalgamated with Nettlefolds, but the manner in which Keen forced Nettlefold's hand caused long term ill-feeling between all members of senior management.

What was thought to be an easy war against the Dutch farmers in South Africa began in 1899 and caused a fervour of patriotism in Cwmbran and elsewhere. Thought to be a short war, the Boers' army of religious rustics would stretch the might of the British Empire to its limits. Men from Cwmbran were soon to be

Arthur Keen 1835-1915.

Cwmbran Works, from the air.

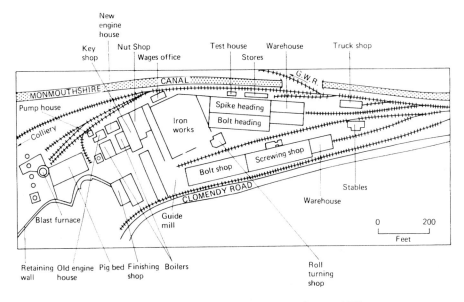

New
engine
house

Key   Nut Shop   Test house   Warehouse   Truck shop
shop   Wages office   Stores

CANAL

MONMOUTHSHIRE

G.W.R.

Pump house

Colliery

Iron
works

Spike heading

Bolt heading

Screwing shop

Bolt shop

Stables

CLOMENDY ROAD

Warehouse

Blast furnace

Guide
mill

0   200

Feet

Retaining   Old engine   Pig bed   Finishing   Boilers
wall   house   shop

Roll
turning
shop

Ironworks and Nut and Bolt Plant at Cwmbran c. 1910.

Guest, Keen and Nettlefold, Cwmbran.

Blast Furnace, Cwmbran.

Coke Ovens, Cwmbran.

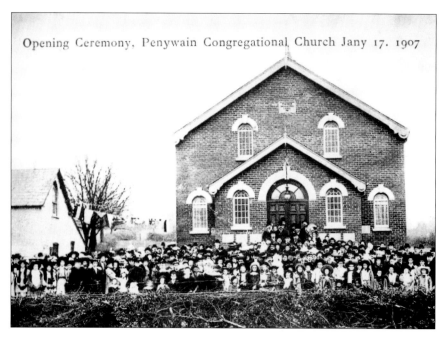

Opening Ceremony, Penywain Congregational Church Jany 17. 1907

St. Gabriel's Church, Cwmbran.

involved. Regular soldiers, who had grown up in the district, heard that their regiments were going overseas, while reservists received orders to report immediately to each depot. Later groups of part-time Volunteers were to be escorted to the local railway stations by large groups of friends with martial music ringing in their ears.

In May 1900, the relief of the gallant garrison of Mafeking caused many people to believe the war was ending and resulted in huge celebrations everywhere. In Cwmbran it would be a time that lived for ever in the memories of those present. Local people were alerted to the unusual happening when in the late evening the screaming of engine whistles, the firing of railway detonators, and the cheering of late night revellers filled the air. All in Cwmbran who heard the commotion hastened out of doors to exchange greetings. The local band soon mustered, and, followed by a large crowd of people, paraded the streets till the early hours of the morning. The next day, a procession of around 900 children with patriotic colours, and every official organisation, toured the district. As darkness descended a huge bonfire and firework illuminations gave a stunning end to the celebrations.

With six of their part-time soldiers serving their Queen in South Africa:

Corporal L. Sketch, Glenhurst, Pontnewydd,

Privates J. Lyons, 8 Spring Street, Cwmbran,

J. Butcher, 10 Spring Street, Cwmbran,

C.H. Butcher, 10 Spring Street, Cwmbran,

W. J. Allsop, 1 Club Row, Pontnewydd,

R.H. Hurley, recently from Somerset,

many Cwmbran folk were keen to hear news of the progress of the war. A military atmosphere prevailed everywhere and it was probably due to this that the long-standing armoury and headquarters at the Cwmbran Gardens began to appear unsuitable in a time of war. In September 1900, the C Company, 3rd Volunteer Battalion, South Wales Borderers, removed their headquarters to the new Drill Hall at Cwmbran. The bulk of the men lived in or very near to the village of Cwmbran and on the opening day around seventy left the old headquarters to march to the new, well-fitted building. They were pleasantly surprised to be met on the way by the Cwmbran Brass Band and Fire Brigade, who joined the procession.

The euphoria of war was somewhat restrained in the Cwmbran district when news came through that one of their soldiers had died of enteric fever in Springfontein on December 17, 1900. Disease, sadly, claimed the lives of many of the British troops during the three year campaign. Private James Farmiloe, a reservist with the 2nd Gloucesters, was formerly employed at the Patent Nut and Bolt Works while residing at Grange Road, Pontnewydd. He is buried at President

Avenue, Springfontein, with a slate headstone over the grave and his name is also on a regimental memorial in Blomfontein.[4] He left a widow and one child.

Amid all the bustle of an enlarged, thriving industrial area, with thoughts on a faraway land where their troops were not faring very well against a wily Boer foe, bad news, as always, travelled fast. Late in the evening of January 22, 1901, the sad news of the death of Queen Victoria reached Cwmbran and quickly spread throughout the district. On January 25, the following entry was recorded in the minutes of the Llantarnam Urban District Council meeting:

'Death of Queen Victoria

'It was resolved that the Clerk forward the expression of the loyal sympathy of this Council, and the inhabitants of their district to his Majesty the King and the Royal Family, in the bereavement they have sustained in the death of Her Most Gracious Majesty Queen Victoria.'[5]

In the days that followed many Cwmbran folk walked the canal towpath to Newport or Pontypool to hear their new king being 'Proclaimed' outside each town-hall. In the days that followed impressive memorial services were conducted in the iron church of St. Gabriel, and the Elim Congregational Church. A large number of schoolchildren attended with C Company, of the Volunteers, and all the various local organisations.

The war continued in South Africa with the enemy proving elusive due to their knowledge of the vast countryside and their sturdy horses. Fresh troops were needed to replace those exhausted while needlessly tramping through the hot land. The Volunteer Battalions, South Wales Borderers, were commanded to supply more men and C Company (Cwmbran) quickly responded. The following men soon entrained:

> Corporal David Watkins
> Lance Corporal T. Field, Rose Cottage, Cwmbran
> Private D.C. Fisher, Stone Row, Cwmbran
> Private F. Ford
> Private John Jones
> Private F. Lewis
> Private C. Morgan, Fair View Terrace, Cwmbran
> Private M. Relihan, Pritchard Terrace, Cwmbran
> Private A. Spanswick
> Private H. Whitby

In May 1901, the first group of Cwmbran Volunteers returned to a very enthusiastic reception following around twelve months service abroad. Bunting and mottoes were displayed in profusion in the vicinity of Cwmbran railway station. Exploding fog signals placed on the railway line gave notice of the much-awaited arrival. The train carrying the local heroes was met by the Cwmbran

Brass Band, and C Co. Volunteers, and as they alighted onto the platform, vociferous cheering by a crowd of between four and five thousand people filled the air. While the band played popular war songs en route, the men were escorted to their homes. The returned soldiers were later guests at a supper and concert where each man was presented with a gold medal, a memento in recognition of their service in South Africa. Similar scenes were later witnessed for the return of single reservists and other groups of Volunteers.

With the war coming to an end the call to arms went out for the last time in the Cwmbran district and Bugler J. Cunningham, Private Charles Oakey and Private Thomas Williams, all of C Co., entrained for South Africa.[6]

On May 31, 1902, the Boers surrendered and all the Cwmbran men who gave service to King and country in the difficult conflict could rightly be proud of their contribution. At the Cwmbran Colliery a fund had been set up for the families of the reservists who had been called up for active service, and the Volunteers who went with them. In September 1902, an interesting ceremony took place in the Upper Cwmbran School when gifts were presented to the soldiers from their work colleagues. Each of the soldiers employed at the colliery received gifts consisting of English lever silver watches, all being engraved with the recipient's name and date of the presentation, a silver chain, and a gold-centred pendant. Those worthy of the gifts were: Milsom Ashton, John Harrington, Alfred Spanswick, Fred Evans, Charles Smith, William Peploe, Hubert Whitby, Ben Pearce, John Jones, William Thomas, Arthur Phillips, William G. Parry, John Allsop, Fred Robinson, Fred Lewis, Albert Parfitt, Thomas Field, W. Collins, John Morris and Matthew Watkins.

Meanwhile, King Edward VII had lain dangerously ill with appendicitis and it would take a surgical operation to save his life. This, coupled with his wish for his Coronation not to be held until the South African war was over, delayed the keenly awaited royal celebration. During August 1902, the Coronation celebrations at last went ahead with a special tea for upward of a thousand children at Llantarnam Abbey Park. The enjoyable proceedings concluded with a distribution of Coronation medals and the singing of the National Anthem. A similar tea for the children of Pontnewydd took place in a field adjoining Holy Trinity Church. Followed by games and entertainments, each child had a wonderful day. At this time streets in the district received names and numbers. Thus, to commemorate the rare royal event, the Cwmbran U.D.C., gave the name Coronation Road to the first houses built by them since taking office.[7]

Life continued in the thriving district with just the occasional distractions. The visit of General Booth, the founder of the Salvation Army caused quite a stir amongst the Cwmbran members. Not since the opening of the local headquarters in 1883, had an event of such magnitude taken place.

Special Council Meeting, May 23rd, 1910.

Present.—THE WHOLE COUNCIL.

King Edward VII.

Resolved, on motion of Councillors Hartley and Thomas, that we the Llantarnam Urban District Council desire to most respectfully express our sincere and profound sorrow at the death of our late beloved Sovereign, His Most Gracious Majesty King Edward the VII., after a short, peaceful, and prosperous reign ; and to humbly tender to their Most Gracious Majesties King George V. and his Consort Queen Mary, and to Queen Alexandra and the members of the Royal Family, our deepest sympathy in their great bereavement, and to assure Their Majesties of our continued loyalty and devotion to the Throne.

Proclamation.

Resolved on motion of Councillors Lawrence and Kelly that Public Proclamation of King George V. be made in this district on Friday next at 6.30.

—That the ceremony be held in the Star Brick Company's Field Llantarnam Road.

—That the Managers of the Schools in the district be requested to give the children a half-holiday on the occasion.

—That Councillor James be requested to take steps for the marshalling of the children, and that the Military, the Clergy and Ministers, and other public bodies and the general public be invited to take part in the ceremony.

—That the Surveyor and Clerk carry out the necessary arrangements for the ceremony.

Another interesting event seized the imagination of not only the Cwmbran schoolchildren, but all of those in the Eastern Valley. In June 1903, an advertisement in the Pontypool Argus gave details of a visit to Newport of the legendary Buffalo Bill and his Wild West Show. For one day only, at the Shaftsbury Park Grounds, people would have the unique opportunity of seeing the famous Indian fighter. Four special trains conveyed his eight hundred employees and four hundred horses through the provinces to visit the principle towns and cities. Extra to the re-enactment of historic events, his congress of rough riders gave a proudly pre-eminent exhibition of unusual interest. Leading up to the special performance it was observed that children everywhere were unable to concentrate on their schoolwork. Some head teachers gave their pupils a holiday to see the show. At the Cwmbran schools this was not to be, but with an exceptional high number of scholars absent on the day, it is believed that not many missed the chance of a lifetime.

By 1906, Penywain Congregational Church was ready for rebuilding. The old farmhouse turned into a house of worship in 1818, could no longer accommodate the large congregation and land was purchased with money raised by a mortgage. With half of the work carried out voluntarily by church members, the impressive opening ceremony occurred in January 1907.

Similar circumstances were present in St. Gabriel's Mission Church found at the top of Commercial Street. The erection of the iron structure in 1881, on a site given by a Miss Griffiths, of Gloucester, an owner of property in the neighbourhood, had cost £400. In 1907, the old iron construction was in a bad state of repair and it was decided to build a new edifice of stone at a cost of between £5,000 and £6,000. October 17, became the day of the stone laying ceremony by Viscount Tredegar, of Balaclava fame, who received a handsome silver trowel in commemoration of the event. Opened in November 1908, by the Right Reverend the Lord Bishop of Llandaff, the attractive structure was of greystone from Cross Keys with Bath stone facings.

The church of St. Andrew at Pontrhydyrun also opened in October 1907, as a daughter church of Holy Trinity. The corrugated sheeting for the building was donated by Isaac Butler, iron master, of Panteg Iron Works, whilst the site for the Mission Church was given by Mrs W. Moseley, Pontrhydyrun. The interesting structure seated two hundred persons.

At the end of 1908, yet another slack time was being experienced in the local ironworks causing many families in the neighbourhood to be in great distress. Fortunately, with experience of the similar situations in the past, the management of the difficulties had become a little easier. The hundreds of hungry children received meals at the Temperance Hall, whilst the Cwmbran U.D.C., found work for a number of the unemployed by offering them stone-breaking work. In 1910, it was the turn of the Cwmbran colliers to feel the pinch. This again gave rise to the frequent use of soup kitchens in the district. While many could do nothing but accept the hard times brought about by recession, around sixty colliers went across to the Western Valley, and to Glamorganshire, in search of work.

Amid the gloom in the Cwmbran district caused by lack of orders in the coal trade, further bad news was received on May 6, 1910, when it became known that the popular King Edward VII had died from pneumonia. At a special meeting of the Cwmbran U.D.C., it was resolved to send a letter of condolence to the Royal Family. Unlike former times, when interested Cwmbran residents travelled to Pontypool or Newport to hear the Royal Proclamation of their new monarch, it was decided that Cwmbran had become so populous that there could be no objection to them holding their own ceremony. Fine, warm weather favoured the proceedings and practically all Cwmbran turned out to witness the ceremony. A long procession containing hundreds of schoolchildren and various organisations formed at Oak Street and proceeded via Victoria Street to a field at the junction of the Grange and Llantarnam Roads. Here a flagpole and temporary platform had been erected ready for the special day. In front of the largest crowd ever assembled in Cwmbran, the Rev. W.E. Robinson offered up an appropriate prayer and Mr. E. Hartley, J.P., read the proclamation. The magnificent display of loyalty on the part of the people present concluded with a reading followed by "God save the King" and the hoisting of the Union Jack. The singing of the National Anthem, and three hearty cheers for the King, brought the historic event to an end.[8]

The following year excited children experienced a Coronation tea and the presentation of commemorative mugs and medals, the latter again being given by Sir Clifford Cory, M.P., of Llantarnam Abbey. A free hot dinner for elderly residents consisted of roast or boiled beef, mutton, potatoes and vegetables with plum or milk puddings. Services in the local churches preceded a large procession walking around the principle streets of the district and games and sports added to the celebration.[9]

Cwmbran continued to play its part in history. No different to other districts it would remain at the mercy of difficult, fluctuating trade cycles. Residents continued to seek solace in their religious worship and the many activities of each church and chapel. The problem of extra office space for the expanding Council was solved in 1912, when the Tennis Court Hotel was purchased for £1,250, and converted. A new band room opened nearby, which provided the opportunity for those of a musical nature to perfect their talent. The movies arrived and would draw large numbers to the Olympia Picture Palace. At Pontnewydd, a new golf course attracted those seeking more leisurely exercise. Life was good in many respects, but most were unaware of the gathering of distant war clouds.

REFERENCES

1. Gwent Record Office, A421 M 1, Llantarnam Local Board Minute Book, 1893-1898.
2. Steer, Pembereton E., *The Monmouthshire Review, The History of the Llangibby Hunt,* Vol. 1, No.3, July 1933
3. Jones, Edgar, Cwmbran Local Studies Library, *The History of GKN -Volume One, 1759-1918,* (1987) pp. 362-3.
4. Watt, Steve, *In Memoriam - Roll of Honour Imperial Forces Anglo-Boer War 1899-1902.*
5. Gwent Record Office, A 421 M 2, Llantarnam Urban District Council Minute Book, 1898-1901, January 25, 1901.
6. Public Record Office, War Office records; Lloyd, W.G., *Call To Arms - A Valley History,* 1999.
7. Gwent Record Office, A 421 M 2, Llantarnam Urban District Council Minute Book, 1898-1901, June 16, 1902.
8. Gwent Record Office, A 421 A M 6, Llantarnam Urban District Council Minute Book, 1910-1911, May 23, 1910.
9. Gwent Record Office, A 421 A M 7, Llantarnam Urban District Council Minute Book, 1911-1912, May 5, 1911.

Chapter Nine

OVER THE RIVER

The land over the Afon Lwyd river in an easterly direction is now an integral part of the large town of Cwmbran, but still commands an individual presence of its own. With the Llanfrechfa parish always divided into two divisions for administrative purposes in years gone by, the lower division appears to commence on the eastern side of the river and extend to Ponthir. To suit this history only intimate knowledge of the districts of Llanyrafon, Croesyceiliog and Llanfrechfa is required.

Llanyrafon Farm, was probably built between 1550-1610, though there seems to have been a house on the site from the Middle Ages. It belonged originally to the Cistercian monks of Llantarnam and was acquired by the Morgan family when they purchased the Manor of Edlogan in 1558. Easily recognisable are features of Tudor and Stuart building in Monmouthshire. Built near the Afon Lwyd, it has been considerably altered over the last four hundred years and thus is an excellent example of the development of the small manor house in the county.[1]

The Griffith family is the first family known to live at the farm. Members of this family resided at Llanyrafon for two hundred years, while actually owning the property for almost three hundred years (from 1616-1886). Walter Griffith is the first recorded member of the Griffith family to have lived at Llanyrafon. Records state that in 1616 Walter Griffith acquired: *"One mansion house, one barn, four gardens, one orchard, one barton and four parcels of land on the road from Croesyceiliog to Caerleon."*

Walter Griffith, an attorney, left considerable property in his will of 1629, including a generous sum of £10 to be distributed amongst the poor of the Llanfrechfa parish. Also, the bequests to his servants proved to be very generous. His property passed on to his son Charles Griffith I. The following generations of the family, Charles Griffith II and III both lived at Llanyrafon Farm, with Charles Griffith III holding the important position of Steward to Edlogan Manor.

Charles Griffith III's grandson, William Griffith, became the last of the family to live at Llanyrafon. Around 1800, he moved to Barton Street, Gloucester, where he had a successful solicitor's practice. Surviving records of business correspondence sent to his son shows that he still maintained close ties with the farm returning regularly to manage the estate. William Griffith died in 1831. The

Llanyrafon Mill c. 1960.

Renovation of Llanyrafon Mill in 1977.

following obituary entered in the August 27, 1831, issue of the Monmouthshire Merlin gives an insight into the benevolent nature of the man:

'On Friday night, at his residence in Barton Street, in the 74th year of his age, William Griffith, of Gloucester and of Llanyravon, in this county, the excellence of whose public and private worth will long remain an exemplary instance of one who in his generation, has not lived in vain. In all the nearer relations of life, the manner in which he discharged his duties bore testimony to the kindness of his heart, and to the devotedness of his domestic attachments; and, whilst constant and uniform in his friendships, a singleness of motive and firmness of purpose pervaded his public character, and marked with a sincerity and steadiness of principle. As a solicitor of the most respectable rank, he passed a long life of undenating integrity; and the ready hand of kindness which he held out to his younger brethren, will long be a source of their grateful recollection. Though busied in the labours of an arduous profession, he was ever alive to the calls of active charity and of public improvement; and the course that he took, as a leading member of a political party, men of all denominations will admit was no less honest than zealous, and that though a warm partisan, he never sullied the cause in which he was engaged, either by a departure from principle, or by the too common, but objectionable practises of ribaldry or personality. A combination of such qualities could not but secure him the love and respect of his friends and fellow citizens. Unostentatious in himself, the tribute here offered to his memory would not overstep the modesty of truth, or do a violence to the feelings of those who survive. Suffice it to say that the calm resignation of his latter days was the best assurance of the motives of his life, and that the firm faith in which he approached his end, is the best consolation of his afflicted family and friends.

Llanyrafon Farm passed to his son, Charles Griffith IV, who died in 1836, without a heir. His wife Jane, (ob. 1880), inherited the estate by right before marrying Frenchman Eugene Jean Baptiste de Solignac. However, the Llanyrafon Farm came much later into the possession of Florence Griffith, sister of Charles IV, who died a spinster in 1886. This marked the end of the Griffith family line.[2]

In 1892, the estate of approximately 1000 acres was broken up before being sold. The house ceased to be a manor house and became the centre of a working farm.[3] Richard Laybourne of the 'The Firs', Malpas, bought the farm containing 235 acres of land for £3,000 and gave it to his daughter for a wedding present on her marriage to Mr. Alfred Massey Pilliner. Alfred Pilliner was the son of Mr. A.C. Pilliner, J.P., of Llantarnam Grange, who before his death in 1887, had been the managing director of Oakfield Wire Works. Alfred junior, went to university, but while there his father died and he left early to look after his father's estate.

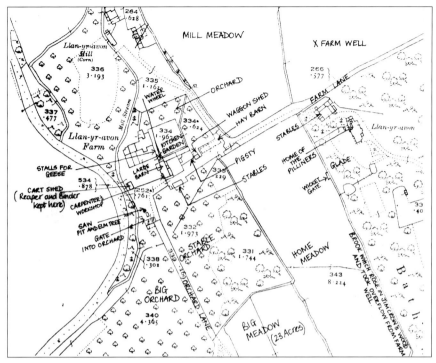

Llanyrafon in 1922

The newly weds lived at the farm for about six months, in 1900, while the nearby Llanyravon House, 'a modern mansion in Gothic style' was being built at a cost of £1,000. The Pilliner family had considered living at the farm, but it had fallen into such bad repair that they decided to build a new home where Mrs Pilliner designed the tile surround of the big fireplace in William Morris style. At the time the original staircase of the old farm was removed to the new house. In later years Llanyrafon House became the Stirrup Cup Club and provided land for building the popular Commodore Hotel.

When Alfred Pilliner owned Llanyrafon Farm, the farmhouse was initially divided into three separate houses. The west wing of the house was originally a cider cellar and granary before being converted into a separate cottage. The gardener, Mr. Evans, lived in this part of the farmhouse from about 1918 until 1928. The Skellet family lived in the main central section of the farmhouse and the carpenter lodged with them. He was a bachelor who had been badly injured in the Senghenydd pit disaster of 1913. The north wing remained part of the central section until Mr. Pilliner converted it into bachelor quarters for the unmarried workers on the farm. The east wing also became a cottage where various bailiffs lived. A kitchen garden was shared by the occupants.

Llanyrafon Farm, 1916.

Llanyrafon Farm was without a doubt a busy agricultural concern. A water wheel, housed behind the large barn was a crucial machine, essential for the running of the farm. In the early 1900's, it powered the elevator that took the hay to be stacked in the barn, and the grindstone which crushed the apples to make cider. It also worked the root pulper, the chaff cutter and the circular saw. Just prior to the First World War there was a plan to provide electricity. Mr. Pilliner's son, Rupert, had constructed plans for this, but sadly he was killed in the war and this had a devastating effect on the family. A hero of the retreat from Mons, he was recommended for gallantry and the Legion of Honour of France.[4] An impressive memorial to him can be seen inside All Saints Church, Llanfrechfa.

A variety of farm animals were kept at the farm. A bull occupied the outhouses adjoining the partly derelict barn, while a sty next to the cowshed held a large number of pigs. After the First World War, all the woods on the estate were fenced in and from then on the pigs were kept in huts in these woods. Working horses were always stabled at the farm while Mr. Pilliner bred pedigree Arab horses at nearby Llanyrafon House.

A herd of Hereford cattle was originally kept and reared for their beef. Sometimes a cross bred herd developed when a Hereford was crossed with Mrs Pilliner's house cow, which was a Jersey. Only occasionally were mountain sheep kept in winter. There were always chickens in the farmyard and geese and ducks swam in the stream behind the hay barn.

The main crop grown was hay and a system of flooding the fields made it possible to obtain an early harvest. Two hundred tons of hay were grown every year. Some of this was used on the farm with the remainder sold to collieries. The large orchards nearby made it possible for a great deal of cider to be produced. It was not made for commercial sale, but consumed by farm workers or given away. During every haymaking season a large amount of free cider quenched the thirst of the labour force.

It was a difficult time during World War One because so many men had joined the army. Several Land Girls worked on the farm to boost the work force. Mr. Pilliner's young daughter Judith helped at the farmhouse by washing up for the girls because they had to go out to work very early in the morning. At the end of the war three prisoners of war came to work at the farm. There were two Austrians, Andrew and Karl, and one Pole called Paul. They were very hard workers. The Polish prisoner of war, Paul, stayed until 1922 and became very attached to the farm, the people and the area. In 1922, however, he was forcibly returned to Poland.[5]

Alfred M. Pilliner became a Justice of the Peace in 1928, before giving up farming because of illness. He died in 1932 and was interred at All Saints Church, Llanfrechfa. The Pilliner family owned the farm until the 1950's, when it was sold with a large amount of land to the Cwmbran Development Corporation. Its condition further deteriorated over the years until the Torfaen Museum Trust took over the Grade 2 Listed Building in 1980, on a long lease for a peppercorn rent. This began a huge programme of restoration, which led to the buildings being used to illustrate a typical late Victorian valley farm.

Due to Health and Safety and financial problems at the farm in recent years, sadly, it is no longer open to the public.

Close to Llanyrafon Farm stands Llanyrafon Mill. The exact date of the building is uncertain, but the old timber work of the mill-house roof and the former mechanical apparatus indicates great age. Evidence contained in the papers of the Griffith family prove that the mill was in existence in 1632 and part of the Manor of Edlogan. Owned by the Griffith family from early times until 1892, the mill would have many tenants throughout the centuries. Similar mills were to be found at nearby Llantarnam and Pontyfelin, but these are all gone and we are fortunate to still have a splendid example of a former small milling industry in our midst.

Sometimes confusion sets in regarding the title of the small Llanyrafon milling industry. An establishment with one grinding stone is known as a mill, but the former local workplace had three stones and was officially known as Llanyrafon "Mills."[6]

At the three-storey corn mill a team of horses was kept to deliver to a wide area with one important customer being the Morgan family, of Tredegar House, Newport. The working day consisted of hoisting sacks of grain to the top floor before being temporary stored in large bins to prevent access by rodents. Poured into chutes the grain fell to the grinding stones on the first floor. Water from a constructed weir in the Afon Lwyd would be regulated to travel along a sluice before hitting the blades or "buckets" causing the former wooden wheel to turn and set the machinery in motion. From here the meal passed to ground floor to be bagged.

Inside the mill could be seen the gearing. Great use was made of wooden cogs. The worn teeth were easily detached and quickly replaced by new ones. By means of belt and pulleys, the same motive power was used to work the flour dresser. This was a skilfully constructed wooden machine consisting of long arms fixed by spokes to a revolving spindle. The "silks" were fixed around this to form a drum with the whole machine enclosed in a box-like structure. The arms rotated at great speed for the ground wheat to be fed by a chute into the drum. The flour was then forced at great pressure against the silk screens and only that which had been forced through could travel down the flour chute. Other grades such as middlings, sharps and bran each had its own chute. Animal feed was the main product in later years.

By the 1940s, the warmth of old wood had given way to gleaming metal with hard steel rollers replacing the stones. The rush of water and the beat of the wheel soon changed to the whine of the electric motor as the local industry strove to keep up with the times.[7]

We often hear of the long, hot summers in years past, but in August 1887, this appears to have been true. Henry Knipe, of Coedygric Farm, had been enabled, thanks to the continued run of fine weather, to have five-and-a-half acres of wheat cut, hauled and threshed, and a large portion of it ground at Llanyrafon Mill in advance of his usual time. In the previous thirty-seven years, he had not transported the crop and had the work at Llanyrafon Mill completed so early!

Following the death of Florence Griffith in 1886, the Llanyrafon Estate was broken up and sold in 1892. Lot 35, the old established corn-mill, in the occupancy of Thomas Francis, at a yearly rent £90, was purchased by Mr. Richard Laybourne, of Malpas, for £1,450.[8]

In 1916, Thomas Wait moved his family from Ty Coch, Cwmbran, and took up the tenancy of the historic mill. They lived in the nearby house. During a heavy flood in the early 1920s, the centre of the Afon Lwyd weir broke and the cost of repairing was too much for the Laybourne family because Colonel Arthur Laybourne had just died. The highly respected Tom Wait was offered the opportunity to purchase the property and he became the first owner to actually carry out milling at the premises.

Extra to the regular work brought to the mill by local farmers, Tom Wait often visited the Corn Exchange, near Newport docks, and negotiated for a load of corn. This would be transported to Llantarnam Railway Station before the back-breaking task of transferring the sacks of corn to a horse and cart. In 1929, he obtained his first lorry which enabled the collection and delivery to a larger area. The mill ceased operating in the early 1950's, and was subsequently purchased by the Cwmbran Development Corporation in 1967.[9]

A fire started by boys in the redundant building during April 1971, caused considerable damage and many thought this to be the end of the historic building. However, in 1977, government money became available to provide a scheme for unemployed people to participate in useful work. This was taken up and the fabric of the building received a complete renovation. The timely intervention undoubtedly saved the Llanyrafon Mill from being lost forever.[10]

Today, a caring group known as the Friends of Llanyrafon Mill are dedicated to restoring the Grade Two listed building to a working facility. This will undoubtably be an asset to Cwmbran town.

With the building of the Monmouthshire Canal in the 1790s, many entrepreneurs in the eastern valley of Monmouthshire realised the usefulness of this new form of quick and efficient transport. George Conway, formerly of Melin-Griffith, Glamorgan, had observed the opening and immediately formulated a plan to utilise the liquid road. He was at the time employed in a senior position at the Caerleon Works, owned by his father-in-law, John Jenkins. George had three sons, John, William and Charles; and daughters, Jane, Sarah, Hannah and Mary. He left the Caerleon Works in 1802, to construct his own iron and tinplate works on the site of a small forge near the banks of the Afon Lwyd at lower Pontnewydd.[11] By this time he and his three sons had become experts in the trade and the eldest son John, would in 1806, start a second tinplate works at Pontrhydyrun *(The bridge over the ford of the ash trees)*. This was the Edlogan Works, which was erected at the bottom of Chapel Lane. During the early years pig-iron brought by canal barges from Pontypool or Newport Docks was unloaded on "the quay" at Pontnewydd and taken thence by mules to the Conways' works to be converted into tin-plates.

During the early days, at the rear of the Ed Logan Works flowed the "dyke", which was the mill-race diverted from the Afon Lwyd and it turned the great wheel, 14ft. by 3ft., a necessary power for the iron mill.

Inside the works the red-hot "pigs" of iron were taken by strong men from the furnaces and flung across the iron floor to other men standing at long iron rolls which looked somewhat like mangles.

These men passed the bars to and fro many times until they became very thin; then they folded the thin plates and rolled them again and again. It was the girls' job to separate the sheets when they were cold. This was followed by cleaning in acid, the most unpleasant task at the works and often harmful to health. Finally, the beautiful process of passing the sheets through boiling tin whence they emerged like silver plates.

Extracts from a Government report into the employment of children during 1841, although lengthy, gives a rare insight into the working lives of the employees at both Pontnewydd and Ed Logan Tinplate Works:

Mr. W. Conway James, managing partner at the Pontnewydd Works, states -

We employ 32 male and 8 female adults; 9 boys between 13 and 18 years, and 1 boy and 1 girl under 13 years of age.

None of our machinery is fenced off; indeed, we do not think it necessary, as since the works was established no accidents has occurred, with the exception of a child four years old (under the care of her sister) being allowed to go near the wheels, by which she was a little injured.

The temperature in the different parts of our works is variable, but neither very hot nor very cold, the exact temperature is not known.

The greatest heat is in the scale-house, but only sufficient to heat the plates "warm red" this is, however, a closed place, as it is necessary to exclude air, otherwise the plates would be injured in the process.

Children are not necessary required in any of our processes, and they are only employed in the lightest work, as men would not work for the wages.

Never having employed very young children, we can hardly answer to a limitation of age for employment. They generally begin light work about 12 years, and we do not find them suffering from it; in general those who begin young are the best workmen.

In some parts (in the mill and scale-house for instance) the men work more than 12 hours on Mondays and Saturdays. They begin early on Monday morning, and work late on Saturday night. In the tin-house, upon emergency, the men have worked 14 hours each day, but very seldom.

We should say the excess beyond the regular hours are unavoidable; because it is so seldom necessary as not to make it worth while employing an extra "watch," or set of hands, by which the wages of the regular workmen would be so curtailed as to render it hardly likely they would stay with us; besides, as men work by the box, or piece, they are always willing to work over-hours on the two days named, if required, for the sake of the extra wages.

Any children (if ours may be so called) we employ, work with regular sets, and of course work the same number of hours.

The greatest number of hours that the same set of children or young persons worked during one day in the last year is in the scale-house, about 14 hours; but this occurs very seldom - only when we are very much pressed; perhaps the next week they have an idle time.

We have not tried relays of hands; but parents sometimes if they have many children change them, to which we have no objection; it has been a system here with parents to work one child while another is in school, and so on changing them continually.

The effect of reducing the hours of children's work would be to reduce the hours of all men who work in our manufactory, the wages would by this means be materially reduced.

In the mill and the scale-house we work day and night; the watches are changed at six o'clock night and morning.

We have employed only two children at night-work, and not more than 12 hours, excepting there may be have been occasions for it, and then not more than 14 hours.

The prohibition of night-work for children and young persons would prevent our employing children; and as men could not be procured to work for the wages it would perhaps in the end destroy our trade.

No processes in our work indispensably require them if men would work for the wages.

No part of our works are continued in operation during Sunday.

With regard to meal-times, the men always regulate this; they work by the box, and they take their meals when they please.

Corporal punishments are never inflicted.

The best workmen are always found amongst those who were taken into the works when young; indeed, we consider it necessary, in order to secure good workmen, to put children to work as soon as we consider them able.

Examinations at Pontrhydyrun Tin Works, belonging to Messrs Conway, Brothers, employing about 50 people.
Samuel Conway, aged 45, "shearer."
I have eight children, four are working in these works, one boy and three girls. The youngest is the little one now with me, she is about eight and half years old; the boy is 13 years old, he is employed raising plates out of the "tin pot." The oldest girl is 17 years old; she is employed in rubbing the tin-plates in saw-dust and lime; the other girl is 15 years old, she works with me in opening the plates after I shear them, and this little one helps her; they both work by my side; the little one has only been at work four months; I do not mean to keep her at work; I have two working,

and I mean to send them to school every other week; I have done this with all my children; when they first come to work I do not keep them long at it at a time, but change them every other week, and they get good schooling in this way; they go to day-school, and I pay 4d. per week for them for reading and 6d. per week for writing, all ages the same. The master is a tolerably good one, but another school is very much wanted in this neighbourhood, and I have been speaking to Mr. Conway about it. The children get, for opening plates, from 3s. 4d. to 5s. 10d. per week; I get for shearing about 25s. per week, and I receive the children's money; they all work from six to six, but go home for their meals, as they live near the works; and as they work by the box, they can go and come when they like, but they cannot do so in the mill, as they must attend fires, and the metal, and other things. I worked when I was eight years old in a copper works rolling mill quite as hard as any of the children do here; it did not hurt me, and I do not think that it hurts any child to put them to light work about eight years old. The dipping of plates in lime is not healthy work; the lime-dust gets into their throats and gives them a short cough; they have not done that work more than two years; it is done by big girls 15 or 16 years old; it agrees with some very well, others complain at first but get used to it.

  Phoebe Conway, aged 8 years and 6 months.

  I work with my father and sister; I open plates from the shears; my father shears them; I help my sister. I have not been long at the works - not many months; my work is not hard; I would rather work than go to school; I have been to school a little, and go on Sunday to chapel school; I can't read, I am spelling; I am going to school again next week.

  Thomas Evans, aged 12 years.

  I am dusting plates with sawdust; I work 11 hours; I have an hour for dinner; about a month ago I worked at the mill behind the rolls, "catching;" it was harder work than "dusting;" it was very hot sometimes behind the rolls; I was at school for three years, and I attend the Sunday-school; I can read; I would rather go to school than work; I don't know how much I get; my father receives my money.

  John Absolem, aged 11 years.

  I am a "lister;" I have been working for four years, but I have only been "listing" for four months; I work in the tin-house; we all work 12 hours; I go home to dinner, but am not allowed an hour, sometimes not ten minutes; they must keep on at the work while the tin and grease is hot and in temper; I do not always work 12 hours; I do not get very tired; I am never ill; I do not recollect that I have lost a day by being sick; before I went to "list" I was putting down plates in the pickle, that was not hard work, but sometimes the pickle burned my fingers, I used "hand-leathers," which saved my hands; I did not hurt them much; I was in school three years, and I go to the Sunday-school now, and can read; I would rather go to school than work; I do not know how much money I get, my father has it; he works in the same place; he is a "scaler" at the furnace.

Statement of Charles Conway (son of the late George Conway) managing partner of the Pontrhydyrun Tin Works:

I have resided in this parish, with little exception, for upwards of 40 years...I have all my lifetime been engaged, more or less, in tin-plate manufactory, and I have had sole management of these works for more than 20 years...Workmen almost invariably stick together right or wrong; they are always suspicious of any interference of the employers. I am not aware of a single person connected with these works being joined to any Chartist societies during the late movement; yet I cannot conceal from myself that they very considerably sympathised with the Chartists...I know not a church or chapel in the district that has not a Sunday-school attached to it; connected to these works is a Sunday-school at Pontrhydyrun Chapel.

George Conway and his family settled at Pontrhydyrun House, which stands at the bottom of Chapel Lane, next door to the site of the Edlogan Works. Later, the younger members of his family would marry and live in four large houses, which stood at the corner of Edlogan Way and Station Road. (These have since been demolished and a complex of flats now occupy the site). In addition to the houses, there were splendid gardens and a magnificent domed ballroom. Opposite these were terraced houses, which became homes for domestic staff and probably some of the works foremen. Known as Conway Terrace, this row of terraced houses is still present.

Throughout his life George Conway believed in the Baptist cause and with his works giving employment in the area, he began to realise the religious needs of the workforce. The first intimation of his caring attitude was when the younger female members of the Conway family commenced a Sunday School for the children in 1807. Held in the Assorting Room of the Edlogan Works, Pontrhydyrun, the project proved a success with full services occasionally held. However, the enterprise would suffer a setback when conditions under which the classes were held became unhealthy and other options had to be considered.

A more substantial place of worship became a priority and inspired George Conway's eldest son, William, to donate a parcel of land at the top of Pontrhydyrun hill. Here, the foundation of a new chapel was laid on May 13,

The First Conway Works at Pontrhydyrun.

Edlogan Works, Pontrhydyrun, c. 1960.

140

Pontrhydyrun Baptist Church

1815, at a cost of £600. The improved place of worship opened on November 15, of the same year.[12]

George Conway died on July 4, 1822, and Rev. Micah Thomas preached at his funeral on July 8. He was interred in the family plot called the 'Conway Yard', at Pontrhydyrun Baptist Church. His descendents took over his profitable business undertakings and continued to manage them successfully.

The first Pontrhydyrun Baptist Church served the followers well, but by 1836, the congregation grew to around one hundred members and again improvements became necessary. The building of the present day impressive edifice commenced in 1836 and opened for worship on August 16, 1837. The cost was £2,000, but it opened free of debt.

The lower Pontnewydd Tin Plate Works ceased trading in 1885 and was dismantled. In more recent years local people will be aware of the presence of the Gwent Pipe Works on this site.

The Edlogan Works at Pontrhydyrun survived well into the 20th century. In 1905, three mills were in operation. Its potential attracted the large concern of Richard Thomas & Company, who took over in 1908. Incidentally, it was one of the last in Wales to transfer from a water mill to steam power. The works eventually closed down during the slump of the 1930s.

Requisitioned for storage by the Ministry of Supply during World War II, the task of dismantling much of the old works began in 1946. It was in October 1949, that many interested bystanders witnessed the demolition of the old chimney stack, which had been a landmark since the earliest days of the works. The site would continue to accomodate many successful small businesses up until the present time.

At the top of the steep Pontrhydyrun hill, the Baptist Chapel continues to serve as a memorial to the good work of the remarkable Conway family.[13] Built like a Greek temple, it provides a profound backdrop to the splendid Lebanese cedar tree found alongside the entrance gates.

Leaving Chapel Lane, and joining The Highway, one may pause to think of the old mail and passenger coaches hurrying through the scattered district of Croesyceiliog while on their way to the staging posts of Pontypool and Abergavenny.

Croesyceiliog, the name given to the village, is of Welsh origin, signifying Cock Cross, and is believed to be derived from curious circumstances: In an adjoining field, on a hillock facing the road, there stood, centuries ago, the figure of a large bird with outstretched wings, in the act of crowing as upon the occasion of Peter denying Christ. By its side was a cross. Local tradition states that this interesting piece of sculpture was destroyed by the Roundheads in 1646, when a band of them swept through the district, breaking to pieces all tendencies to superstition and "pious" monuments of an interesting past.[14]

Another version of its origin, more probably the correct one, is based on the name of an ancient hostelry alongside the road and now known as the *"Upper Cock."* The hostelry formerly had a sign with a painted cockerel and a rhyme in Welsh with an English version on the other side:

> Dyma dafarn Croes y Ceiliog
> Groesaw i bob un am ei geiniog
> Cwrw da i bawb trwy dalu
> Dewch i mewn, chwi gewch ei brofi.

> Here is a tavern, the Cross of the Cock
> A welcome to each one for his penny,
> Good ale to all for his payment
> Come in, you can taste it.[15]

It was at this hostelry that the Chartists stopped after marching through New Inn before reaching Croesyceiliog about 11 p.m. The year was 1839, and the ill-fated attack on the *Westgate Hotel*, Newport, would come to nothing. The wet weather had not deterred the marchers from seeking out every able-bodied man to forcibly join them since leaving the top of the eastern valley. In Croesyceiliog it was no different when they met Brough, a brewer, and a currier named Watkins, who were both on their way home. These were later released, but there was dire consequences at the later trial of the main abductors. Inside *The Upper Cock* hostelry the Chartists sheltered and depleted the stock of alcohol. Their gunpowder had by this time become damp, so they placed it in a oven to dry! The inn-keeper wisely sheltered in a wood nearby. The illegal actions continued when a house on Turnpike Road was forcibly entered. Here, John Lewis, a baby of three days rested in his mothers arm. His father had also taken shelter in the dark under a yew tree nearby. With no respect for property the Chartists searched the house. Entering the bedroom, the exhausted mother held her baby towards them saying with contempt, 'Here's the only man in the house, take him with pleasure.' John Lewis grew up to be a miller at Llanyrafon Mill and a regular winner of foot-races.

The eastern valley Chartists, as part of their strategy, avoided confrontation at the homes of the county gentry with the intention of returning when Newport had been captured.

Thus, the newly erected pseudo Elizabethan house of Llanfrechfa Grange was passed by. Owned by Charles Prothero, Clerk to the Peace of the County of Monmouth, the land it was built on belonged to a much older estate. It was he who, in 1835, had built the handsome grey stone house in the middle of the estate, and turned the fields surrounding it into parklands. It stood in 140 acres of rich agricultural land, with fine trees and wonderful views on all sides.

As the years passed Charles Prothero continued to improve his home. Probably, his last building project was in 1855, when, with numerous workmen, he added a new wing to his already magnificent mansion. So pleased with the result, he arranged a splendid supper at the *Greenhouse Inn* for the large workforce. In 1860, he sold the property to Frank Johnstone Mitchell.

The new owner was born in 1824, and lived at Upper Wimpole Street, London. He came to live in Monmouthshire during 1855, at the age of thirty-one. His purpose was to work on the managerial side of Messrs Cordes and Company, at their works familiar to all Newportonians as the "Dos Works." He appeared a presentable young man being tall, fair and handsome, and soon became very-well known in the county. Before long he became engaged to be married, his chosen bride, Elizabeth Harcourt Rolls, being the eldest daughter of John Etherington Rolls, Esquire, of The Hendre, Monmouth, a well-known family whose name is engraved in history.

Before the marriage took place Frank bought Llanfrechfa Grange, which included Whitehall Farm, The Lodge, the Gardener's Cottage, The Laundry Cottage (the scene of the unsolved murder of Mr. W. Richards, the Churchwarden), Chestnut Cottage and the Park.

He and Elizabeth were married on January 15, 1860, at the little village church of Llangattock-Vibon-Avon. However, alterations had to be made to the house,

Llanfrechfa National School, built 1862.

Datestone

so, whilst these were being put in hand, the happy couple travelled until 1864, before finally settling down at the Grange. Both were highly intelligent people, interested in humanity, history, archaeology and all aspects of church life. They had two daughters - Hilda Mary, who later became Mrs Tyler, and Gwladys Elizabeth, who married Brigadier-General Cleeve, before spending a great part of her life in India.

As early as 1862, Frank and Elizabeth had begun to do wonderful things for the community. On a day at the beginning of March, they entertained a number of dignitary to a special luncheon in their new home. In order to celebrate the opening of the new National School at Llanfrechfa, the day had begun with the Bishop attending a service at the parish church before everyone proceeded to the educational establishment for the short service for opening schools. The new edifice consisted of a schoolroom 40 feet by 20 feet, a class-room, and the residence of a school mistress. Built in the style of the 15th century, it was constructed of grey stone with Bath stone dressing, and a roof of red Bridgewater tiles. Nearly a hundred children were treated to tea and buns.[16]

It was they who were the pioneers in the rebuilding and enlarging of All Saints Church, Llanfrechfa, in 1873, with Frank subscribing thousands of pounds towards the cost.

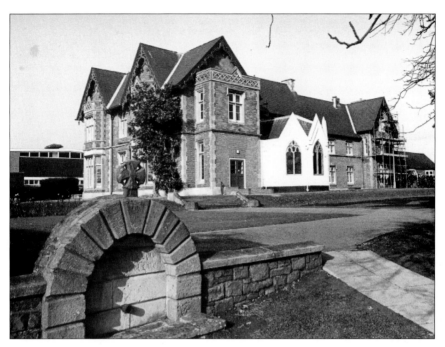

Llanfrechfa Grange

No. 6827 "Llanfrechfa Grange", Locomotive.

Mr and Mrs Mitchell continued to travel a great deal, and after a visit to the Holy Land, added a small, but very beautiful chapel to the east side of the house.

The gates of the main entrance were of wrought iron, standing on beautiful stone pillars. These stone pillars came from the parish church for, when it was rebuilt in 1873, Mr. Mitchell bought the stones of the old vicarage as well as those of the old church and used them to build gate pillars and garden walls. The front entrance to the grounds had the most southerly approach. Nearby, a handsome fountain was erected by Mr. and Mrs. Mitchell after they had bought out the licence of the Crown Inn, found at the top of Crown Lane. The fountain was put in to compensate weary travellers for the loss of the inn. It was also created to supply water to the horses whose job it was to haul heavy loads up the steep slope of Crown Lane and at the same time supply water for nearby cottages. The back entrance was from the west, passing through the Parklands to the house and grounds, which were again closed.

The front door of the house opened to a large hall, and to this was added a conservatory where ferns and flowers were always to be seen. Over the beautiful fireplace were three plaques, hand carved in wood. The library leading off from it contained old and interesting books. The dining-room and staircase were made of oak and the furniture designed to harmonise with the woodwork. The drawing-room had a lovely Adams fireplace, whilst the ceiling held a moulded plaster picked out in gilt. The windows of this room commanded a vista of the well-planned rose gardens, the front drive and parklands beyond. As well as roses, there was a glorious tulip tree, a mulberry tree and a wonderful rhododendron maze, which took you to the woods beyond.

A large hall behind the servant's quarters, was used for all festivities and celebrations in the Parish, such as those connected with Jubilees, Coronations and Harvest Festival suppers. Hundreds of books, covered in blue linen and numbered in white, lined the room; these were borrowed monthly by members of the Mother's Union and Guild of the White Cross, who met there regularly.

The Chapel had a carved wooden altar, some lovely stained-glass windows and beautiful hand-made frontals. A beam had been especially erected across the Chapel to hold the figures of Christ on the Cross, John and Mary. These were obtained in Southern France and were bought for the Parish Church but, failing to obtain a space for their erection, a temporary home was made for them in the Chapel. Later, they were placed in the Parish Church where all can see these wonderfully carved figures. Also in the Chapel was a blue and gold painted candelabra, which was no longer required in the old Parish Church when it was restored.

In 1903, the Mitchells were also instrumental in the founding of St. Mary's Church, Croesyceiliog. The church, built entirely of red brick and standing in an elevated position, was intended as a mission church to relieve All Saint's Church.

The cost, including furnishing and a small American organ, amounted to £2,000.

Mr. and Mrs. Mitchell celebrated their Golden wedding at the Grange in January, 1910. Gifts were numerous and at the village celebration the following address was given to them by the inhabitants of the parish of Llanfrechfa:

> *"We cannot tell you all that we think and feel about the exemplary lives which you have lived in our midst. Your tender care and sympathy for the sick and needy, your thoughtful interest for everything affecting the welfare of the Parish, and your splendid generosity - these things are so familiar to us that we have ceased to wonder at them, but we wish to assure you that they are precious memories, and, will not soon be forgotten."*

Elizabeth died eight months later. It was a rare sight at the large funeral when an unfamiliar Rolls Royce vehicle transported the body, followed by eight horse-drawn coaches. Frank lived on until October 11, 1913.[17] After his death the house was occupied for a time by their daughter, her husband, Brigadier General Cleeve and their children. In 1922, Brigadier General Cleeve died and his mortal remains was transported on a Union Jack covered gun carriage to the nearby All Saints Church.

Sir John Cecil Davies, a Swansea industrialist, purchased the property in 1922, but he did not stay long, a matter of two years, and in 1924, the house was sold to Sir Leonard Llewellyn, Baronet, who died in October of the same year. His family lived there for a while. For a period of time the house was empty, but in May, 1936, the Boy Scout's Association took it over and, for many years, it changed its character by becoming a centre for boys from the distressed areas who were sent there to be trained as domestic servants, waiters etc.

It was at this time several interesting events took place. Firstly, prior to his abdication, King Edward VIII visited Llanfrechfa Grange as part of his South Wales tour. Here he showed tremendous enthusiasm for the work carried out to improve the lives of young people. The publicity generated by the visit immediately jogged the memory of Miss Florence M. Winsor, a valued Griffithstown railway employee. Miss Winsor, knowing that a series of Great Western Railway locomotives were being built, and to be named after "Granges", suggested to the authorities that it would be appropriate if one of them was named "Llanfrechfa Grange." The idea met approval at headquarters, and when the new locomotive (No. 6827) appeared it bore that name for the extent of its working use.[18]

Not long after World War Two began, the Grange provided emergency home facilities, in the first instance, for expectant mothers evacuated from London and other bombed areas of England. Later, with the reduction of the evacuee incidence, the facilities were made available for expectant mothers of the Monmouthshire County.

In May, 1947, the Monmouthshire County Council purchased the property from Sir Leonard's estates. Its use for maternity purposes was continued until October, 1950, when, with the opening of a new maternity wing at the County Hospital, Griffithstown, it was no longer needed for this purpose.

In October, 1958, it was re-opened for the care of persons of incomplete psychological development, with accommodation for fifty-seven residents. Early in 1956, plans were drawn up to extend the accommodation for four hundred residents. The building programme was to be carried out in two stages. The first stage consisted of two villas for women, two villas for men, an administrative block with staff accommodation, residents' workrooms, main kitchen, boiler room and laundry, all of which was commenced in December, 1957. The cost of this building was approximately £450,000. The second stage, amounting to around £540,000, consisted of four extra villas, assembly hall with canteen, shops, infirmary, sports pavilion and recreation ground, mortuary and a Chapel of Rest.[19] Commendable work by the staff gave the residents an improved quality of life for many years to follow.

For over a century and a half Jim Crow's cottage caught the eye of travellers as they were about to ascend The Highway at Croesyceiliog. Described as an example of the mock-Tudor Gothic revival school of architecture of the period 1840-1860, its pleasant appearance sometimes appears out of place, even in the previous rural setting. It still is the only local example of this particular Victorian Gothic, but many examples can be seen in the Home Counties and around London.

The 1840 tithe apportionment shows Squire Capel Hanbury Leigh, of Pontypool, owning the cottage with Benjamin Evans paying rent to live in the dwelling and for the use three fields nearby. Jim Crow, an itinerant English seafaring man lodged at the cottage with the Evans family during the 1840's. In the 1841 Census Return, Benjamin Evans, age 55 years, is found to be living in Croesyceiliog with his wife Temperance, and three daughters. He was employed as a gardener and his cottage was unnamed. However, in the 1851 Census Return his cottage is named after Jim Crow and Evans is employed as a sub-postmaster. He would later add the occupations of schoolmaster and shopkeeper to that of postmaster. Evans and his wife became fond of the old sailor and when he died they immortalised him by naming their rented cottage and fields after him.

Throughout the years the picturesque mock-Tudor Gothic cottage would have a number of owners and in 1927, it remained part of the Pontypool Park Estate. A 1940 sale document described the property set in 1 acre 0 roods 35 perches, as containing a living room, back kitchen, pantry, store, two bedrooms, with garden and two useful paddocks.

Cwmbran Development Corporation later purchased the cottage and land for future modern redevelopment and intended to demolish the old building. Many local people had become fond of the charming little house and contacted the offices of the Development Corporation to explain their concern.

An understanding chief architect immediately became aware of the feelings of local people and worked out a special scheme into which the building would fit. This included restoring the cottage, and putting in a special landscaped garden, followed by the building of three new houses nearby to form a miniature housing scheme.[20]

In the late 1870s, the population of Croesyceiliog had increased to the point that a local school for young children had to be erected to prevent them having to travel long distances during inclement weather. A Board School was duly built on the The Highway and catered for the young for many years. The old infant's school closed in 1955, but in 1959 it re-opened for a while because of the many children brought to the district by the New Town housing estate.

The pleasant land of Croesyceiliog would later become the site of important building projects as the new town of Cwmbran became established.

REFERENCES

1. Fox and Raglan, *Monmouthshire Houses,* 1954,
2. Bradney, Sir Joseph, *A History of Monmouthshire - Llanfrechfa*. pp. 286-287.
3   *Pontypool Free Press*, October 7, 1892, Sale of Llanyravon Estate.
4. Lloyd, W.G., *Roll of Honour,*1995, p.19.
5. Interview with Mrs Judith Lesley, of Whitehall Farm, Dingestow, near Raglan, 2nd July, 1987.
6. Interview with Mr. Arthur Wait, BEM., 5 August, 1987.
7. Dovey, F. and Walters, H.F., *Llantarnam,* 1953, pp. 91-95.
8. *Pontypool Free Press*, October 7, 1892, Sale of Llanyravon Estate.
9. Interview with Mr. Arthur Wait, BEM., 5 August, 1987.
10. *South Wales Argus,* October 19, 1977.
11. Gwent Record Office, D1605.4, p.44.
12. Garwood, Derek, Newport Reference Library, pq M290 286, *God Our Fathers - The Story of Pontrhydyrun Baptist Church 1815-1965.*
13. Lloyd, W.G., *Tales of Torfaen,* 2000, pp. 20-22.
14. Jones, Adolphe George, *Half Hours in Monmouthshire,* 1906.
15. Evans, C.R.O., *Monmouthshire - Its History and Topography.* 1953.
16. *The Reformer and South Wales Times,* March 7, 1862.

17. Hockey, Primrose, Newport Reference Library, pf M290 726.5, *Stories in Stones,* 1975.

18. *Free Press of Monmouthshire,* September 9, 1955.

19. Hockey, Primrose, Cwmbran Reference Library, *Presenting Monmouthshire*, No. 12 (Autumn, 1961)

20. *Free Press of Monmouthshire,* May 19, 1967, and April 11, 1969.

Chapter Ten

WORLD WAR ONE

The wail of GKN hooter could be clearly heard in Cwmbran village and surrounding districts. This became more sinister when people began to realise that it was not the usual time of day for it to be heard. Almost immediately other industrial hooters joined in the relentless chorus and with church bells ringing, railway warning detonations signalled a similar noise that many Cwmbran men would soon hear in a distant land.

The people of Cwmbran were not prepared for war. Most had been enjoying the fine summer at the beginning of August, 1914. For several weeks the main topic of conversation had been the strike action at Cwmbran Colliery. New machinery for improving the sifting of small coal broke a thirty year old agreement and caused the men to lose 6d a day. With such excellent weather the short, unplanned holiday would not have done the colliers much harm. This was all to be forgotten when people came out of their houses and workplaces as the news of war with Germany circulated at an unhesitating speed.

The morbid excitement of what was believed by many to a brief, successful war in Britain's favour gripped the people of Cwmbran. In only a short time mobilisation began. A crowd of several hundred assembled at the railway station to see the men of the National Reserve leave for their various depots. A number of Territorials were not slow in travelling to Pontypool or Newport to report themselves. Telegrams were received by the Chemical Company and Star Brick Company informing them to blow their hooters to hurry up late Territorials in their employ. This was done immediately. All of the men not away on holidays were on the railway station an hour later.

In the weeks that followed recruiting continued to be brisk. The Cwmbran veteran Sergeant John Williams, VC, had been appointed recruiting agent for the district. Immediately he began enlisting likely young men before being seen at the railway station giving advice to the recruits before they entrained.

At Messrs GKN and Company, generous notice had been given that they would pay ten shillings every week to each of their employees taking up military service with the Regular Army, as Reserves, Territorials or recruits.

Regular recruitment meetings began to take place with Colonel Cleeves, of Llanfrechfa Grange, playing a leading part. 200 free tickets were given to possible recruits to attend the Olympia Cinema and see a film of the famous first naval engagement in the North Sea. Patriotic music played in the street by the Cwmbran Brass Band greeted the cinema-goers.

The meetings were highly successful with Cwmbran soon providing its quota. Over 120 recruits had been presented from the St Dials Schools Recruiting Office, and more than 80 accepted at the Central Station, Newport. After an ordinary meeting in the Salvation Army Hall, presentations were made to five young men of the corps. Band-Sergt. H. Ross, Deputy Bandmaster W. Birchley, Bandsman W. Chapman. Messrs P. Hood and Tom Lewis, were each presented with bibles before they left for the front. For the following scholars formerly connected with the Cwmbran Wesleyan Sunday School, bibles had already been forwarded: Sapper E.W.G. Kelly, Royal Engineers, BEF; Pte. Tom Jones, 24th Batt. South Wales Borderers, BEF; Ptes. A.W. Kelly, Stan Kelly, Reg Stiff, Bram Scott, all of D Co., 5th Batt. South Wales Borderers; Ptes. Will Scott and Archie Tilney, R.A.M.C; Ptes. Harry Perrett and Will Smith, 8th Batt. South Wales Borderers; Lce-Corporal Edgar Steed, 4th Batt. South Wales Borderers; Ptes. George Scull, George Maggs, Lewis Davies, Edward Smith, Arthur Robinson, Clarence Stiff, Lce-Corporal W. Tilney, 2nd Batt. Monmouthshire Regiment; and Pte. Alfred Cousins, 4th Batt, Royal Field Artillery.

At a special meeting of the Llantarnam and Llanfrechfa Urban District Councils, sub committees of the National Relief Fund were formed. This resulted in collection boxes being placed in shops and public houses. Letters sent to various companies regarding the possible future distress amongst the families of their employees, met with a favourable response. The larger firms promised to attend to any distress among their employees without troubling the UDC in any way. The ladies as usual were quick of the mark. Clothing items, either collected or knitted, accumulated before being forwarded to various organisations and hospitals.

By the end of August concerns were growing for the state of industry in the district. GKN were fortunate to receive a large order from a French firm as a consequence of the war. The production of 60 tons of nails extra to their existing orders would keep them going for a while. Although a number of tin mills in South Wales had already closed the Avondale Company managed to continue. Unfortunately, the Redbrook Company's mills had temporarily stopped immediately at the outbreak of hostilities because their orders were chiefly from Germany.

As the German army killed many innocent civilians while smashing its way through Belgium, the British Expeditionary Force, although hopelessly outnumbered, fought a courageous rearguard action at Mons in an attempt to hold up the well-planned advance.

Private Alfred Clift, of Wesley Street, was in the thick of things. In an interview he said, "We were just billeted when the Germans surprised us...they were all around us in no time and we were constantly firing at them. It was a terrible experience. Men all around us were falling, and we had to keep retiring from one place to another, but there was no disorderly retreat." Nearby was a young man from Llanyrafon. 2nd Lieutenant Rupert Pilliner, RFA., would be mentioned in dispatches and recommended for coolness, gallantry and resourcefulness. Sadly, he would be killed-in-action a short time later. Another casualty during that September was the eldest son of the Cwmbran recruiting officer Sergeant John (Fielding) Williams VC. Tom Fielding, of the South Wales Borderers, had been cut down by a sniper's bullet.[1]

Slowly, the news trickled through of the death and capture of a number of Cwmbran's regular soldiers. The plight of the Belgium refugees also became known. Immediately, a patriotic concert at the Olympia Cinema raised subscriptions for the Refugee Fund. Spare clothes were parcelled up to be sent to the fund organisers, while a public meeting considered the purpose of raising money to accommodate Belgian refugees at Park House, Upper Cwmbran. Kindly placed at the disposal of the committee by Messrs Guest, Keen and Nettlefolds Ltd, the large house could accommodate twenty-five men, women and children. Occupying a prominent position some 600 feet above sea level, on a clear day it commanded a wide view of the valley below.

It was hoped to have a quiet arrival for the Belgian refugees, but this did not go according to plan. Due to the well-circulated secret, which everyone seemed to know, the platform of the railway station was jammed solid by the time the new arrivals stepped down from their railway carriage. Two large motor cars, commandeered for the day, held the flags of the allies. Fluttering prominently in the breeze, the yellow, black and red of the Belgian nation appeared most appropriate as the motor vehicles slowly moved off through the large cheering crowd.[2] However, this arrangement did not last long due to the refugees being re-housed at Newport.

The war that was thought to be over by Xmas continued into 1915 and turned into a conflict of stalemate with both armies deeply entrenched and facing each other.

Recruitment continued. Much excitement prevailed on a Monday morning when fifty men from Cwmbran and Pontnewydd, who had enlisted in the Gwent Battalion, entrained for Colwyn Bay. Hundreds of men, women and children witnessed their departure from the lower station. As the train steamed away cheer after cheer was sent up for the noble band of men who, like others, were determined to do their duty. One of the recruits was Charles Cole, brother of Private Raymond Cole, 2nd Mons., who had recently been killed at the front.

Patriotism was running high among the teaching staff of St. Dial's School with an eastern valley record about to be broken. By May, 1915, seven male teachers had enlisted in H.M. Forces: W.S. Davies, Devon Regiment, Percy J. Hood, R.F.A., Claude J. Davies, 2nd Mons., Richard H.L. Griffiths, Motor Machine Gun Section, J.B. Griffiths, Royal Marines, Arthur E. Smith, SWB, and Mr. J. Roxburgh, assistant headmaster, completed the record number.[3]

Another fine example of patriotism occurred when Mr. William Scott, of 62 Wesley Street, gave six sons to serve their country since the outbreak of war: John Scott, 1st Mons., Joseph Scott, SWB., Fred and Bramwell Scott, 5th Batt. SWB., William Scott, a playing member of the Cwmbran Cricket Club and member of the Liberal Club, joined the Royal Army Medical Corps, and Tom Scott, the youngest son, joined the 2nd Monmouthshires. It was a complete surprise to their father when he received the following letter on behalf of King George V:

> *"I am commanded by the King to convey to you an expression of his Majesty's appreciation of the patriotic spirit, which has prompted your six sons to give their services at the present time to the Army. The King was much gratified to hear of the manner in which they have so readily responded to the call of their Sovereign and their country, and I am to express to you and to them his Majesty's congratulations on having contributed in so full a measure to the great cause for which all the people of the British Empire are so bravely fighting."*

All six male members of the Scott family fortunately survived the war. By transferring battalions five of the brothers served together in the 4th Battalion, South Wales Borderers, at the Dardanelle and the Middle East. All received their campaign medals and local presentation watches when they returned home. John worked at the Cwmbran Postal Depot and Bramwell became a well-known and popular postman in the district for many years.[4]

Everyone in the Cwmbran village and district did their part for the war effort. Garments were knitted at St. Dial's School and parcelled before being sent to the front. Cigarettes were regularly requested in letters sent home and a special effort made by local people caused these to be added to the parcels. A National Egg Fund became a welcome diversion for the young scholars of St. Dial's School. On each egg would be written the name and address of the scholar making the donation before it went to the collection depot at Newport. Because of this many interesting postcards and letters would be received by the youngsters from home and abroad. During the term ending July 30, the girls had brought in 662 eggs for the fund. With the price of eggs later increasing, the numbers dropped considerably. News that a good home had been found for a donated egg often reached the scholars. Seven year old Ivy Beech, of Star Street, was thrilled to receive the following picture postcard:

Dear Miss Beech,

> *I am sending you many thanks for your kind wishes and your very nice egg. It was the nicest egg I have tasted since I left New Zealand. I belong to the New Zealand Expeditionary Force, and was silly enough to get in the road of two bullets. I was wounded at the Dardenelles.*
>
> *Well thank you again for your share in my tea.*
>
> *I am a grateful New Zealander,*
> *Lance Corporal L.E. Walker.*

By the middle of 1915, hardly a week would pass without the news of a serious casualty becoming known to the Cwmbran people. Many were buried in the corner of some foreign field while some had to be invalided home only to die months after sustaining their injuries. Private George Ashworth died from wounds received in Gallipoli and is remembered at Cwmbran Cemetery, while Private Penry Morgan, 1st Grenadier Guards, was wounded in France, but died at a West London hospital. He is buried at St. Michael's Churchyard, Llantarnam. His brother Corporal Ernest Morgan, of Wooden Houses, Upper Cwmbran, had sadly died earlier in Hammersmith Hospital, while another brother Phillip, lay seriously ill in a Nottingham Hospital with a severe wound. In June, the Wesleyan Chapel was crowded for a memorial service for three Sunday School scholars who had recently left for the front. Clarence Stiff, Lewis Davies and W. Leyshon would be the first to be placed on the chapel's roll of honour.

Pontryhdyrun Baptist Church World War I Memorial

Another big steel order from France for GKN Ltd, at the beginning of 1915, helped stabilise employment in the local iron industry while the tin trade was hard hit throughout the year. This occurred mainly through cancellation of exports to both Allies and the enemy, who were engaged in the war. It was not until December that trade suddenly

155

improved and local tinplate reached its highest price for thirty-five years. America had the monopoly in tinplate trade until recent improvements in transporting the finished product placed the South Wales tinplate trade at an advantage.

It was not long, however, before remunerative business had to be declined for anything more than a few months ahead. With the Government and Allies requirements having to be met first, a tin-bar shortage was a distinct possibility, abetted by a shortage of male labour. To monitor this situation, all tinplate works in South Wales and Monmouthshire were taken over by the Government from January 1, 1916, and continued as controlled establishments.

The 1914-18 war was not just a war of explosives, but equally a war of entanglements. The Allies used barbed wire in front of their trenches while the enemy did the same. Either side had to cut through the wire to come into close contact with the opposing forces. All of this meant the making of a vast mileage of wire. The amount produced at Messrs J.C. Hill, Oakfield Wire Works, Cwmbran, proved astonishing. As production greatly increased, female labour had to be introduced to cope with the work. Energies were chiefly concentrated upon the manufacture of French wire entanglements, which were used by the British forces in Salonika, and the Eastern theatre of the war. For this extra work, new machinery and plant had to be laid down and other arrangements made at the works. Often the need for men during the various crises of the long war depleted the staff, but all had jobs when they returned.

In pre-war days the sulphuric acid, which was made by the Cwmbran Chemical Works went to the tinplate works, to the galvanising sheet works, and to the local coke ovens and gas works, where it was used in the manufacture of sulphate of ammonia. In 1915, the need of shells became so urgent that the works which needed the acid had to be rationed, and an appeal was issued to increase the output for more high explosives. The firm received instructions from the Government as to the amount expected from them, and it is to the credit of the Cwmbran Chemical Company that they did not fail to turn out the quantity required.

This in the main was due to the loyalty of the employees. Although the staff had been depleted by about 40%, they succeeded in keeping the works going thanks to those who remained and the new men who were called in. Special mention should be made of the foreman, William Anslow, who only previously had received such severe burns in the course of his work as would have permanently incapacitated many men. Throughout the war he showed initiative, perseverance, skill and resource in maintaining the output of sulphuric acid. For his devotion to duty, and on behalf of his Majesty the King, at a large meeting of the residents of Cwmbran, Lord Treowen presented him with the O.B.E.

With the war continuing, food shortages proved considerably and ration cards became a priority. With a shortage of potatoes local newspapers soon began giving gardening hints to it readers.[5] Never seen before queues were now a regular occurrence outside Cwmbran shops and consisted mainly of the womenfolk. High prices were often demanded for meat and poultry with some local shopkeepers amassing a small fortune during the war years.

Recruitment continued with an adverse effect on industry. Cwmbran pride was on a high when it became known that seven young men who emigrated to Australia four years before the war had voluntarily joined the overseas forces. All resided at the town of Lithgow, Australia, and many remembered Mr. John Magness Fisher, who took with him a splendid record as a tenor vocalist.[6]

The long four years dragged on for the Cwmbran folk with many receiving the dreaded communication of the loss of a loved one. It seems small recompense to know that many of the local men received bravery awards, while others simply did what was asked of them by King and country.

At last it was all over. On November 11, 1918, the armistice was signed and the news announced by the sounding of the various works hooters in the Cwmbran district. Many of the industries ceased for the day and with the excitement of the children being so high, school holidays were immediately granted. A quickly formed procession toured the Cwmbran streets and consisted of members of the U.D.C., the fire brigade, and boy scouts and girl guides. Headed by the joint bands of the Salvation Army and Cwmbran Brass Band, the procession enticed the remainder of people who were not already out of doors. In the evening, thanksgiving services were held in all parts of the district.[7]

REFERENCES

1. Lloyd, W.G., *John Williams VC - A Biography,* p. 66.
2. Lloyd, W.G., *Roll of Honour,* p. 37.
3. *Free Press of Monmouthshire,* May 14 and May 28, 1915.
4. Author's six uncles.
5. Gwent Record Office, Llanfrechfa U.D.C. Minute Book, A422 A M 11. 1916-20.
6. O'Brien, Dave, Lithgow, Australia.
7. Gwent Record Office, Llantarnam U.D.C. Minute Book, A421 M 16, 1917-18.

Chapter Eleven

THE SLUMP

At last the war was over. The battle-scarred soldiers came home and were feted by their districts while each received a wristwatch from the people as a token of their esteem. Local employers kept their promises and men returned to their former occupations. With a shortage of manpower this was easily done. For a short time there was talk of houses being built that would be fit for heroes. The sadness caused by the terrible four years of war would remain with many all their lives.

For some time an enormous Peace Day Celebration had been planned everywhere and in July 1919, Cwmbran and district joined in with a commendable show of festivity. Regardless of the inclement weather crowds collected near the Cwmbran Council Offices. A monster procession formed headed by the Brass Band, the Fire Brigade, under Captain Derby, decorated wagons with tableaux, Scouts, Girl Guides, and the Bugle Band. These were followed by hundreds of competitors in fancy and comic dress. The streets were paraded until the large procession arrived at a field in Oakfield Road. Here, a huge marquee provided the venue for 1,800 school children to receive a first rate tea. Various competitions were entered and the following day a successful athletics meeting was well attended. Similar celebrations occurred everywhere. With the districts of Henllys, Llanfrechfa Upper and Llanfrechfa Lower showing colourful decorations, the park at Llanfrechfa Grange was thrown open for similar entertainments.[1]

In the immediate years that followed the question arose everywhere concerning the erection of memorials to those who gave their lives for freedom. Each Cwmbran church and chapel provided a memorial plaque with the names of their late parishioners suitable inscribed. For district memorials the task became more complicated with considerable planning required to get the best results. At a meeting of the Llantarnam U.D.C., in May, 1919, it was resolved that members consider the possibility of a public clock as a memorial. However, the members of the Cwmbran British Women's Temperance Society had already showed great determination in raising money to provide a suitable building in memory of the fallen, and it was decide to let the scheme take its course. Regardless of the commendable effort to raise the large amount of money for the building project, the required amount fell short of its target. In a generous gesture in 1935, the ladies donated their collected money to the Council to help with the original plan of erecting a War Memorial Clock. The clock tower was erected by the Cwmbran U.D.C. in February 1936, and later in June, the electric clock was unveiled amongst a large crowd by Mrs Annie Kelly, the oldest member of Cwmbran B.W.T.A.[2]

The idea of providing a large German field gun for every district as a triumphant memento had not been thought through properly and only served to remind people of the terrible consequences of the war. The Cwmbran gun arrived and did service in front of the Council Offices for a short time. Soon it was relegated to stand in the cemetery until an application from the Cwmbran Comrades Club requested that it should adorn their premises.[3] This was granted until all the guns nationwide were eventually withdrawn.

Slowly things got back to normal. Coal fires were again lit in the Cwmbran railway station's waiting rooms and Llanfrechfa Upper Council purchased a horse which had served at the front from the Army Remount Dept. A great favourite with the children, the cob horse was a valued member of the Council's workforce for many years. Gradually new building projects took shape. In 1922, at Llantarnam village, a new Mission Hall was well underway with the purpose of providing a social institute for the children attending the nearby St. Michael's Church. In the same year plans were commenced to build a new Catholic school in Coronation Road. The dual purpose of church and school built in Oak Street, in 1882, was no longer practical. Completed by November, 1925, the new school allowed the Cwmbran Catholic Church to be re-opened.[4]

Times were changing dramatically for the Cwmbran and district workforce since the end of the Great War. A serious depression in trade would slowly have appalling consequences on the hardworking families of the area. It was thought to be a good sign when news of the re-start of the Coke Ovens and By-product Works of Cwmbran Colliery became known in 1923. Capable of giving around sixty men employment, the works had been idle for two years. However, the hopeful re-opening was short lived. The following year great anxiety was felt at the prospect of the temporary closing down of Messrs J.C. Hill & Co. Ltd., wire works and nail factory at Oakfield. Employing around four hundred men, for some time past the lack of orders intermittently put the men on short time. The exceptionally prosperous time of producing the famous "Acorn" brand of wire and nails was over for the time being.

By September, 1925, it became the turn of Cwmbran Colliery to feel the pinch. 711 men employed at the colliery received twenty-four hours notice to terminate their contracts, owing to the fact that parts of the undertaking were said to be unremunerative. At this time the colliery employed 1,100 men, who had been on day-to-day contracts for some months. This poor situation continued until the 15th November, 1927, when a deputation visited the Llanfrechfa Upper Council with news of complete closure of the colliery by the end of that week. Despite the holding of a public meeting and Council representatives attending a meeting with the Directors of GKN Ltd., the colliery closed completely and was dismantled the following year.[5]

Another blow for an ailing Cwmbran and district occurred when in March 1930, workers and clerical staff at the Coke Ovens and By-product plant received a fortnight's notice. The plant had managed to keep operating with the production of coke and the manufacture of a wide range of by-products, but, alas, around one hundred men were thrown out of work by the down-turn of trade. With many redundancies also in the iron works of GKN Ltd., employment at Cwmbran was in a bad way.

So favourably situated, being only five miles from a port, Cwmbran had been a centre of industry with an ironworks, coke ovens, a colliery concern, tin works, a blast furnace foundry and about five brick works, all always in full swing. The whole local atmosphere was smoke-laden, while by night the red glow in the sky indicated a prosperous state of affairs. In earlier days, while passing by train from Pontypool, the forge of Messrs GKN Ltd could be seen aglow and the noise from the busily engaged blast furnace works became familiar to everyone. Long trains of coal, coke, scrap iron, ore, and boxes packed with nuts and bolts, filled the large railway sidings. A number of locomotives were busy engaged in shunting operations until one had the impression from the railway carriage that he was nearing some large port. Further down the railway track the steam hammer at the wire works pounded out its message while the busy hum of the machinery from the nail factory, the galvanising department and mill was further evidence of industrial prosperity.

At William's Brick Works, and The Star Brick and Tile Works, trucks laden with bricks, pipes and terra cotta items were dispatched daily. The output from the Henllys Brick Works also helped swell the complement of laden trains steaming away from Cwmbran.

All of this had changed by 1930. Practically the whole of the industries were closed down, or on short time. Woodside Road Brick Works had been closed down for some time, while the next to follow was William's Brick Works, which gave employment to about one hundred men and boys.

At the Oakfield Wireworks, a rescue package by the well-known firm of Whiteheads, was in trouble. The puddling had disappeared long before, while the nail factory, galvanising department, rolling mill, steam hammer and wire drawing department were almost at a standstill. Hundreds of men and girls formerly engaged there had by this time become unemployed.

The Star Brick Works, which operated two clay holes in the district, had closed except for the limited manufacture of pipes, the main activities of the firm having been removed to Ponthir.

The difficulties which fell on Messrs GKN seemed inexplicable at the time, but it is now known that these were brought about by other countries developing their own industries. Large sums of money had been expended in alterations and extensions, and in the introduction of the most modern machinery, yet nearly the whole works was at a standstill. Where there was four mills working full time night and day only one remained engaged and that intermittently. The puddling furnace industry had become extinct, and the production of rods for the manufacture of bolts and nuts was, by 1930, a rare occurrence.

The key and cotter shop was idle most of the time, while the men's factory remained almost at a standstill. The blast furnace stood like a gaunt black spectre, idle and useless, never to be used again.

Further up was the foundry, a large works, which for some years had done little or nothing, the only orders being those of maintenance from the Great Western Railway. Previously, large orders were worked from here for the Indian and Egypt State railways. Orders of this class had disappeared despite the improvements and up-to-date methods of production.

With the men of the Chemical Works receiving their notices in February 1931, the plight of the district became extremely serious. Upwards of seven hundred of the workers were on the dole, and no jobs could be found for them. To some it appeared that the districts were becoming derelict with no future hope of family life. Many families after the payment of rent and other bare necessities had to exist on a penny per meal at the rate of three meals per day. This state of affairs had for many lasted since 1921, and things continued to go from bad to worse. Day by day hope grew more faint and starvation was always waiting around the corner.

The slump in industry continued into the nineteen-thirties. At the Elim Chapel a soup kitchen served around fifty gallons of soup to the children on specified days. A ton of parcels received from the Congregational Union consisting of clothes and boots was most gratefully accepted. The limited number of boots were given immediately to the most needy. Despite the local Councils trying their best to introduce schemes to provide work, they could not cope with the mass unemployment. Many men left the area to seek work elsewhere.

As could be expected, the poverty caused by unemployment brought other difficulties. Health problems from lack of a good diet became common place. Problems with sanitation also caused concern. This was a time when many of the old Victorian houses had become worn out and needed upgrading. Unfortunately, funds were not readily available for these building projects. Regardless of all the concerns, the Cwmbran folk kept their dignity and gradually both Council and population appear to have begun to adjust to the changing times.

It was a set back to the recovery of Cwmbran when the popular manager of GKN Ltd., Mr. Joseph Pitter Bayley, passed away on 24 April, 1931. He had been appointed general manager of GKN Ltd., Cwmbran in 1921. During his time as manager he completely re-organised the works and foundry and as a result they probably became one of the most up-to-date in the country. It was due to this man, who cared for the welfare of his employees, and took a great interest the social life of Cwmbran, that the GKN works did not go under like so many of it competitors. Funds raised by the more wealthy of the district's inhabitants led to the building and opening of the J.P. Bayley Memorial Hall. Found alongside St. Gabriel's Church, the opening ceremony took place in September, 1933.

Further gloom descended on Cwmbran in 1932 with the passing away of one of its heroes, John Williams, VC, who won the coveted award at the defence of Rorke's Drift, South Africa, in 1879. At Cwmbran he had a happy upbringing in a strong Catholic family and courted a young lady who lived nearby. When just short of his twentieth birthday, he suddenly joined the army and changed his name from Fielding to Williams to avoid being traced. The young lady he had courted subsequently gave birth to a baby girl nine months after his enlistment. Upon discharge from the army six years later he immediately married his former sweetheart, who had a daughter approaching six years of age. However, due to joining up under the name Williams, whenever he was on military duty in later years, he would always be known as John Williams VC, the name under which he had won the award. It is understood by most enlightened people that the famous initials, 'VC,' should never follow the name of Fielding.

He had been active in his later years attending the opening of the Territorials new drill hall in Malpas Street, Cwmbran, in May 1925, and also the impressive unveiling of the Pontnewydd War Memorial in November of the same year. At the age of 75 years, the greatly esteemed old soldier gave up the ghost and past into legend. An enormous number of people attended his funeral and it is said the cortege extended from Cwmbran village to the burial ground in St. Michael's Churchyard, Llantarnam.[6]

In March 1935, the last meetings of the old Councils of Llantarnam and Llanfrechfa Upper took place before they amalgamated into the more effective Labour controlled Cwmbran Urban District Council. The elected members were: W.E. Brown, J.P., chairman, Tom Miller, Pontnewydd, vice chairman, Rev. John Donne, Mrs Fanny Carver, Messrs Arthur Kelly, Alex Jones, Fred Gifford, James Williams, W.G. Thomas, Joseph Daley, Alfred James Perrett, James Griffin, Arthur Edwards, Herbert J. Lewis, William H. Hill, John Williams and Ernest E. Moule.[7]

Gradually times were improving for the Cwmbran folk commencing with electricity replacing gas lighting in 1930. New recreational parks came into being and the area resumed its reputation for producing useful local sportsmen. The Cwmbran Harriers Athletic Club boasted a number of Welsh Cross Country champions and continued to win competitions against other more wealthy clubs. Always a favourite in the summer months, Cwmbran cricket continued its long history. Each of the industries had in the past its own team with keen rivalry always displayed. Often Whiteheads would thrash the Chemical Works with the more junior side vowing revenge next time. By 1935, new clubs had been introduced to their fixture list. With the introduction of the new parks it was not long before the Cwmbran and Pontnewydd bowling teams were giving a good account of themselves against the well established clubs.

By 1935, the popular King George V had been on the throne for twenty-five years and although money was scarce, the Cwmbran people were determined to join in the Silver Jubilee celebrations. Any coloured paper was procured and the ladies became busy with scissors and string in preparation for streets to be decorated. In no time the enthusiasm spread with individual houses competing to be the most colourful on show. Brilliant sunshine accompanied the special day when it finally arrived. In the new urban area of Cwmbran the day began with a Thanksgiving Service in the various churches and chapels along similar lines to that relayed from St. Paul's Cathedral. Following a tea in their schools and the distribution of chocolates and souvenir beakers, the children all headed to the nearby parks behind the local bands. Here, sports, fireworks and community singing were enjoyed by young and old alike. The senior citizens were not left out of the festivities and sat down to a splendid tea. In many Cwmbran streets dancing extended long into the evening with a huge bonfire on the mountainside of Twm Barlwm lighting up the night sky. Absenteeism was rife the following day in the Cwmbran schools due to children being tired from staying up late watching the bonfires.[8]

The memory of the recent royal celebration would remain with many Cwmbran folk all their lives, but sadly King George V passed away on January 20, 1936, at Sandringham, aged 70 years. A letter of sympathy was immediately sent from the Cwmbran Council to the royal family.[9] Within a few days a large gathering of village people assembled outside the Cwmbran Council Offices to hear the Royal Proclamation of King Edward VIII, read by Mr. W.E. Brown, J.P., chairman of Council. Mr Brown reminded the Cwmbran folk that by their many personal sacrifices and hardships in recent years, they had fully carried out their duty with the peoples of the Empire. At All Saints Church, Llanfrechfa, a new bell was already being dutifully inscribed "King Edward VIII Coronation 1937."

Perhaps as a sign of changing times, in May 1935, the old GKN blast furnace at Forge Hammer, which had been out of commission since 1919, was at last demolished with the hope that extensions to the works could be commenced.

A further glimmer of hope for the future of the district occurred when the Whitehead Iron and Steel Company Ltd., purchased a sixty acre farm adjoining their wire works at Oakfield in February, 1936. The reason for this was to diversify into the manufacture of high quality bricks. On farmland, next to their works, there happened to be an extraordinary good bed of clay. Trials were soon carried out and it was pleasing to find that the quality of the bricks, the colour, and their crushing strain exceeded practically any in the country. This new, unexpected industry gave employment to a large number of men in the immediate area. Within a few years the Llandowlais Brick Works trebled its orders and as a consequence had to duplicate completely their brick-making plant. Such was the success of this venture that part of the freehold site was allotted for the men employed at the wire and brick works to have a sports field. This included a fully equipped sports pavilion, cricket and football fields, tennis courts and other recreational facilities. It is interesting to record that this sports club, in its first year, entered the Cwmbran and District Inter-works Tournament and was awarded the Challenge Shield for the greatest number of events won.[10]

Cwmbran, at last, was now beginning to show the ability to help itself. This became apparent when a local man with ten employees, in 1936, set up the firm of Metalitho Works Ltd., decorators and art printers of enamelled and lacquered tinplate for packing food, fruit, and canned beer. By 1939, the small firm had become highly successful employing over a hundred workers.

On November 18, 1936, the uncrowned King Edward VIII toured the Eastern Valley of Monmouthshire in an attempt to give a boost to the distressed areas. After an overnight stay of the royal train in Usk, His Majesty commenced his tour at Cwmbran. In readiness, streets and shops had been colourfully decorated in National colours and even the Memorial Clock received a dignified adornment.

As the train steamed into Cwmbran Station the crowd burst into *"Hen Wlad fy Nhadau."* This was followed by the *National Anthem.* After a few minutes the King emerged from the train and walked along the bridge to the station approach. The first sight of a figure in a grey overcoat, with a bowler hat in hand, passing through the station gate was the signal for excited and almost deafening cheering. The King shook hands with a number of people and spoke at some length to the waiting war veterans. The royal tour began with hundreds of cheering Cwmbran inhabitants lining the roads as he passed in his car. From Cwmbran the King travelled via Llantarnam, Road to the road junction at Llantarnam, up the main road to Turnpike House, and thence to Llanfrechfa Grange, where he inspected the junior training centre for boys. Leaving about 10.30 a.m., his car proceeded through Croesyceiliog and along the Straight Mile, before continuing its climb up the valley.[11]

164

Cwmbran Roman Catholic Schoolchildren in Operetta, 1938.
T. Kennedy, M. Rowlands, J. Elsmore, D. Gibbon, P. Coleman, J, Cunningham,
B. Fisher, E. Chamberlain, J. Rowlands.

Richmond Road Baptist Church Operetta, 1939.

J. Blakesley, Captain, receives Cwmbran Works Cricket League Sheild, 1939.

Mrs. Fanny Carver, Cwmbran Council's first woman Chairperson, 1939.

Saunders Valve Administrative Block.

Saunders Valve Athletic Team, 1939.

Dr. F. Carlton-Jones investing Mr. Joseph Daley, JP, Chairman of Cwmbran Council, with Chain of Office.

On December 10, 1936, Edward VIII abdicated after a reign of only 325 days and his younger brother, The Duke of York, became King George VI. Soon, another Royal Proclamation Ceremony was to take place. There was a representative attendance of the general public outside the Cwmbran Council Offices on the occasion of the Proclamation of King George VI by the chairman of the Council, Mr. Tom Miller, J.P. The Rev. John Donne, B.A., offered prayers for the King, the Queen, and the Royal Family, and the ceremony concluded with the singing of the National Anthem.

Although doing little to improve the economic situation of Cwmbran, the interest taken in Royal events seems to some extent to have helped to lift the psychological depression, which had been suffered for over a decade by the Cwmbran people. This was further evident during the coronation of King George VI, which had been planned and looked forward too for some time. On May 12, 1937, Cwmbran inhabitants entered wholeheartedly into the celebrations and mothers were determined that the children would have a time they remembered for the rest of their lives. In the morning a civic church parade was largely attended and headed by the Cwmbran Town Band. Father Reidy conducted mass and Canon Jarvis preached an appropriate service. Prayers were offered for their Majesties and the service concluded with the singing of the National Anthem.

Streets were colourful with an abundance of bunting and flags. A tea for the children was served in the schools throughout the district and coronation books

168

and beakers were distributed before they were let loose in the parks to enjoy various sports and entertainments.[12] The Salvation Army and Town Bands gave a magnificent musical rendering throughout the day. The elderly also received excellent attention while thoroughly enjoying the celebration. In the evening Cwmbran Park was electrically illuminated for dancing on the green. As an added bonus, special Coronation medals were presented to both Dr. Frank Carlton-Jones, M.O.H., Cwmbran, and J. Daley, J.P., Cwmbran Council, in recognition of service in the Eastern Valley. The indomitable spirit of Cwmbran was made manifest on the special day, when, notwithstanding the difficult time through which they had past, the people indeed rose grandly to the memorable occasion.[13]

The only problem which remained was what to do with wrongly inscribed new bell about to be hung in All Saint's Church, Llanfrechfa. The answer was quite simple - Edward was chiselled out and the name of his brother George substituted.[14]

By 1937, the Redbrook Tinplate Company had, at their Pontnewydd premises, recently opened a tin box works containing considerable extensions in building and machinery. This was soon employing 300 men and girls. A further development to their main plant at Pontnewydd, in December 1938, also helped their workmen. Two new steam driven tinplate mills gave added work to the 250 regular workers, which was particularly helpful just before Christmas.

At Llantarnam there was also an interesting development that augured well for the future. By June 1937, Weston's Biscuit Company, Ltd., had purchased a triangular piece of land about nine acres in extent, and only around two hundred yards from Llantarnam Railway Station. A planned new factory would be one of thirty-four which the company had established in the country. At an estimated cost of £100,000, it was expected to employ 450 men and women. Work of building began in October 1937, and the opening took place towards the end of the following year. The new factory was a Nuffield National Trust-assisted new project and in the presence of Mr. Garfield Weston, Lord Nuffield performed the opening ceremony.[15]

This trend of new industries continued with the arrival of Mr. P.K. Saunders to the Cwmbran area. He had earlier gone to South Africa, his mother's native country, and commenced work in a gold mine. A series of deaths meant rapid promotion for him and at 27 years he became manager of one of the richest mines in that country. With his prospects increasing, he unfortunately contracted a miners' illness and was forbidden to work underground any more. Before long he put his previous mining experience to good use and took up compressed air research. His new work resulted in the invention of the successful Saunders

Valve. In 1935, he set up a small manufacturing company in Wolverhampton and by 1937, the factory was overflowing with orders. His good fortune continued when he heard on the wireless the announcement of a new Special Area Act with its facilities for manufacturers who would set up industries in special areas. He hurried to London and was the first applicant under the Act. With the loan of a very considerable sum of money he established his second factory in Cwmbran

The new £100,000 engineering works was officially opened in March 1939, by Alderman Arthur Jenkins, J.P., M.P., for Pontypool, in the presence of over three hundred guests. Situated alongside Grange Road, the new factory occupied a site of about four acres, and was the only one of its kind in South Wales. Employing 200 workers at first, the Cwmbran company would expand until almost three thousand local people found regular employment. On April 21, 1966, among the British firms who won the Queen's Award for outstanding achievement, either in increasing exports or technological innovation, appeared the name of Saunders Valve Company, Ltd., of Cwmbran. A successful and popular place of work since 1939, the firm was recently taken over by Alfa Laval and is presently the premises of the prestigious Crane Company.[16]

Despite the new industries springing up and the raised morale of the Cwmbran people, unemployment still remained relatively high. Perhaps this was partly due to the rise in births as shown in demographic figures over the previous twenty years.

By the beginning of 1939, Cwmbran showed all the signs of a gradual progressive move towards prosperity. However, many had by now began to recognise the gathering of distant war clouds once more and the possibility of again adding the names of young people to the districts already lengthy war memorials.

REFERENCES

1. Gwent Record Office, Llantarnam U.D.C. Minute Book, A 421 A M 18, 1919-1920; Llanfrechfa Upper U.D.C. Minute Book, A 422 A M 11, 1916-1920.
2. Lloyd, W.G., *Roll of Honour,* 1995, p.162.
3. Gwent Record Office, Llantarnam U.D.C. Minute Book, A 421 A M 19, 1920-1921.
4. *Free Press of Monmouthshire,* November 27, 1925.
5. Gwent Record Office, Llanfrechfa Upper U.D.C. Minute Book, A422 A M 14, 1927-1928.
6. Lloyd, W.G., *John Williams VC - A Biography.* 1993, pp.83-98.
7. Gwent Record Office, Llantarnam U.D.C. Minute Book, A 421 A M 32, 1934-1935; Llanfrechfa Upper U.D.C. Minute Book, A 422 A M 21, 1934-1935.

8. Gwent Record Office, C.E. A52.4, May 6, 1935, St. Dials School Log Book, 1921-1943.

9. Gwent Record Office, Cwmbran U.D.C, Minute Book, A420 A M 2, 1935-1936.

10. *News and Weekly Argus,* February 27th, 1936.

11. *Free Press of Monmouthshire,* November 13, 1936.

12. Gwent Record Office, C.E. A52.4, May 5, 1937, St. Dials School Log Book, 1921-1943

13. *Free Press of Monmouthshire,* May 14, 1937.

14. Guy, John R., and Smith, Ewart B., *Ancient Gwent Churches.*

15. Newport Local Studies Library, fm 310 641, Commemorative Booklet: *The Official Opening of the Weston Biscuit Factory by Viscount Nuffield, at Llantarnam, Monmouthshire, November 1st, 1938.*

16. Garnish, Ian, Newport Local Studies Library, pf M275 620, *Profile of Saunders Valve Company;* pq M275 620, *A Move That Spelt Success.*

Chapter Twelve

WORLD WAR TWO

As Adolf Hitler continued his expansionist policy in Europe, it was obvious to everyone in Britain, by late 1938, that war with Germany had become a reality. The Home Office immediately advised Councils to have large trenches dug at a distance from schools and public buildings to prevent falling masonry causing injury if air attacks occurred. Soon, men carrying picks and shovels were seen making their way to the Pontnewydd Labour Exchange. It was suggested that Cwmbran Colliery Adit would make an excellent bomb-proof shelter for the people living nearby, and the old clay level pit could also be easily converted.

Next came the Government plans for each house to have its own air raid shelter in the nearby garden. Designed to accommodate six persons, the trench would be covered with corrugated iron with the floor sloped towards one end to allow water to collect before being easily removed. Due to the huge dread of mustard gas, arrangements were made for the supply of 14,000 gas masks to be quickly distributed to the inhabitants of the area. Public meetings gave out local information, while many volunteers were obtained to act as air raid wardens, auxiliary firemen, and to man first-aid posts. Helpful lists were drawn up of those willing to drive their own vehicles, which might be improvised as ambulances. Each Cwmbran workplace received instructions of the warning and 'all clear' signals to be given by their sirens. With Air Raid Precaution (ARP) courses well attended by both men and women, many received their certificates and badges of proficiency. When war was declared between Britain and Germany on September 3, 1939, Cwmbran was as well prepared as any other district in the country.

Probably, due to the experience of shortages during the Great War, food immediately became a priority. Within days of the outbreak of hostilities a Cwmbran and District Food Control Committee was formed and headed by Mrs Fanny Carver, J.P., the chairperson of the Cwmbran Council. This resulted in an even distribution of food among the local inhabitants, although it is still remembered that some local tradesmen became wealthy due to the difficult times. A further appeal on the radio encouraged local farmers and gardeners to produce more food to feed not only themselves, but also others.

There was a definite buzz of excitement when it became known that Cwmbran would receive its quota of young children evacuated from some of Britain's major cities. Due to the fear of immediate bombing by German planes of the tightly packed large cities, by the end of the first week of the war, young evacuees prepared to say a tearful goodbye to their parents before leaving for the safety of less populated districts. Some parents who could not bear to be parted from their children as the trains began to leave, quickly retrieved them and took them back home. The remaining children, with gas masks slung over their shoulders and identification labels attached to their clothing, bravely boarded the trains while anxious not to be separated from brothers or sisters. At Cwmbran, the reception of these young children was nothing less than marvellous. Their arrival at Llantarnam Railway Station, the feeding at Weston's Biscuit Factory canteen and considerate despatch to foster parents, was an experience never to be forgotten. The few teachers accompanying the children were heard to say that they expected everyone to be sleeping in churches and schoolrooms on the first night, yet as darkness fell, all were tucked up in beds with caring people looking after them. When billeting the large number of children great care was taken not to separate brothers and sisters. The evacuees found Cwmbran very clean after Birmingham. Many had a dreary outlook in their home towns and no experience of the countryside or mountains. A child, when gazing intently at the Myndd Maen, was heard to ask, "Where is the snow." In no time the children began to settle. The boys soon began playing marbles and exchanging cigarette cards with their new friends. Countryside rambles organised for the youngsters were eagerly anticipated with many tasting their first blackberries before eating as many they could. Soon the boys had climbed Twm Barlwm, visited Roman Caerleon and sensed the beauty of Llantarnam. Prior to their first Christmas in their new homes, the senior evacuees produced the colourful pantomine, '*Ali Baba and the Forty Thieves,*' in St. Gabriel's Hall. This was intended as a 'thank you' for the kindness they had been shown. However, there were times of great sadness. The abandoned water-filled clay pits in the area again claimed another life when a young Birmingham boy regrettable drowned.[1] The descendents of those Cwmbran inhabitants, teachers, drivers, and the ladies in charge of the canteen, who opened their hearts to children, can be justly proud of their actions on that remarkable day when the first Birmingham evacuees arrived. Many were later to treasure the Birmingham School Magazine containing an account of the master in charge expressing his sincere thanks for all that was done. He ends his account thus: "*We went to our beds with a silent prayer for those who had helped us so kindly and generously in our great adventure.*"

Cwmbran appears to have got off the mark very quickly with the ladies organising collections for war comforts. A Pontnewydd lady actually presented a converted ambulance to the district. Men in uniforms left the Cwmbran railway stations at frequent intervals. There would be no military music played or loud cheering as the trains departed; the memories of the Great War were still fresh in the minds of many of those present.

With Cwmbran servicemen fighting with the British Expeditionary Force in Belgium and northern France, it was news of some of the local men serving in the British Navy that was first to become known. On December 13, Able Seaman John Jones, of *H.M.S. Exeter,* survived the thrilling battle of the River Plate in the South Atlantic. The cruiser *Exeter* was badly damaged by the German pocket battleship *Graf Spee,* whilst being driven into Montevideo Harbour by *HMS Ajax* and *Achilles.* Five days later the *Graf Spee* was scuttled in Montevideo Harbour. The young man from Ty Coch had come through the terrifying ordeal without a scratch. While home on a well-earned leave at the end of March, 1940, he was presented with a wristlet watch at a large gathering in the Yew Tree P.H., by his friends and workmates of the forge works. Later, he was the guest at his old school, St. Dials, where he gave a talk of his experiences during the famous battle. The next day the scholars walked to the nearby St. Gabriel's Hall where, amid loud cheering, the young hero received a suitably inscribed cigarette case from Brynley James, one of the young scholars.[2]

In April 1940, three Cwmbran seamen took part in the ferocious First Battle of Narvik, an engagement which convinced the Germans that they had a serious enemy. A destroyer flotilla went out, *HMS Hardy, HMS Eclipse* and *HMS Bedouin* among it, and courageously attacked a far superior German naval force off Narvik, Norway. A snowstorm raged that day as Captain Warburton-Lee led the five destroyers, his mission was to prevent the German occupation of Norway's ice-free port. The German U-boats and destroyers guarding Narvik were taken by surprise. On the way in, *HMS Eclipse* came under attack from five enemy aircraft and received two glancing blows from their bombs. Signalman Reg Cooper, who lived at Llandowlais Street and had previously played rugby for Cwmbran, was uninjured, but the damage to his ship caused it to retire. On board *HMS Bedouin,* Supply Petty Officer Bert Tanner, of Two Locks, also a former scholar at St. Dial's School, and schoolboy international footballer, survived the battle. As soon as was possible he would write to his wife informing her of his safety. The *Hardy* opened fire, sinking and damaging three destroyers and six merchant ships. Suddenly, from a neighbouring fiord, five previously unseen German destroyers emerged with their guns blazing before sinking or damaging four of the Royal Navy attackers. Signalman Bernard Francis Mostyn Kennedy, of Cocker Avenue, told of the third and final time *HMS Hardy* entered the fiord with guns blazing only to receive severe damage before running aground. With others, Signalman Kennedy swam ashore and the Norwegian people immediately got them to safety.[3]

When arriving in Britain all the survivors had a thrilling reception at the Horse Guards Parade, London, where Winston Churchill, First Lord of the Admiralty, addressed the survivors. On his return home, Signalman Kennedy gave an interesting talk of his recent adventure to the scholars of Cwmbran's Roman

Catholic School before both staff and children presented him with a splendid cigarette lighter as a memento of his visit.

All the Cwmbran inhabitants pitched in to do what they could for the war effort. Despite certain disruptions, every effort was made for life to continue normally. There became an understanding that the continuation of the social life in the district did not indicate any lack of concern for those fighting for their country, in fact many servicemen advocated this cheery approach to the new difficulties. Concerts continued and there was no curtailment of sports events, although Cwmbran Cricket Club did run only one team due to lack of player power.

Throughout 1940, Cwmbran's war effort slipped into a higher gear with the Council first arranging the sites for twenty-two air raid shelters. Lectures were given instructing people how to deal with incendiary bombs, and large quantities of sand arrived to assist in extinguishing the deadly menace.[4] Many more evacuees arrived. Servicemen came home on leave and were feted by their districts. Some, more daring than others, visited their old schools. Various campaigns commenced. Several members of the public approached Cwmbran Council with the wish to open a 'Spitfire Fund', which would be separate to any other similar enterprise. This was successfully carried out. A letter to the Cwmbran Council from the Ministry of Agriculture suggested a 'Dig for Victory Campaign'.[5] Due to so many proficient gardeners already in the area, this was easily implemented. The children of St. Dial's School also showed interest in the campaign when they attended St. Gabriel's Hall to see a film on the subject. With all the local energy now being voluntarily diverted into assisting the armed forces, Cwmbran residents must have been very proud when hearing that Mr. Sam J. Chaney, of Cocker Avenue, a member of the Home Guard, had six sons serving in H.M. Forces. Mr. Chaney had served with the 4th, South Wales Borderers for over four years in the last war and was severely wounded whilst fighting at the Dardanelles.

Industrial Cwmbran answered its country's call commendably. The men in the foundries at GKN Ltd worked all hours producing sections of military Bailey bridges and other equipment. Another industry had by this time opened alongside the Saunders Valve Works and required a limited number of specialist workers for the project to get off the ground. The newly opened engineering firm of Lucas had moved much of its production from Birmingham to Cwmbran to avoid probable damage by air raids. In February 1941, a letter received by the Cwmbran Council from Messrs Joseph Lucas Ltd, Grange Works, stated that in all probability they would be transferring 150 skilled and semi-skilled men from their Birmingham Works. This became the total number required when their peak output would be reached some months later. For the necessary new staff re-locating, it was estimated that the Council would have to provide houses for 100 families and lodgings for at least fifty single persons.[6] These were only a small number of the workforce as many of the out-of-work local people finally had regular employment. The Grange Works operated during the war for the Ministry of Aircraft Production. Its war effort involved reconditioning guns from the turrets of aircraft. Some were badly damaged and covered with blood. Many remember the noisy testing area at a safe distance from the workforce and seeing those participating with suitable ear protection in place. Soon to be known as Girling, Ltd., the workforce quickly grew to over 3,000.

The voluntary work continued at a greater pace in 1942. Comforts of all description were regularly sent to the servicemen, particularly the prisoners of war. Cwmbran people had began to make savings investments with the hope that several military aircraft could be purchased from their efforts. Plans were also in hand to purchase a tank. If this was not enough, plenty of support went into Cwmbran's Warship Week. Soon, £70,000 raised by investors enabling the trawler-minesweeper, *HMS Turquoise,* to be adopted by the area. A letter received by Cwmbran UDC, from the Secretary of the Admiralty, gave rise to the following entry in the minutes of their monthly meeting:

> '...that the Lord Commissioners of the Admiralty desired to express their pleasure at the result of the successful Warships Week in the Council's Urban Area, thus enabling it to adopt HMS Turquoise, and stating instructions had been given for the preparation of a replica of the Ship's Badge for presentation to the District, and asking if the Council had in mind to present in return a commemorative plaque to the ship.'[7]

This was carried out at the end of the year when the Council's Chain of Office went to Swansea in order to present the district's plaque to the ship. The gesture was pleasantly reciprocated when some of the crew attended a social evening in Cwmbran and subsequently presented a replica of the ship's badge to the Council.

While planning for the future, in April, 1943, the Cwmbran British Legion opened a more commodious premises in Commercial Street. Not only would the new club be a "home from home" for the men on leave, but when victory was won it would serve as a place of recreation for many years to follow. The Cwmbran branch of the British Legion had established in Ventnor Road in 1928, before carrying out a great deal of useful work for ex-servicemen throughout the years. With many people in attendance, the larger premises was opened by Mr. S.J. Chaney, chairman.[8]

Another opening with a military connection occurred later in the year when Cwmbran's Air Training Corps established in Ashley House, Pontnewydd. Ashley

House was originally the residence of Mr. Henry Parfitt, JP, a local industrialist. The new headquarters was formally declared open by Air Commodore J.A. Chamier, CB, CMG, DSO, OBE.[9]

This seemed appropriate for the Cwmbran members of the Royal Air Force had already achieved fame. Flight Sergeant John Appleby received the Distinguished Flying Medal and Polish Cross of Valour, and Flying Officer B.A. Rowe-Evans, the Distinguished Flying Cross. In October 1943, the Director of Education granted the pupils of St. Dial's School a half day holiday because four old boys of the school had been awarded further decorations: Warrant Officer B.J. Thomas, Distinguished Flying Medal, Flying Officer A.E. Wheeler, Distinguished Flying Cross (deceased), Pilot Officer A.T. Casely, Distinguished Flying Medal, and Flight Sergeant M.L. Rowland, Distinguished Flying Medal.[10]

Much more visual evidence of a major war taking place was to be seen at Llantarnam Village, sited on a major road leading from the north to the seaports of Newport, Cardiff and Swansea. It is to the young pupils of Llantarnam School we must give thanks for recording the following unique events which, but for them, would now be lost in the mist of time. In 1972, wartime events were much fresher in the minds of local people and while carrying out interviews for a school project, the impact of war on the quiet, picturesque village was revealed to be nothing short of amazing:

> 'Anti-invasion precautions were taken and sturdy blockhouses erected near the Greenhouse P.H. The Home Guard manned these posts and checked all travellers at night.
>
> We well remember the British troops, at the outbreak of war, travelling in convoy singing optimistically about the "Siegfried Line" and with dire threats to Hitler and his kind chalked on their vehicles.
>
> Later military convoys of all kinds thundered by. They were often several miles long, all other traffic was stopped and crossing the road made impossible for long periods. Tanks, armoured cars, guns, landing craft, aeroplanes, in fact every conceivable item of military equipment went rumbling by.
>
> There were convoys of American troops and many packets of chocolate, chewing gum and candy were thrown to the children watching spell-bound from garden gates. Sometimes a convoy would halt for a rest or for food and much money must have changed hands during the dice games they played on the roadside and many local children enjoyed drinks of fruit and other tit-bits for these warm hearted men always had "something for junior." In addition, Canadians, Australians, New Zealanders and Indians passed our way en-route for war.
>
> A military camp existed at Croes-y-Mwalch. In the fields of Pen-y-parc

were stationed Indian troops with mules. They were very friendly people and on Sundays opened the camp to visitors who were invited to partake of a curious flat cake, which they made. The cake was most unpalatable, but the people enjoyed the friendliness of it all. The R.A.F. took over the Abbey and used it as a huge storage place for uniforms. We saw rooms stacked to the ceilings with clothing. It was a striking contrast to a previous visit when Sir Clifford Cory had been in residence.

The name of the local church hall was covered for security reasons and part of the hall used as a Air Raid Wardens' Post. The old wheelwright's shop was used as a garage for ambulances. The petrol filling station near the Blackbirds Cross was taken over by the military authorities and the nearby "Homestead" was used to accommodate Ministry of Aircraft Production personnel. The Three Blackbirds Inn was filled nightly by soldiers from nearby camps. The right of way through the Abbey grounds was closed for a time.

We had our air raids, but not of a serious nature and there were no casualties. Incendiary bombs were dropped near the Afon Lwyd and no damage was done. An oil bomb fell in a field near the river bridge. Its object was to spread fire by scattering oil over a large area and ignite it. A string of bombs fell in a line near Cottage Farm towards Bettws. One fell a few yards from Old Station House. Here, a little damage was done to ceilings, but no harm came to the inhabitants. In fact Mrs Miller was so calm about it all that she insisted on preparing cups of tea for Air Raid Wardens who had rushed to help. A few of us witnessed the machine-gunning of the old mineral line by enemy aircraft. Quite a stir was caused by the finding of a strange object in a field of Pen-y-parc Farm. It proved to be a flute from a "screaming bomb" which had fallen in open space beyond Llanfrechfa. A barrage balloon, which had broken loose came down close to the Cider Mill Farm and R.A.F. personnel were called in to deal with it...This was a strange Llantarnam.[11]

Bitter fighting throughout 1944, and the early part of 1945, witnessed the growing list of casualties in the Cwmbran area. On May 8, 1945, the end of the 2nd World War against Germany was officially declared. When the news came through the relief for the local people was enormous and St. Dial's School closed for the immediate victory celebrations. In June, the Council provided a Victory Tea for the children, however, these celebrations were limited until Japan surrendered to the Allies on August 14, 1945. This was the signal for Cwmbran to hold a long-awaited Thanksgiving Service, and to discuss plans for a final peace celebration. After much deliberation, June 8, 1946, was set aside for the victory celebrations in the urban area.[12]

Albert Booth, M.C.

Leonard John Cunningham, M.M.
Croix de Guerre

Murrell Chatwin, M.M.

Morgan Waters, M.M.

John W. Bevan, M.M.

Reginald Ivor Manning, D.F.C.

Signalman Reg Cooper, HMS Eclipse

Signalman B.F.M. Kennedy, HMS Hardy

The Cwmbran men came home from war to be feted by their districts. It was a great relief for the families who had prisoners of war returned to them and a great effort followed to give them all the support they needed.

By the end of the war, Cwmbran had a remarkable savings record worthy of mention. In six special efforts since 1941, the Cwmbran urban area had subscribed enough to purchase eight Wellington bombers, three fighter planes, three tanks - two of which carried the areas name into battle - one minesweeper, and the cost of moving a Monmouthshire Division from Wales to Germany.[13]

At this time the Cwmbran Home Guard also came in for a lot of well deserved praise. As a last line of defence they had worked hard and by now these older part-time soldiers were up to a high standard. Many of the men worked long hours and returned home, donned their uniforms and went on military duty. Often they would be seen marching around the countryside or expertly throwing make-shift bridges over the canal or Afon Lwyd during training. Some volunteered to be guards at prisoner-of-war camps, while others manned anti-aircraft guns on the coast while acquitting themselves with credit. Fully aware of their excellent contribution, and the reassurance their presence gave the local people, a 'thank-you' letter was forwarded by the Council to their commanding officer.

1946 brought about the winding up of war efforts and the holding in June of the final Victory Day celebrations. Huge plans had been made for impressive entertainments, but heavy rain put paid to most of the events. A short break in the weather allowed the carnival to parade, while lesser festivities were quickly organised indoors.

Such was the events of that frightening time, which is still in the memories of many Cwmbran folk.

REFERENCES

1. Gwent Record Office, A420 M-9, Cwmbran UDC Minute Book, June 25, 1940.
2. Gwent Record Office, C.E. A52.4, March 18, 1940, St. Dials School Log Book, 1921-1943.
3. *Free Press of Monmouthshire,* May 3, 1940.
4. Gwent Record Office, A420 M-9, Cwmbran UDC Minute Book, January 14, 1941.
5. Gwent Record Office, A420 M-9, Cwmbran UDC Minute Book, October 22, 1940.
6. Gwent Record Office, C.E. A52.4, March 12, 1940, St. Dials School Log Book, 1921-1943.
6. Gwent Record Office, A420 M-9, Cwmbran UDC Minute Book, February 18, 1941.
7. Gwent Record Office, A420 M-10, Cwmbran UDC Minute Book, March 31, 1942.
8. *Free Press of Monmouthshire,* April 9, 1943.

9. *Free Press of Monmouthshire,* October 1, 1943.

10. Lloyd, W.G., *Torfaen Heroes of World War Two,* 2003; Gwent Record Office, C.E. A52.5, October 20, 1943, St. Dials School Log Book, 1943-1970.

11. Dovey F., and Waters, H.F., *Llantarnam.* 1956, pp. 157-162.

12. Gwent Record Office, A420 M-14, Cwmbran UDC Minute Book, February 26, 1946.

13. *Free Press of Monmouthshire,* November 30, 1945.

Chapter Thirteen

A GARDEN TOWN

The slump of the nineteen thirties appeared to be over with post war Cwmbran looking forward to a better future. New industries brought hope to the workers by considerably reducing the unemployment figures. Some problems still remained and this was compounded by the lack of rented houses in the area. Due mainly to the shortage of building materials, houses could not be built causing new workers, in many cases, having to travel long distances to their place of employment. Easily erected prefabricated or aluminium buildings did little to reduce the growing waiting list of those in urgent need.

However, in August 1948, residents thoughts were elsewhere as a former Upper Cwmbran farm boy stood on the starting line of the London Olympic Marathon. Well known as a Pontnewydd Harrier, Tom Richards had already represented Wales eight times in cross-country events. On that memorable Saturday, Tom thrilled the 82,000 people at Wembley Stadium by passing a competitor on the final lap to gain the silver medal just sixteen seconds behind the winner. Many folk remember seeing his great effort on the silver screen of the Cwmbran cinema. When the local man entered the stadium for the last lap everyone in the cinema stood and applauded vociferously. A non-sports fan would have thought he was winning the race! His achievement was later recognised by the inhabitants of his birthplace at a presentation ceremony when he received a radiogram purchased out of a testimonial fund.

At the end of the year a twenty five foot high illuminated Xmas tree, erected in the street outside the Cwmbran Police Station, became a sign of the district's recovery that everyone understood.

Towards the end of the war a government committee had been set up to consider a planned decentralisation of the population by the building of new towns, which produced the New Towns Act of 1946. This did not necessarily apply to Cwmbran as the situation was not one of moving residents from large, congested cities, but that of providing homes and other amenities for the thousands of workers who were travelling to Cwmbran from adjoining valleys, this problem having developed from the rapid growth of new industries. A proposed large building project was also hoped to provide housing for workers at British Nylon Spinners, Pilkintons, Pontypool, the Royal Ordnance Factory, Glascoed, Richard Thomas and Baldwins, Sebastopol, and later, the Spencer Steelworks, Llanwern. It was believed to be only a short distance for Cwmbran inhabitants to travel to these satellite industries

In May 1949, the Minister of Town and Country Planning decided to proceed with the preparation of a Draft Order designating an area in the neighbourhood of Cwmbran as a site for a new town.

In July 1949, it was announced that the Draft Order had been issued for the new town of Cwmbran. The area designated for re-development included the built up areas of Pontnewydd, Cwmbran, Croesyceiliog, Upper Cwmbran and Llantarnam, and comprised of 3,157 acres, of which 2,550 acres were in the Cwmbran Urban District and 610 acres in the Pontypool Rural District. This huge building project was one of 22 planned for Britain and the only one in Wales.

The New Town would be built and organised by a Development Corporation who had the power to acquire any land or buildings within the designated area, but acquisition of land could only take place in stages, as and when needed. People living or carrying on business on the required land would be given an opportunity to obtain suitable accommodation on other land belonging to the Development Corporation if they so wished.

Life went on in Cwmbran with many people oblivious to the enormous changes about to commence. Sponsored jointly by the British Legion and Cwmbran Council, a splendid new garden of remembrance in Cwmbran Park was dedicated by Rev. John Donne in 1949. As the formalities concluded, a volley was fired by a party from the 2nd Monmouthshire Regiment. A short time later a memorial cross consisting of Portland stone was unveiled by Lord Raglan, J.P., Lord Lieutenant of Monmouthshire. A simple cross, 5 foot 3 inches high, served the two purposes of remembering those who died in both World Wars. All that was required to honour the fallen was the following dignified inscription:

1914-18

To The Fallen

1939-45

As the going down of the sun

and in the morning

we will remember them.

Those members of the British Legion and related groups who worked so hard in those bygone days to raise the money for this dignified memorial must be appalled at the desecration of the site in recent years.

What was hoped to be the happy fifties began with a dreadful air disaster on March 12th. Eighty people died in what was then believed to the worst air disaster known. The plane, an Avro Tudor V, with a crew of five and carrying seventy-eight Welsh rugby supporters, was returning from the international match at

Belfast. Wales had won the Triple Crown the day before and all were in high spirits as they carried their gifts for loved ones. Approaching Llandow airfield the plane crashed killing all but three of its occupants. Those local residents who tragically lost their lives were:

> Bert John Butcher, (61) licensee of the Greenhouse Inn, Llantarnam.
> David Jones, (46) New House Farm, Cwmbran.
> William Nicholas, (40) Penywain Farm, Cwmbran.
> John Williams, (34) Court Farm, Cwmbran.
> Arthur Williams, (32) Court Farm, Cwmbran.
> Squadron Leader William H. Irving, DFC, (32) Llantarnam and Pontnewydd.
> William Stevens, (25) Llantarnam Road, GKN worker.[1]

The success of Cwmbran industry continued with the ever-present trade cycle at that time most definitely in its favour. The old Redbrook Tin Stamping Company had recently extended their Pontnewydd works, which doubled the output capacity and the number of employees. Further expansion at GKN Ltd in 1951, resulted in more men joining the workforce. To this was added a new foundry extension in July 1954, built on the site of an old blast furnace used until 1919. Field Marshal The Viscount Montgomery of Alamein opened the new foundry and was greeted by cheering schoolchildren en-route. Even the old flock factory at Pontnewydd was doing well. For a quarter of a century Mr. Cliff Parker, of Llantarnam, had depended on the rag-and-bone man for his cast-off garments. These were quickly sterilised before being turned into soft fluffy flock ready for the padding of mattresses, furniture, cushions and other articles. Mr. Parker's deserving claim to fame was that he owned the only flock factory in Wales. With more work available in the Cwmbran area and the population steadily growing, the need for good housing had by now become a necessity.

The plan to establish a new town at Cwmbran was finally approved early in 1951 and the first sod cut at Tynewydd on 12th April, 1951. The first house, in Yewtree Terrace, Croesyceiliog, was completed on the 2nd February, 1952. With good transport links, the site was further enhanced by the magnificent backdrop of the Mynydd Maen to the west and the undulating countryside to the east. An understanding had been reached regarding the preservation of buildings of special architectural or historic interest. This reassured many people when the building program gained momentum.[2]

When any new project begins it seems to be human nature that the doom mongers immediately start their carping. Those comfortable in their long established homes and without any concern for the homeless, particularly the young married people, soon began to heard condemning the new site as a 'concrete jungle.' In answer to these damaging comments, a very wide range of architect-designed dwellings soon emerged. These ascended in size from bed sitter flats to five bedroomed houses, whilst the corporation also built houses specifically for sale in selected areas. It was even possible for the individual who wished to build a house to his own requirements, to obtain a building plot from the Corporation. Perhaps the military backgrounds of many of the senior members of Cwmbran Corporation gave rise to a certain amount of regimentation in those early days. Each street had its doors painted in the same pleasant colour while the next street would display a different, yet also eye-catching colour. An innate sense of discipline also surfaced among the tenants. Probably due to the delightful surroundings, most people creating beautiful gardens surrounded by well-manicured box hedges. It also seemed like the many excellent gardeners raised the performance of those less skilled until all gardens had reached a high level of scenic delight. The only thing lacking in this utopia was the absence of friendliness brought about by so many strangers suddenly coming together. It would take a long time for these new communities to have the warmth experienced by the older settlements.

Landscaping the area would in time add to the already pleasant site. Influences of the Garden City style of landscaping, in vogue during the first half of the twentieth century, soon became apparent as the project took shape. Initially, efforts were made to preserve the greatest number of trees, in addition to which the Corporation planted almost one tree for every house built. A lot of success occurred with the difficult task of transplanting of semi-mature trees. This centuries old method of stealing time from nature quickly enhanced the area. Apart from the trees, thousands of shrubs, bushes and plants, miles of hedging and acres of grassed open spaces became a pleasing feature.

In time the layout of the town consisted of a central commercial and residential area (Northville and Southville), which was surrounded by five large estates. The older sectors, although gradually absorbed into the new residential estates, never lost their old individuality, but this appears to have strengthened the binding of the much larger vision. The five large estates had, for all purposes, been designed with the intention of being self sufficient for the primary necessities such as schools and social and recreational centres. The town's chief commercial, shopping and business areas were to be situated in the new Town Centre.[3]

When built, the modern Cwmbran Town Centre became without a doubt the most attractive shopping centre in Monmouthshire. Based on the pedestrian precinct principle - which means one can shop without contact with vehicular traffic - all shops were to have permanent, illuminated canopies for weather protection. This was an advanced concept at the time, but now is seen in all parts of Britain. Over 4,000 free multi-storey or surface parking spaces near the shops, further added to the modern concept by encouraging visitors from outside the area.

As the landscape changed, the nineteen-fifties brought a modern way of life to not only Cwmbran, but the whole country. The war had previously plunged Britain into debt and ration books allowed only the purchase of the necessary amount of food each week. All of this began to change as clothes, meat, milk, and eggs became more plentiful. Life had become easier particularly for the young housewives who understandably wished to live in a modern house, with nice surroundings, and near a school. In the new town both private and rented houses looked alike and this added to the natural desire to settle. For the new tenants chic ideas of interior decoration became a must and modern style furniture began to be shown in the shops. Gadgets, also, were to open up a better way of life for the housewife. New inventions like the washing machine took much of the hard work out of housework, leaving more free time for other pursuits. Soon, all had a vacuum cleaner. Frozen goods became more widely available in the mid-fifties, and a new refrigerator, while keeping food fresh, made frequent journeys to the shops unnecessary. In the new town houses hot water could be miraculously drawn straight from the kitchen tap and no longer had to be warmed on a stove. In Cwmbran today, the use of all these machines are regarded as the expected way of living, but to the new settlers of the fifties, it was a whole new world opening up for them.

During this time national and local events were far from being ignored. No one realised in July 1951, that the colourful Festival of Britain, with its street parties, flags and bunting, served as a trial run for an even greater ocassion about to take place. Sadly, in February 1952, King George VI died and memorial services were held in the Cwmbran churches and chapels. Many witnessed the Royal Proclamation of the new monarch outside the Council Offices. The following year Cwmbran streets vied with each other for prizes for the best decorated creations as a young Queen was crowned. Colourful outdoor parties were held everywhere in the district on Coronation day and elderly folk had the chance to view the historic ceremony on televisions temporarily placed in the Cwmbran Catholic Hall. Amid stiff competition, blue eyed Gabrielle Willis, an attractive 17-year-old, became the Cwmbran Coronation Queen and performed her duties exceedingly well.[4]

Two recent world wars meant military action was never very far from the thoughts of the Cwmbran folk and it came as no surprise when Britain's strong alliance with America caused a number of young, local men to serve in the Korea war. Most were National Servicemen and within a short time of leading a comfortable life in Cwmbran, they were shocked to find themselves involved in bitter fighting in a foreign land. Private Ken C. Richards, formerly of Ton Road, remembers the bitter cold weather causing the land on which the savage conflict

Left to right: Pat Strawford, Marilyn Samuel, Gabrielle Willis (Cwmbran Coronation Queen), Sybil Tonks.

Cwmbran Locomotive

was taking place to be frozen. As a member of the Royal Welch Regiment he tells of how they hoisted their battle flag on the summit of Hill 355 on April 18,1952, when they relieved an American unit. The flag was immediately used for target practise by the enemy. During one of the many engagements with the enemy, Ken received a gunshot wound to the foot and was flown to Kure, Japan for hospitalisation. This was far from the end of his active service for as soon as he recovered, the long journey back to the front began. Thankfully, he and other local representatives, Keith Howard, Abbey Road and Barry Roberts, Penyparc, Pontnewydd, returned safely home. Ken worked most of his life at Girlings Ltd, while his friend Keith Howard later emigrated to Canada.

Throughout the nineteen sixties Cwmbran continued to expand with a number of much needed schools opening. Problems again began to surface with the districts old industries being casualties of the modern market. In 1957, the Avondale Tinplate Works finally closed while employing around 250 people and having been in existence for almost seventy years. Demolition of the site began in 1960. Nearby, the works of the Redbrook Tinplate Company was also forced to close in 1961.[5] Other old local industries by this time were also struggling and the call for the introduction of new industries of the smaller type went out. In preparation to receive future light industry, the twelve acre site of the old chemical works was at last about to be levelled and cleared. It was a noisy few days when explosives had to be used to break up more than two hundred

Private K.C. Richards

separate pieces of concrete, which were the remains of the foundation of the old works. However, despite the setbacks there was no serious break in Cwmbran's prosperity.

A future disruption to the everyday life of local people became apparent when the gloomy news concerning the valley's railway service was announced. Despite the opening of small halts and dramatically cutting fares, the G.W.R. continued to lose a substantial revenue in its competition over the years with the omnibus companies in the Eastern Valley. On his appointment as chairman of the Railway Board, Dr. Beeching announced the withdrawal of the railway passenger service, which had served the valley since 1852. Although a last attempt to attract customers included the introduction of diesel multiple units, passenger services were finally withdrawn on April 30, 1962. Mineral traffic continued to pass

Guest Keen & Nettlefolds (Cwmbran) Limited. Long Service Awards, 1959.

through the town and Cwmbran railway station remained very busy receiving parcel goods, particularly for the large shops in the Town Centre. Unfortunately, Beeching had his way and railway goods traffic ceased in 1966. The old railway line became 'ribbons' of jungle with only the rare, nostalgic train journey occurring. Complete closure of the line occurred on October 8, 1979, prior to the whole system being dismantled.

Cwmbran continued to grow with many new buildings helping to add more quality of life for the local people.

1966 saw the opening of Llantarnam Grange as a successful valley arts centre. Said to have originally been a farm for the Cistercian monks of Llantarnam Abbey, the building had many owners throughout the centuries until purchased by Alfred C. Pilliner, a director of the Oakfield Wire Works. It was he who converted the ancient building into a comfortable, roomy Victorian house. The 'Grange' remains the sole survivor of buildings which formerly stood in Cwmbran's town centre area. Purchased by the Cwmbran Development Corporation in 1951, and leased several times, it was later remodelled as the excellent social meeting place and arts centre that we know today.

The following year witnessed the opening of what was at the time the tallest residential building in Wales and Monmouthshire. It had been suggested that Cwmbran needed a landmark easily recognisable for first time visitors to the area. All those dignitaries present at the opening observed that the 210 feet high, 22 storey block of flats, commanded a magnificent view of the countryside. In the same year the Cwmbran Stadium and Sports Centre also opened. The stadium held the only running track of international standard in Wales and made possible for Cwmbran people to see many famous sporting stars competing.

Many young people were thrilled on November 12, 1971, when H.R.H. Princess Anne made her first visit to the county for the opening of the impressive new Gwent Police Headquarters and Llanyrafon Boating Lake. When she dropped out of the sky in a royal helicopter it was quickly confirmed that she added a welcome dash of colour to an otherwise cloudy day.

Local people believed it would go on for ever, but in April 1971, the British Steel Corporation decided to close the Whitehead, Hill Wireworks at Oakfield. Employing ninety-six people at the time of closure, the hundred year old works had been producing twelve thousand tons of wire annually in recent years. For those who wanted it, alternative employment was found within the Steel Corporation.

Cwmbran wholeheartedly participated in another royal celebration, the Silver Jubilee of 1977. It seemed like all of Cwmbran made a great effort to give the children a wonderful time. At the Congress Theatre, the result of the Cwmbran

Nightingale Row - Old and new housing.

Diane Jenkins, Cwmbran's Silver Jubilee Queen, 1977.

West Rodin, Coed Eva, Cwmbran , Silver Jubilee Party 1977.

Tynes, Coed Eva, Cwmbran, Silver Jubilee Party 1977.

Silver Jubilee Queen contest would be a dramatic affair. Diane Jenkins, of St. Dials, only turned up to watch the proceedings, but was persuaded to enter the contest. In a borrowed dress, she deservedly won her first ever beauty contest. Chosen as her court attendants were Lyn Stanley, of Greenmeadow, and Gail Thomas, Croesyceiliog.[6] With the Silver Jubilee celebrations fresh in the minds of local people, in April of the following year, many travelled the short distance to see the Queen Mother open the impressive new County Hall at Croesyceiliog.[7] It became yet another memorable occasion in the now long history of Cwmbran.

October 4, 1979, proved to be a significant date in the still growing Cwmbran New Town. It was the occasion of the official twinning ceremony between Cwmbran and Bruchsal, which took place in the castle of the West German town.

The Railway Station, Cwmbran.

LLANTARNAM STATION

The Whitehead Locomotive

Llantarnam Grange Arts Centre

Lord Raglan, the popular chairman of Cwmbran Development Corporation presented a silver cigarette case to Dr. A. Bieringer, Oberburgermeister of Bruchsal, on behalf of the Cwmbran delegation, which travelled to the function. In reply Dr. Bieringer presented a plaque to Lord Raglan. During the pleasant ceremony, Mr. Ronald W. Howlett, general manager read out the text of the twinning document. A short concert followed.[8]

The grim news in November 1980, of Cwmbran's remaining GKN Works closing down because of the current economic recession was undoubtedly a blow to the 230 employees about to join the increasing dole queue. It was the last of the old industries and had been Cwmbran's biggest employer for many years. Some were glad to see it close. There was nothing romantic about working in iron, it had been dirty and heavy with many employees having their health ruined. Thanks to the brilliant strategy of the Cwmbran Development Corporation, chaired at the time by Lord Raglan, the building of a good number of factory units for immediate rental proved very popular. This soon brought about the introduction of a number of new, progressive, small industries to the area. Cwmbran became the first area to implement this new approach to providing local jobs and it would later be copied everywhere.

The closure of the Guest Keen and Nettlefold Works, which developed from the early works of R.J. Blewitt and John Lawrence, alongside the canal at Clomendy, and was so instrumental in the development and survival of the Cwmbran we know today, brought to an end to the old days that have been. These times and people who gave us our future will forever remain as fond memories in the mind's eye. Today, Cwmbran is a bright, bustling healthy town full of vibrant people and a wondrous place for young people to grow up. Gone is the lack of warmth that existed sixty years ago. With churches and chapels still bringing people together, assisted by the commendable organised social activities that many inhabitants participate in, we can be sure that Cwmbran will grow stronger and meet any new challenges with the same brave resolve as our ancestors. Long may Cwmbran flourish!

REFERENCES

1. Lloyd, W.G., *Torfaen Heroes of World War Two,* 2003, p. 74.
2. Pound, Carl, Presenting Monmouthshire, No. 18 (Autumn 1964), *"Into the Valley of the Crow",* pp. 28-33.
3. Scholefield, C., *This Is Where We Live,* 1972. p. 234. A prize winning study of Cwmbran and its environments by pupils of Croesyceiliog School.
4. Lloyd, W.G., *The Golden Jubilee of Queen Elizabeth II and Torfaen,* 2002, pp. 65-66.

5. Clark, Arthur, Presenting Monmouthshire, No. 32, (Autumn 1971), *Monmouthshire v The Twentieth Century.*

6. Lloyd, W.G., *The Golden Jubilee of Queen Elizabeth II and Torfaen,* 2002, p.80.

7. Newman, John, *The Buildings of Wales/Gwent/Monmouthshire,* p. 200.

8. *Free Press of Monmouthshire,* October 12, 1979.

SEAL OF MARY MAGDALEN
AND THE
HOMILIES OF ST GREGORY MANUSCRIPT

The seal of St Mary Magdalene on whose feast the Llantarnam Abbey was founded. This is to be found in the National Museum of Wales. It shows a monk who could possibly be Bernard, the Cistercian founder, blessing three people. This dates back to the 14th century. Photographs of the seal will be seen in the British Museum Catalogue of Seals, at the National Library of Wales, Newport Museum and Pontypool Museum.

Another authenticated item is a manuscript copy of the Homilies of St Gregory, dating back to the late 12th or early 13th century. This unique manuscript has a very chequered history.

The Llantarnam Abbey manuscript is not a beautifully illuminated text similar to other examples of the time, but nevertheless it is an important tangible link with the past. This manuscript still possesses the original medieval wooden covers although the vicissitudes of time and damp have damaged the vellum leaves.

This manuscript, which is certainly the only remaining one from Llantarnam Abbey, actually sheds light on the Abbey's relative stability and prosperity at that time. The manuscript was given by Llantarnam Abbey to Hailes Abbey in Gloucestershire in 1248. The evidence is to be found on the front fly leaf of the manuscript, where written in green ink is a record of the donation.

Hailes Abbey had been found two years earlier in 1246 and probably requests were made for donations to their new library. At a time when no printing presses existed and producing manuscripts was such a skilled, and perhaps laborious task, this probably indicated that Llantarnam Abbey was reasonably wealthy since such a gift was an expensive item.

On the rear leaf of the manuscript are some notes, obviously made before the book left Llantarnam. They both appear to be dated 1204 and refer to building and maintenance work. The first concerns the expenses of Brother Jewaf Talrein for digging around some pasture land and the second is a record of the building of a mill on the Grange of Maestir Kanvawr, a property belonging to the Abbey.

The manuscript also has the signature of one Thomas Bristow in a style of writing which can be dated at c.1500. How the manuscript survived the ravages of the Reformation is unknown. By 1850, it was in the possession of Job Walden

Hanmer from whom it was bought by Sir Thomas Phillips, Baronet of Middle Hill, who died in 1872. In 1955, Eric G. Millar wrote to the British Museum informing that he had bought the manuscript together with a second unrelated document, in 1947, for £1000 from a firm by the name of Robinson. It came into the possession of the British Museum and, since the separation of the British Library from the Museum, it is now kept in the British Library.

Several framed photographs of pages from the manuscript can be seen in the entrance hall during an extremely interesting organised tour of Llantarnam Abbey.

APPENDIX II

DAYS THAT HAVE BEEN

Can I forget the sweet days that have been,
When poetry first began to warm my blood;
When from the hills of Gwent I saw the earth
Burned into two by Severn's silver flood:

When I would go alone at night to see
The moonlight, like a big white butterfly,
Dreaming on that old castle near Caerleon,
While at its side the Usk went softly by:

When I would stare at lovely clouds in Heaven,
Or watch them when reported by deep streams;
When feeling pressed by thunder, but would not
Break into that grand music of my dreams?

Can I forget the sweet days that have been,
The villages so green I have been in;
Llantarnam, Magor, Malpas and Llanwern,
Liswerry, old Carleon, and Alteryn?

Can I forget the banks of Malpas Brook,
Or Ebbw's voice in such a wild delight,
As on he dashed with pebbles in his throat,
Gurgling towards the sea with all his might?

Ah, when I see a leafy village now,
I sigh and ask it for Llantarnam's green;
I ask each river where is Ebbw's voice -
In memory of the sweet days that have been.

W.H. Davies.

CWMBRAN CATHOLICS WITH THE COLOURS - 1915

2nd Monmouthshire:	Sergeant P. Cunningham, Lance Corporal Conelius Love, Privates W. Sullivan, R. Crimmins, W. Thomas, D. Desmond, J. Munroe, Jas. Crimmins, P. Kilday, P. Desmond, R. Caffary, E. Purcell, L. Kennedy, Jas. Meenham, G. Floyd, T. McCarthy, Albert Powell.
Kitchener's Army:	Lance Corporal J. O'Brien, Privates D. Fielding, J. Simms, D. Driscoll, M. O'Brien, T. Cunningham, T. Crowley, W. Crowley (junior), J. Harrington, P. Mahoney, J. Crimmins, Jas. Kennedy (junior), W. Hurley, J. Nolan, Jas O'Conners, J. Reardon, Charles Cordier (junior), J. Virgo, T. Murphy, T. Larder, F. Crimmins, W. Conners, D. Sullivan, D. Cunningham (junior).
South Wales Borderers:	Sergeant John Williams, VC, Privates W. Roach, J. Roach, E. Purcell, P. Doolan, Tom Fielding, Harold Sly, Jas. James, John Morris (junior).
Special Reserve:	Privates James Desmond, D. O'Brien, H. Cordier, H. Driscoll, T. Sullivan.
Royal Field Artillery:	Privates W. Sullivan, M. Relihan, J. Mevrick, D. Mahoney, T. Ephraim, W. Ball, John Ryan, J. O'Brien, J. Rowland.
1st Monmouthshire:	Private J. Desmond.
Royal Army Medical Corps:	Private A. Waters.
Dorsets:	J. Fielding (junior).
Royal Engineers:	Sapper D. Beek.
Coldstream Guards:	Private T. Relihan.
Grenadier Guards:	Privates D. Relihan, P. Mynham.
5th Welsh:	Private J. McCarthy.
H.M.S. Canopus:	M. Crimmins.
R.I.R.:	Private M. Dowling.
National Reserve:	Corporal O.J. Stanley, Privates John Travers, J. Sullivan, D. Cunningham, J. Delaney, W. Crowley (senior).

ST. GABRIEL'S CHURCH, CWMBRAN,
MEMORIAL
To The Glory of God And In Proud Memory Of
The Men Of Llantarnam And Cwmbran Who Made
The Supreme Sacrifice In The Great War 1914-1918

Austey T.J.	James T.W.	Skyrme J.
Atkins Jas.	Johnson J.	Skyrme M.
Atkins Jno.	Jones C.	Spanswick D.
Bate A.	Jones J.W.	Spanswick J.
Bennet W.	Jones K.	Steer G.P.
Bishop W.H.	Lawrence H.	Stiff C.
Bumstead L.	Lewis H.W.	Tamplin J.
Butcher J.	Lewis T.	Thomas C.
Chapman W.H.	Leyshon W.	Thomas C.F.
Cole R.H.	Luffman W.	Thomas W.
Collier C.	Lyons T.	Tomkin W.G.
Cook S.	Martin T.	Trotman W.A.
Cumberely R.C.	Meredith J.	Turner H.R.
Davies A.G.	Morgan J.	Vaughan E.
Davies I.	Morgan P.	Wall R.
Davies L.J.	Morgan W.F.	Watkins D.J.
Dawson W.E.	Orpwood W.S.	Waygood P.G.
Desmond J.	Parker G.F.	Weeks H.J.
Driscoll D.	Parker W.	Weldon F.
Drummond T.	Pattemore S.	Whatley C.E.
Fielding T.	Phillips E.	Whitby G.
Fisher R.	Reece L.	Williams A.E.
Flello J.	Richards A.	Williams C.G.
Heastie W.K.	Richards W.J.	Williams R.
Hinton A.G.	Rowlands J.	Williams W.E.
Holmes G.	Salter C.	Wood W.J.
Howells C.	Scammels W.F.	Woodward C.R.
Hunt S.G.	Seymour S.	Woodward H.
James J.	Skillman F.	

APPENDIX V

HOLY TRINTY CHURCH MEMORIAL, PONTNEWYDD.

Memorial Tablet Inscription:

"The Electric Light was installed in the Church to the Glory of God and as a Memorial to the Men who gave their lives in the Great War, 1914-1918. A.D."

Charles Butcher, Jack Butcher, Henry Newman Carter, Samuel Cook, William Edgar Daw, Noel Alfred Hayles, Charles Hale, Charles Llewellyn James, Clifford Linney, Reginald Morris, Charles Morgan, Alfred Stephen Nurden, Thomas Alfred Payne, Albert Pinches, John Ramsden, A.C. Rawlings, Ivor Herbert Tucker, Jack Williams, William Watts, John Watts.

PONTYRHYDYRUN BAPTIST CHURCH MEMORIAL

ERECTED
IN THE MEMORY
OF
THE GLORIOUS DEAD
OF THIS CHURCH
AND CONGREGATION
WHO GAVE THEIR LIVES
FOR KING AND COUNTRY
IN THE GREAT WAR
1914 - 1919

CLIFFORD BOWLES
RAYMOND DART
RALPH FISHER
LIONEL JOHN GEORGE
FRANK HOLCOMBE
WILLIAM JONES
DANIEL JONES
BERT KING
ARCHIE LEE
LEWIS LEIGH
T.J. LEWIS
CHARLES MORGAN
JOSEPH MORGAN
GEORGE OSBORNE
RAYMOND PAULING
ROBERT PASK
ALFRED PRICE
CLIFFORD THOMAS
RICHARD VIZARD
ARTHUR WASSEL
TOM WATERS
JOHN WATKINS
WILLIAM WILLIAMS

ALL SAINT'S CHURCH MEMORIAL, LLANFRECHFA.

To The Glory Of God And In
Grateful and Honoured Memory
Of The Men Of Llanfrechfa Parish
Who Made The Supreme Sacrifice
In The Great War

MAJOR E.S. WILLIAMS
LIEUT. R.C.L. PILLINER
2nd LIEUT. H.H. STEPHENS
2nd LIEUT. C.L. JAMES

Q.M.SGT. G. ROWLANDS   SGT. D. INR. W. KNIGHT

SGT. G.M. GARRETT	PTE. E.G. JOHN
CPL. J. MORGAN	PTE. P.I. LESTER
CPL. A.A. LEE	PTE. A. WHEELER
CPL. T.J. LEWIS	PTE. E. ROBERTS
L.CPL. A.R. BOSWORTH	PTE. G. PRICE
L.CPL. S. BERROW	PTE. T.E. NICHOLS
L.CPL. ALBT. CORDING	PTE. A. KING
L.CPL. R. FISHER	PTE. G.H. BRAIN
L.CPL. A.W. PRICE	PTE. S. PATTIMORE
L.CPL. J.REES, MM	PTE. C. BOWLES
BOMBR. M. ROBBINS	PTE. H.G. LOWE
GNR. ARTHUR CORDING	PTE. J. WATKINS
GNR. S. DALLEYMOUNT	PTE. R.C. VIZARD
PTE. R.C. DART	PTE. A.J. WASSALL
PTE. C.MORGAN	PTE. T. HARDY
PTE. E. WAY	PTE. A. NURDEN
PTE. W.H. BISHOP	PTE. W.J. PROSSER
PTE. IVOR LEWIS, MM	PTE. R.J. CARPENTER
PTE. F.J. LEWIS	
PTE. A. LLOYD	
PTE. L.J. GEORGE	
PTE. C. PASSANT	

INDEX